What people are saying about
The Quiet Millionaire

The book contains many valuable insights, and Wilder does an excellent job of facilitating a more informed advisor-client relationship. Advisors would do well to introduce clients to the complexities involved with financial planning by presenting them with this book.

—NAPFA Advisor, The *Journal of the National Association of Personal Financial Advisors*

Wilder offers sage advice about loans, college funding, and retirement income calculations; his preliminary retirement cash flow analysis detail is a dandy. This book is obviously a labor of love.

—*Life Insurance Selling* magazine

If you're truly serious about developing an understandable and comprehensive financial vision for the future, *The Quiet Millionaire* by Brett Wilder is the right book for you. The author literally guides you step-by-step through how to develop a million dollar financial future. When you finish, you'll have a powerful and workable plan for becoming and remaining *The Quiet Millionaire.*

—Sharon Michaels

This book is an excellent work for retirees. The approach is pure common sense absent the usual theoretical dialogue. Critically important financial decisions are addressed in terms that are understandable, workable and practical for any retiree.

—Gordon D. Butler

This is probably one of the best books I've ever read on personal finance, investing and just understanding the overall industry. The college funding section was so eye-opening, even though my children are past this need, I wish I would have read it when they were younger. It would have changed my planning. Thank you. This is a great resource and a life-changing book.

—Rene Steinkamp

It's a great big doorstopper of a book, but don't be intimidated. The approach is accessible. The language is direct and the advice is sound. You won't be disappointed with *The Quiet Millionaire*.

—John Eckberg

If I had this book twenty years ago, I'd be in much better shape financially. *The Quiet Millionaire* not only describes a solid financial philosophy for investment, it is also a guide thru the heady issues associated with college financial planning, business ownership, insurance, ESOP and retirement planning.

—R. Himmel

The Quiet Millionaire dissects the complexity of wealth management in easy to understand, layman terminology. What makes this financial advisory book unique is that the reader first learns how to define their *true* life values and goals before creating their financial plan. This ensures a successful navigation through the various life stages of wealth management with conviction and commitment.

—Jan Kesselring, Retired School Superintendent

The Quiet Millionaire is an easy-to-read, practical guide to achieving financial security. The advice given is grounded in common sense, and it works. In fact, the sooner that this book is read the better, and should be mandatory 'Reality 101' reading for all students *before* graduating from their school to work life. It's a required read for all of my children!

—Jay Johnson, Managing Director with a global energy company

Brett Wilder does a superb job of introducing the reader to his professionally proven financial management strategies in *The Quiet Millionaire*. The book offers a solid, well-reasoned framework for mapping a customized path to personal wealth building. It even explores topics that, at first glance, might not strike the reader as important financial planning issues. This is a valuable resource for knowing how to work diligently towards the status of a quiet millionaire®.

—Vikki L. Kociela, Long-Time Client

Insightful reading! If you are looking for stock tips, hedge funds, or venture capital schemes, get real! If you want to methodically build your house of wealth, get *The Quiet Millionaire*.

—Larry Askren, President and Chief Executive Officer, Askren Designer Homes

The Quiet Millionaire is an extremely thorough and well thought out book that's loaded with experiential wisdom about how to become and remain a millionaire. It's invaluable reading for anyone regardless of current net worth.

—Robert L. Dinerman, Former Vice President of Administration, Pierre Foods, Inc. Cincinnati, OH

The Quiet Millionaire is a comprehensive, clearly-written guide for making wise and practical financial decisions that are beneficial for persons of any age, including those of us who are retired.

—Rev. Caroll and Ann Wood

The Quiet Millionaire contains useful information for both the novice and experienced investor who are motivated to achieve their investment and comprehensive lifetime financial planning goals. I recommend this book to anyone who is in the process of searching for a financial advisor and as well to someone who wants to confirm the value of their existing advisory relationship.

—Sue Morrissey, Associate Professor Emeritus,
Indiana University School of Nursing

The Quiet Millionaire

The Quiet Millionaire

Eliminate Financial Stress and Accumulate Wealth for a Lifetime of Security and Independence

Brett Wilder, Certified Financial Planner™

**President and Chief Executive Officer,
Financial Management Group, Inc.**

FMG Publishing, Inc.
Cincinnati, OH

Disclaimer This book is intended to provide information in regard to the subject matter covered. Although the author and publisher have made every effort to ensure the accuracy and completeness of information contained in this book, we assume no responsibility for errors, inaccuracies, omissions, or any inconsistency herein. Any slights of people, places, or organizations are unintentional. Names and identifying details have been changed to protect confidentiality, and events describing real-life situations have been compressed and combined.

This book is sold with the understanding that the author and the publisher are not engaged in rendering tax, legal, accounting, investment, or other professional services. If legal or other expert assistance is required, the services of competent professionals should be sought. The purpose of this book is to educate. The author and the publisher shall have neither liability nor responsibility to any person or entity with respect to any loss or damage caused, or alleged to be caused, directly or indirectly by the information contained in this book.

If you do not wish to be bound by the above, you may return this book to the publisher for a full refund.

ATTENTION CORPORATIONS, PROFESSIONAL ORGANIZATIONS, UNIVERSITIES, AND COLLEGES: Quantity discounts are available on bulk purchases of this book for educational, gift purposes, or as premiums for increasing magazine subscriptions or renewals. Special books or book excerpts can also be created to fit specific needs. For information, please contact FMG Publishing, Inc. 10979 Reed Hartman Hwy. Suite 209, Cincinnati, OH 45242.

Published by FMG Publishing, Inc.
10979 Reed Hartman Hwy., Suite 209
Cincinnati, OH 45242

Publisher's Cataloging-in-Publication Data
Wilder, Brett.
The quiet millionaire : eliminate financial stress and accumulate wealth for a lifetime of security and independence / by Brett Wilder. – Cincinnati, OH : FMG Pub., Inc., 2009.

p. ; cm.

ISBN: 978-0-9787720-1-7

1. Finance, Personal—Handbooks, manuals, etc. 2. Saving and investment—Handbooks, manuals, etc. I. Title.

HG179 .W529 2009
332.024—dc22   2008937586

Printed in the United States of America
13 12 11 10 09 • 5 4 3 2 1

Contents

Acknowledgments

For me, writing a book is comparable to raising a child in that it requires a relentless commitment and you do not know for sure how it is going to eventually turn out and when to let go. My journey for writing *The Quiet Millionaire* started five years ago, and many people have accompanied, supported, and guided me along the way to reach the final destination.

Foremost, I want to acknowledge my loyal, supportive, and skilled ensemble of work associates at the Financial Management Group Inc. for enabling me to have the quiet time away from the daily business operation that I needed to write and produce *The Quiet Millionaire*. Thank you—Dave Wilder, Rob Siegmann, Brock Dexter, Chrissie Smith, Jon Andre, Kristin Wiechert, Amy McKiddy, and Michaela Marquardt—for being the very special people that you are both professionally and personally. I feel so blessed to have each of you by my side every day.

I wish to thank René Steinkamp for traveling the road with me from the very beginning to the end even though she has her own busy road to travel. She provided creative thinking and emotional support all along the way and guided me through endless rewrites and edits. Her generous presence when I needed it made the overwhelming challenge of writing a book manageable.

I want to express my gratitude to Jerry Jenkins and his team of professionals at the Jenkins Group Inc. In particular, to Leah Nicholson for making me be accountable to produce by certain deadlines new material for her review. Her encouraging feedback helped me get beyond the times when I doubted whether I could meet my expectation for writing a quality book having a worthwhile message. She rekindled my motivation when I lost direction and enthusiasm for the journey. At one very critical crossroad, Leah removed all my immobilizing self-doubt when she said, "What I see is good and needs to be written. So, just do it." That, coming from her as a writer and a professional in the book publishing industry, encouraged me to continue with confidence.

Additionally, I want to express my appreciation to the two very talented editors who transformed my disorganized, raw manuscript into a polished book. Thank you, Diana Morris, for your creativity and organization and for the idea to brand the concept of the *quiet millionaire*® throughout the book. Thank you, Devon Ritter, for your incredibly detailed editing to professionalize my writing and make it conform to the rules for book publishing.

Regrettably, because of limited space I cannot begin to acknowledge individually the scores of other people who contributed their time and talents to provide me the feedback and direction I sought as I traveled the lonely course but never alone. You know who you are, and I am so very appreciative for your thoughtful and enthusiastic responses to my requests for your help. I am truly humbled and deeply honored by your willingness to help me and have done my very best to make all of you proud of the part you played in the development of *The Quiet Millionaire*.

Introduction

Achieving millionaire status used to be a noteworthy financial accomplishment. Today, it is necessary to be a millionaire in order to have a financially independent and secure lifestyle. Everyone's life is unique, yet there are common elements to the financial and investment management process in order to be successful. This book will share some true-life situations derived from my experiences with clients (whose confidentiality has been preserved). Their stories help explain issues and motivate you toward taking appropriate action for being financially successful without having to experience some of the unnecessary trials and tribulations.

Being a millionaire is a realistic aspiration if you are knowledgeable and diligent about becoming one. This book is about how to become and stay the quiet millionaire® in the twenty-first century. It will guide you through the opportunities and pitfalls you face in managing today's fast-changing and challenging lifetime issues with respect to your financial life. The financial journey of the quiet millionaire® can be your journey if you so wisely choose.

In order to be secure about not outliving your financial resources, you are responsible for accumulating and keeping greater amounts of money than the previous generations. Furthermore, you must invest very wisely in order to assure that your returns outpace inflation. During the twenty-first century, many of the old "tried and true" ways for accumulating money are worthwhile and can still work. However, there are also new and previously unknown ways and opportunities for achieving financial success—yet with more hazards for suffering failure and hardship.

The financial topics selected for this book cover all the areas that should be included in a comprehensive financial management review. Some areas discussed will be more applicable than others, or they may not apply currently to your situation. However, it is likely that at some point in your life, the information will apply to you, and therefore it will be relevant for how to become and how to stay the quiet millionaire®. Also, the content is arranged in a sequence that logically tracks your financial progression while showing you how to set and work toward your financial goals and objectives. In order to focus your attention on the gems of the quiet millionaire® approach to accumulating and keeping wealth in the twenty-first century, throughout each chapter there are **Quiet Millionaire® Wisdom** highlights, and at the end of each chapter, there is a **Quiet Millionaire® Summary**.

In today's technology age, we are constantly being bombarded with financial information from many sources, which you must be able to discern and distinguish as being beneficially useful or as being harmfully useless to your financial life. The quiet millionaire® is one who stays informed yet has learned how to tune out the daily financial noise that can be confusing and contradictory. Proven financial management strategies are discussed. At times, they might be contrary to the typical advice being given out by unregulated, ill-informed, and often irresponsible media and by the many different types of financial advisors. You should be aware that this misinformation exists, and you will be alerted on how to spot it.

Financial and investment management must be approached in a knowledgeable, comprehensive, and coordinated manner. The information presented in this book provides you with a clear big-picture overview about how to become and stay the quiet millionaire®. Therefore, while the book is comprehensive in scope, the material is presented in a concise manner, is straightforward and honest, and is without the hidden agendas that can often occur in the financial services industry.

You may decide that as a result of the complexity and long-term ramifications of your decisions, you need the assistance of a professional financial advisor. Seeking a financial advisor is similar to seeing a doctor about maintaining your physical health or an attorney to solve complex legal matters. As with any professional advisory relationship, you must believe it to be trustworthy, competent, and objective, with no agenda other than to do the very best for you. While there are very good and dedicated professionals competently advising people, you must go through an intelligent and thorough due diligence process in order to find the right trustworthy advisor for your particular financial situation.

If you follow the advice in this book, you will be properly prepared to select, and work with, a professional advisor before you hire one. You will know what to look for in a good financial advisor, and you will know whether your situation justifies paying for an advisor's help. Working with the right advisor can, and should, enhance your financial situation and provide you

xiv ■ The Quiet Millionaire

with more comfort about money matters. Moreover, your money will better serve you and your loved ones.

Financial miracles do happen, but the quiet millionaire® does not wait for a miracle in order to become financially successful. Depending upon what and how much you want, you need to commit to taking action and to making some well-thought-out, informed choices regarding what is really important to you and your financial life. This may require you to throw in some willing sacrifices, steadfast perseverance, and rolled-up-sleeve hard work.

Use the knowledge you learn from this book as the engine for becoming and staying the quiet millionaire® and the money you gain from implementing the recommended strategies as the fuel. By applying the same knowledge to your situation, you will have more control over your financial life; by using the same strategies, you will have more peace about your financial security.

And last, after reading **The Quiet Millionaire**, I would be interested in having your feedback. You can contact me at *brett@quiet-millionaire.com*. May you become and stay the quiet millionaire® with a life of enriched personal happiness in the twenty-first century!

—Brett Wilder

CHAPTER ONE

What Is Important about Money to You?

The quiet millionaire's® life has a purposeful direction, and it is pointed in the direction of a planned, charted course. The quiet millionaire® does not live just for today, drifting aimlessly, being consumed by life's daily activities, or mistakenly thinking that tomorrow will take care of itself. Rather, the quiet millionaire® does give thought about tomorrow and knowingly commits to funding goals and objectives and to being protected against that stormy day. A financial course is carefully mapped out to assure arrival at specified destinations in life. The quiet millionaire® is intelligent and mindful about how to have financial independence and security in order to flow with the happy currents of the life he or she chooses to pursue.

The ways to become and stay the quiet millionaire® in the twenty-first century apply equally to both men and women. However, too often married women are disinterested in finances

> **QUIET MILLIONAIRE® WISDOM**
> *If you do not know where you are going, you will not know how to get there.*

and assume a passive role in preparing for their financial future, which can be a costly mistake because statistics reflect that married women have a high probability of becoming either divorced or widowed in their lifetime. This combination of circumstances is why some women become overwhelmed and vulnerable in the event of having to manage their own financial affairs. Therefore, women, whether married or single, can benefit as well as men from the financial management wisdom set down in this book.

Think carefully about this:

■ If you had all the money you needed now and in the future, what would you be doing differently from what you are doing today?

■ If you knew that you had only a few years to live, what specifically would you change about your life now?

■ If you had complete freedom to decide, what unfulfilled dreams would you pursue, and which people would you choose to enrich your life?

■ If you had to refocus your life in order to pursue your unfulfilled dreams, what meaningless activities that waste your time would you eliminate, and what people who you do not enjoy would you avoid?

The quiet millionaire® knows the answers to these questions and makes sure that his or her time is spent wisely and meaningfully in order to live life to the fullest extent without regrets.

**Discover who the *real* you is and
what you *really* want out of life.**

How you spend your time should reflect what you truly want from life. Mistakenly, people often are too busy with the daily activities *in* their lives to devote the necessary time and energy to working *on* their lives. Figuring out who you are and what you want from life requires some serious devotion to the task. In essence, you should establish a sense of true identity for yourself.

This means stepping back and taking time to contemplate and figure out what the "gut meaning" of life is for you, what your burning desires are, what your greatest fears are, and in what ways you want to be enriched and satisfied. You need to delve into your inner soulful self in order to figure out what enlightens you and what will sustain your commitment toward making happen what you want to happen.

Furthermore, these questions need to be addressed repeatedly throughout your life to make sure that you are staying true to your course and that your ideals and core desires have not changed. Only by periodically taking time to think about and internalize honest responses to these questions can you chart a course and make adjustments along the way to achieve what it is that you *really* want.

Be aware that there are blockages that can sidetrack your thought process. Procrastination is a major roadblock, as is finding private uninterrupted time. Yet, in order to truly experience your feelings and listen to your inner voice as you evolve through the discovery process, you must find quiet space and time.

You can also choose to become more conscious about how you are spending your time. Are you allowing distractions, disruptions, and commitments to interfere with what you need to be doing? Are television, movies, computer games, and other "easy" forms of escape robbing you of quality quiet time? If so, then focus on ways to change being in those ruts. Remember that the often-used definition of "crazy" is doing the same thing over and over and expecting a different result.

While in this self-discovery process, you also need to manage the expectations of others on you. This includes family, friends, and work associates, who may unknowingly rob you of time during this evaluation process. One way to manage this is to include family members into your thinking. Schedule meetings for discussion, and focus on what the family's direction and objectives are and what the overall dreams and expectations are for each individual family member. Then, address in order of importance everyone's dreams and goals.

Only by working together can the family as a whole see what conflicts of interest there may be and what goals need to be evaluated and changed and then as a group determine and resolve any discrepancies that could hinder the success for achieving each other's goals. In order to have a better opportunity for attaining your own goals, you must derive harmonious consensus and support from those around you. With priorities set for desired goals and objectives, planning can be done accordingly and strategies can be implemented harmoniously without incurring unnecessary conflict and stress.

Friends and social commitments can consume your time also. Most of us need to be social and participate in activities with others in life. However, often it gets out of hand and can consume a disproportionate amount of your time. Pay attention to the purpose and quality of outside friends and activities. Learn to say "no" sometimes. Also, be more selective about who you invite into your life. Do not become a "slurpee to the slurpers" who tend to pull you down instead of enrich your life. This does not mean you should not be available to help others who might be struggling with a particular difficult issue. However, there are those who choose to whine and gossip their way through life, and you are better off avoiding them.

With respect to your employment, when you go to work, work! Make the best use of your time and do so efficiently; get done what needs to be done within a normal workday. This way, you can structure a more balanced life and avoid a potential "burnout" situation. Work can always demand more of your time if you let it. However, in the end, you will not feel satisfied by having worked more hours than anybody else, resulting in leading an empty, unfulfilled life full of regrets outside of the workplace. People will not come to your funeral and say, "I'll always remember him—he was a great guy, and he worked more hours

> QUIET MILLIONAIRE® WISDOM
> *True personal self-discovery requires access to your subconscious thoughts.*

than anybody." All of us are dispensable, as it should be, but our egos do not want us to believe that. Yet, it is amazing how things can in fact go on nicely when you are not there, and if for some reason things do not, then it is most likely an ineffective work management issue.

Two Methods for Personal Self-Discovery

Here are two methods for personal self-discovery that can help you learn more about your inner self. Both methods serve a different purpose and provide a different outcome.

Listening to Yourself

The first method is termed "listening to yourself." This process will help you to become more *honest* with yourself. I came upon this while I was trying to decide what to do about my financially rewarding but unsettling career in banking. I wanted to make a change but was anxious, uncertain, and immobilized about what to do. I had bought the book titled *What Color Is Your Parachute?* by Richard Bolles (updated annually), and it provided me with thought-provoking exercises to structure my career change thinking. However, I was struggling to commit with conviction about making the changes. I would sit and talk to myself out loud about the changes I wanted to make. By chance, I decided to tape record some of what I was thinking in order not to forget my thoughts.

An interesting thing happened when I played my words back. I did not recognize the ideas that I was hearing as mine. It was like someone else was saying the words, and some of it sounded like pipe dreams, while other ideas sounded wonderful. Listening to myself forced me to speak more truthfully about what I wanted and how I was going to get there.

The tape recorder revealed the dishonesty I had with myself. At the time, I was seriously considering an offer from an investment advisory firm located in California. The firm wanted me to join, and I was excited about the offer. However, listening to myself discuss the opportunity revealed my honest feelings. I did not really like the person in charge, and I did not feel comfortable with the firm's investment approach or business culture. It was my ego that had been ruling my thinking. The result of my tape-recorded self-conversation was that I turned down the offer much to the firm's and my surprise.

Continuing with this "listening to yourself" approach, I came to realize without any doubt that I could never work for another employer in the financial services industry. I had to be the employer so that I could function entirely on my own inner convictions and "modus operandi." I became ready to commit to that course no matter what the sacrifice. That was when I began my company, the Financial Management Group, Inc. Today, I love what I do. I help people and get paid for it. What better combination can you ask for than that?

Writing to Yourself

The second self-discovery method is termed "writing to yourself." This process has helped me with enhancing my *creativity* and with deciding honestly who I am and what I want to do with my life. The idea here is to develop a free-flowing stream of consciousness, a "just let it rip" approach through writing or journaling. You will realize that this provides structure, consistency, and continuity to your thinking. Every day, in the early quiet morning with a fresh mind, sit down and write out in longhand anything that comes into your mind as quickly as you can without interruption until you have filled up three spiral-bound 8½-by-11 pages. Sometimes, this activity is termed a "fast write," with the writing limited to twenty or thirty minutes.

I emphasize the importance of doing this in written longhand rather than using a computer or typewriter in order to energize the most creative output. Writing longhand stimulates the flow of creative juices from within that are closer to the heart, which will help you to find out what makes you feel happy and fulfilled. Write down anything that enters your mind, and do not worry about punctuation, correct spelling, or complete sentences. This is for your eyes only. It is personal. Here is where you do your whining, list personal to do's, and let out your fears, your anger, your dreams, your ambitions. It does not matter what you write; just write whatever comes out as fast as you can without interruption or inhibition.

Remember, these writings are your private thoughts and not for anyone else to read. Therefore, in order not to inhibit your written content, keep it private and well hidden so that you can feel completely free to "let it all out." Although many times you may not feel like doing this spontaneous writing, and you can make tons of excuses for not following through (procrastination), I cannot stress enough how important it is that you write every single day without fail. You will be amazed at how much creative output and perspective will come forth to reveal your inner desires and excite you into taking action.

If you are truly motivated to learn about your inner self and not just drift through life aimlessly, you will figure out your own most productive ways to use these techniques, to overcome immobilization and blockages, and to make the necessary changes. Furthermore, you will be surprised at your newfound energy and will become more committed over time as you think more and more about what is *really* important to you, your life, and your money.

**Money is the fuel for achieving your
life goals and objectives.**

Money is emotional and reflects many of our inner needs and desires. Knowing your own money values helps to chart the directions you need to take in making life choices. Every choice made for using money, whether it is for capitalizing a career or structuring a happy home environment, a joyous family lifestyle, or a secure retirement, depends upon how you *personally* value money. You must make sure your values are harmonious with your goals and objectives. Otherwise, there will not be a burning desire to set down and commit to achieving those desired goals and objectives.

How to Know What Is Important about Money to You

Because everyone thinks differently about the importance of money, these differences can often cause financial conflict with others as well as within you. The importance of money goes beyond the goods and services it can provide. It plays a critical role in our ability to pursue goals, dreams, and desires. Attitudes about money vary according to each individual's personality and ideals typically formulated and influenced by family background experiences involving the availability and usage of money.

Knowing what is important about money helps you make sure that your specified objectives and goals in life are in sync with your attitude toward money. If this is out of sync, then you will have inner conflict, which decreases your likelihood for rewarding financial success. This will cause you to be insufficiently motivated to commit to the financial strategies required for accomplishing your goals and objectives.

There are also psychological reasons, some healthy and some unhealthy, as to why you feel the way you do about money. Your financial decisions—good and bad—throughout life reflect your money personality. Starting during childhood, your family, your peers, and your society influence your attitude about money in general. Your success or failure with money depends upon how well you understand and assimilate and respond to these influences. You need to know your "true money self" in order to be financially comfortable with your money.

Learning what is important about money to you involves a building block–type self-questioning process. The following story about Walter's background and how his own particular questions evolved to pinpoint his true money self exemplify the way the process works.

> *Walter is a quiet millionaire®. He grew up as an only child in a blue-collar neighborhood and always heard his parents arguing about money. His father worked varying shifts in a paper mill and was frequently laid off and called back until the company eventually closed. When Walter's father was home, he was usually drunk and physically and verbally abusive. Walter's mother always accused his father of being a "poor provider," and his father would say that their financial problems started when Walter was born. He also told Walter, "You will never amount to anything."*

The following were the building block questions that Walter went through to flush out the *most* important reason why he truly values money.

Q: When you think about **money**, what is important about money to *you*?

A: *It provides financial security.*

Q: Why is having **financial security** important about money to you?

A: *It eliminates worry about money.*

Q: Why is **eliminating worry** about money important about money to you?

A: *I can spend without financial stress.*

Q: Why is **spending without financial stress** important about money to you?

A: *I can live a comfortable and peaceful lifestyle without concern.*

Q: Why is living a **comfortable and peaceful lifestyle** without concern important about money to you?

A: *I am being a good financial provider.*

Q: Why is being a **good financial provider** important about money to you?

A: *My family loves and respects me.*

Q: Why is having your family's **love and respect** important about money to you?

A: *I feel a high sense of self-worth.*

As you can see, the importance of money for Walter evolved from financial security to discover that the *real* value of money for him is that it provides **self-worth**. This is what really drove him to become a quiet millionaire® and most influences how and why he accumulates and spends money.

Some Reasons Why Money Is Important

Everyone's self-discovery about the importance of money is unique. The questioning process builds a personalized set of evolving questions and answers until no further answers are forthcoming. The following are some examples of what is important about money to people:

- **Security:** Having enough money to live without the fear of becoming impoverished is comforting, especially for anyone who has lived through or been preached to about tough financial times. Fear is a powerful emotion that can highly motivate some people to focus on saving as much money as possible but also possibly can cause them to be too risk adverse with their investments to keep up with inflation.

- **Freedom:** Being able to have enough money to live a meaningful life the way you choose, as well as occupationally work with enthusiasm and bliss, is healthy and exciting. Intelligent financial management allows you to be a money master, not a money slave.

- **Gaining love:** There's an old cliché that says, "Money can't buy you love." However, in a money-driven world, some people are, in fact, driven to have money in order to attract the opposite sex into their lives and find genuine love.

- **Respect:** Because money is respected, people often equate having money with a means for having the respect they strive to receive from others.

- **Power:** Money is a powerful force that can influence and control other people in either a positive or negative way.

- **Happiness:** While money may or may not bring happiness, it certainly can help to make life more enjoyable. However, spending money sometimes is merely a temporary mood elevator and can lead to financial trouble. Living for the present moment can create short-term excitement at the expense of long-term peace of mind and financial security.

- **Self-worth:** Some people measure their self-worth by the amount of their net worth, while other people may have a high sense of self-worth that in no way correlates with the amount of money they have.
- **Accomplishment:** Money is often used as a scorecard for achievement and success.
- **Entitlement:** Some people feel that having money is an earned right because of past struggles and disappointments in their life.
- **Helping others:** Very often, money enables people to give back to help others because they themselves were given to and feel fortunate.

Remember that your own self-discovery about what is important about money to you may evolve to some facet of money importance that is beyond this list. The objective is to discover what you really feel and truly believe is important about money to you in order to understand the reasons behind your earning, saving, and spending activities, which can be financially healthy or unhealthy and may require adjustments to be made.

Start your own Q&A process with the first question: When you think about money, what is most important about money to you? Then, with your answer, build your next question, Why is (answer) important about money to you? Continue until there are no more answers.

Once you have discovered the *most important* reason that is important about money to you, then you can determine what lifetime events in your background may have influenced your current attitude and emotions about money. You will learn whether your motivations for having and spending money are truly healthy, positive, and worthwhile or whether they are negative and troublesome. This knowledge can help reduce conflict about money within yourself as well as with significant others, and you can then properly prioritize and focus with motivation how you earn, accumulate, manage, and spend money.

The following Q&A money self-discovery process for Lola serves as an example of how important it is to learn as early as possible why money is important to you.

Q: When you think about *money*, what is important about money to you?
A: *I like to own nice things.*

Q: Why is the ability to *own nice things* important about money to you?
A: *My surroundings are important to me.*

Q: Why are *your surroundings* important about money to you?
A: *It makes me feel happy.*

Q: Why is *feeling happy* important to you?
A: *I deserve to feel happy because I've always had to work hard and sacrifice for money.*

Lola's money self-discovery process revealed that money is important to her because of **entitlement**. She felt strongly that she had earned the right to spend money and be happy. However, this ingrained belief became unhealthy when uncontrollable impulsive spending resulted, which created an overwhelming amount of unmanageable debt and financial conflict that destroyed her marriage. The good news is that by understanding her money self, she was able, with professional help, to adjust her attitude about money, rebuild her life, and find real happiness.

As Walter's and Lola's money self-discovery outcomes show, we all have different psychological and emotional reasons for the importance of money. I personally discovered that money is most important to me because I want **financial freedom** to live an independent life by choice rather than by obligation. This attitude started as a very young child when I mowed lawns, shoveled snow, sold Christmas cards, and worked underage for a grocery store *and* a hardware store at the same time. I hustled around to earn as much money as I could in order not to be dependent upon a whimsical weekly allowance. I rushed through childhood to become an independent adult and my own master of money.

> **QUIET MILLIONAIRE® WISDOM**
> *Let money be your servant, not your master.*

For me, money is not about acquiring a lot of "things." That causes money to become my master. Instead, I feel more comfortable being able to have things of value and to give without obligation being expected. Being able to do this is what makes money important for me and drives my thinking about the way I choose to live and manage my priorities.

Be a Master over Your Money

In order to be a master over your money and to control your own future rather than let money be the master over you, you must learn to manage your money and let it be the fuel for building a life of happiness and fulfillment. Only then will you know how to best balance living for the present moment while planning for the future.

There are times when some people may seek help to understand their money self from professionals such as financial advisors and psychologists. However, there are some professionals who do not take the time themselves to learn what is important about money to them. Furthermore, some financial advisors often base their financial review and recommendations for you in a manner that can be biased toward what is more in their best self-interest or beliefs than what is in line with yours. So, make sure that any professional guidance relates to your true inner self and why money is important to you in order to take the best direction in life for you.

Where are you going, and how are you going to get there?

Knowing where you are going and how you are going to get there require more than vague statements such as, "I want to be rich" or "I want to own my own business." These are wishes, not specified goals and objectives.

> *"If one advances confidently in the direction of his dreams and endeavors to live life which he has imagined, he will meet with a success unexpected in common hours."*
>
> **—Henry David Thoreau**

While this is a wonderful famous quote and it is OK to dream and imagine, the "unexpected success" requires that you take motivated action based upon honest and much more specific answers than mere dreamful wishes. *"You have to be specific in order to be terrific"* is an easy way to remember that you need to quantify specifically your direction and how you are going to get there. For example, if sending your children to college is important, then you need to know the amount of money required in order to make that goal happen, and you need to know how you are going to set aside enough money in the proper time frame.

Knowing the specifics can make any necessary sacrifices more palatable. The previously discussed daily journaling can help you unlock the best and most specific direction for you to take. If you are highly motivated to accumulate what is necessary to achieve a specified goal, you will more likely be committed to living more simply today in order to save like crazy for that future goal such as buying your dream house, going into business for yourself, funding college for children, or retiring by a certain age. And, most important, you will be well on your way to becoming and staying the quiet millionaire®.

Quiet Millionaire® Summary

■ Discover who the *real* you is and what you *really* want out of life.

■ Use the two methods for personal self-discovery to tap into your subconscious thoughts for truth and creativity.

■ Use the building block questioning process to determine what is important about money to you.

■ Plan to make sure money is your servant, not your master.

■ Be specific about where you are going and how you are going to get there in order to become and stay the quiet millionaire®.

CHAPTER TWO

The Financial
Management Review™

If you want to become and stay the quiet millionaire®, you must plan and manage your financial way of life. You need to implement the most appropriate strategies for achieving the results you want and then monitor and measure the actual results against your expected results. You must be proactive in order to attain the financial life you want. By doing this, you will overcome the seven major obstacles to financial success.

The Seven Major Obstacles
to Financial Success

1. **Undisciplined Spending:** Spending impulsively, spending more than you make, and not tracking where your money is going.

2. **Materialistic Thinking:** Preoccupation with owning physical assets and things rather than pursuing intellectual and spiritual endeavors to enrich your life.

3. **Burdensome Costly Debt:** Irrational, unintelligent, compulsive, wealth-robbing borrowing.

4. **Taxes:** A governmental levy that should be proactively reduced in magnitude at all times.

5. **Inflation:** The silent erosion of wealth and purchasing power.

6. **Poorly Structured Investment Portfolios:** Undiversified investments possessing an unjustifiable amount of risk relative to the potential for reward.

7. **Unforeseen Life-Changing, Financially Devastating Events:** The major financial risks we all share in life: catastrophic medical expenses, divorce, job loss, disability, death, lawsuits, and long-term health care expenses.

The Financial Management Review™ (FMR)

In order for you to proactively overcome these obstacles and be organized to knowledgeably map out your path to financial success, I recommend that you use a personalized, comprehensive, and fully coordinated planning process I developed called the **Financial Management Review™ (FMR)**. By understanding and using the tools for this review process discussed throughout this book, you will become aware of what is required to build a well-constructed financial house and how to become and/or stay the quiet millionaire®.

To help you get started with the FMR process, there are sample FMR worksheets in this chapter for you to use in order to gather and input your own financial data. For your convenience, the worksheets are also available for you to print out at the Web site *www.quietmillionaire.com.* You can develop your own system for

organizing your FMR data and information, but one way to organize it is
to put the material in a binder separated according to the chapter topics
for your ready use and referral as
you read about the financial and

> **QUIET MILLIONAIRE® WISDOM**
> *Use qualified professionals to make certain your financial house is well constructed.*

investment management topics being discussed and as they apply to
your situation in each of the chapters.

While you might be able to build your financial house on your
own without the guidance of a professional, the final construction may be shoddy, the required maintenance may be poor, and
therefore the results may not be the best ones for you. For these
reasons, you should seriously consider working with a qualified
professional who possesses all of the necessary tools in his or her
financial tool kit and the right skills to advise you on how to
build and maintain your complete financial house.

In any event, working with a professional financial advisor is for
you to decide upon as you learn what is required to do the job
right. Remember that this is not intended to be a "how to do it
yourself" book, although there is a lot of the FMR process that
you can do by yourself if you devote the required amount of time
and purchase and properly use the required tools. By reading
this book and completing the data gathering worksheets, you will
be ready with "blueprints" to use yourself or to show an advisor
who can help you with the construction of your financial house.
Furthermore, if you decide to use a financial advisor, you will
also learn by reading the material how to hire a financial advisor
who is right for you and how to know whether the advisor is
worthwhile, as well as what results you should expect.

Financial Management Review™ Worksheets

Document Gathering Checklist Figure 2-1
Financial Management Review Questionnaire Figure 2-2

Cash Flow Planning Worksheet Figure 2-3
Financial Statement Planning Worksheet Figure 2-4
Insurance Planning Worksheet Figure 2-5
College Planning Worksheet Figure 2-6
Retirement Planning Worksheet Figure 2-7
Estate Planning Worksheet Figure 2-8

If used properly, the Financial Management Review™ never becomes stale or useless. It serves as an ongoing informational tool that incorporates any adjustments required as your financial situation changes and monitors and measures the results of strategies you have implemented and put in place. In the appendix at the back of the book is a sample of a completed Financial Management Review in order to give you a visual snapshot of the review's format and results that are produced from the information gathering and review process. The ultimate purpose of the Financial Management Review is to determine whether your current financial position is relative to what you need to do in order to become and stay the quiet millionaire®.

> QUIET MILLIONAIRE® WISDOM
> *No goals, no plans, no strategies, no perseverance, no financial success!*

The review process begins with comprehensive information gathering. Use the **Document Gathering Checklist** as shown in Figure 2-1 to do this for your own situation. Be aware that the checklist is comprehensive in order to cover as many different situations as possible, so disregard the listed items that do not apply to you. The gathered information should include all that is applicable to both partners in a couple's relationship.

As you assemble the listed document gathering checklist items that apply to you for the preparation of your Financial Management Review, use this opportunity to organize and weed out the information and the documents according to "what you need to keep" and "what you can get rid of." The result of this financial "house cleaning" is to give you more control over your financial situation. Furthermore, you might even find long-forgotten items, such as not so valuable lapsed life insurance policies, as well as some very valuable items, such as stock certificates and government E Bonds.

FIGURE 2-1   Document Gathering Checklist

Employment Information
❏   Two Most Recent Detailed Paycheck Stubs

Employee Benefit Manual Descriptions
❏   Group Life Insurance
❏   Group Medical/Dental Insurance
❏   Group Disability Insurance
❏   Pension, Profit-Sharing Plans
❏   Stock Option, Deferred Compensation Plans
❏   401(k), 403(b) Plans
❏   ESOP, Employee Stock Purchase Plan
❏   Tax Sheltered Annuities (TSAs)
❏   Most Recent Account Statements for above Plans
❏   Annual Benefits Summary Statement

Individual Policies and Most Recent Statements
❏   Life Insurance
❏   Annuities
❏   Disability Income
❏   Hospitalization/Major Medical
❏   Automobile
❏   Homeowner/Renter's
❏   Other Property Insurance
❏   Personal Liability Umbrella

Individual Tax Returns
❏   Two Most Recent Federal and State Tax Returns

Investment Account Statements
❏   Bank Accounts, CDs (with Yield and Maturity Date)
❏   Brokerage Accounts
❏   Mutual Fund/Dividend Reinvestment Accounts

(continues)

FIGURE 2-1   Document Gathering Checklist (*continued*)

❏ IRA/Keogh/Pension Accounts
❏ Real Estate (Original Cost, Market Value, Date Acquired, Original Mortgage Amount, Term, Interest Rate, Taxes, Payment)
❏ Real Estate Rental Properties (Same as above)

Loan Schedules
❏ Residence (Original Mortgage Amount, Term, Interest Rate)
❏ Autos
❏ Line of Credit, Second Mortgage
❏ Business, Other

Legal Documents
❏ Wills, Trusts, Living Wills, Durable Powers of Attorney for Financial and Health Care, Prenuptial Agreement

Business Documents
❏ Two Most Recent Tax Returns, Federal and State
❏ Articles of Incorporation, Limited Liability Company, or Partnership Agreement
❏ Two Most Recent Financial Statements
❏ Buy-Sell, Stock Redemption, Split Dollar, and Other Agreements
❏ Value of Business and Stock or Ownership Percentages
❏ Plan Documents and Most Recent Statements for Qualified Retirement Plans, Deferred Compensation Plans, Business Insurance Coverage

In order to prepare the Financial Management Review, you will also need to complete the various data input exhibits for the **Financial Management Review Questionnaire** and the **Planning Worksheets**. As another reminder, for your convenience, you can go to the Web site *www.quietmillionaire.com* and print the document gathering checklist and the Financial Management Review questionnaire as well as the various planning worksheets. The planning worksheets will be referred to as the specific worksheet topics are discussed in various chapters. By gathering your data and completing the Financial Management Review questionnaire as well as the planning worksheets as they are referred to, you will gain a perspective for the comprehensiveness of the Financial Management Review process.

FIGURE 2-2   Financial Management Review™ Questionnaire

Your Name _____	U.S. Citizen	Yes ❑ No ❑
Home Address _____		
Home Phone _____	Home E-mail _____	
Employer _____	How Long _____	
Occupation _____	Work E-mail _____	
Work Phone _____	Birth Date _____	
Spouse Name _____	U.S. Citizen	Yes ❑ No ❑
Employer _____	How Long _____	
Occupation _____	Work E-mail _____	
Work Phone _____	Birth Date _____	

Current Financial Management Status
(Please circle your answers)

CASH FLOW MANAGEMENT

Do you have a spending plan or budget?	Yes	No	Don't Know
Do you monitor your expenses?	Yes	No	Don't Know
Is your cash flow positive?	Yes	No	Don't Know
Are you saving enough for future funding requirements?	Yes	No	Don't Know

MORTGAGE and OTHER DEBT MANAGEMENT

Do you own your home?	Yes	No	Don't Know
Do you plan on moving?	Yes	No	Don't Know
Do you plan on buying another home?	Yes	No	Don't Know
Do you need or plan to refinance your home mortgage?	Yes	No	Don't Know
Have you had a mortgage or refinancing analysis done?	Yes	No	Don't Know
Do you have a home equity line of credit?	Yes	No	Don't Know
Do you have multiple credit cards?	Yes	No	Don't Know
Do you pay off credit balances monthly?	Yes	No	Don't Know

TAX PLANNING

Are you satisfied with the amount of taxes you pay?	Yes	No	Don't Know
Are you using all the legal tax loopholes to reduce your taxes?	Yes	No	Don't Know
Do you know the difference between tax preparation and tax planning?	Yes	No	Don't Know
Do you prepare your own tax returns?	Yes	No	Don't Know

INVESTMENT PLANNING

Do you feel you need better financial organization?	Yes	No	Don't Know
Has your current portfolio been reviewed by an independent advisor?	Yes	No	Don't Know

(continues)

FIGURE 2-2   Financial Management Review™ Questionnaire (*continued*)

Do you have sufficient cash flow to meet your monthly expenses?	Yes	No	Don't Know
Do you feel that better budget planning would be helpful?	Yes	No	Don't Know
Does your portfolio protect you from financial disaster?	Yes	No	Don't Know
Is your portfolio safe from a stock and bond market crash?	Yes	No	Don't Know
Do you have adequate investment asset diversification?	Yes	No	Don't Know
Does your portfolio protect you from inflation?	Yes	No	Don't Know
Does your portfolio match your risk and tolerance?	Yes	No	Don't Know
Do you plan on making additional investments in the future?	Yes	No	Don't Know

RISK MANAGEMENT/INSURANCE

Do you feel you are paying too much for your insurance coverage?	Yes	No	Don't Know
Do you have the right kind and amount of insurance coverage?	Yes	No	Don't Know
Has all current insurance had an objective, independent review?	Yes	No	Don't Know

EMPLOYMENT BENEFITS

Are you taking full advantage of all of your company benefits?	Yes	No	Don't Know
Have you done proper planning with your company stock options?	Yes	No	Don't Know
Do you expect an increase in income?	Yes	No	Don't Know
Do you plan on changing jobs?	Yes	No	Don't Know
Do you know whether your company retirement plans are adequate?	Yes	No	Don't Know

BUSINESS OWNERSHIP PLANNING

Are you using all of the tax loopholes available for your business?	Yes	No	Don't Know
Is your business tax planning coordinated with your personal planning?	Yes	No	Don't Know
Will you be acquiring a business in the future?	Yes	No	Don't Know
Will you be selling your business in the future?	Yes	No	Don't Know
Do you know your business value?	Yes	No	Don't Know
Have you done business succession planning?	Yes	No	Don't Know

EDUCATIONAL PLANNING

Do you have children?	Yes	No	Don't Know
Do you plan on having more children?	Yes	No	Don't Know
Do you have sufficient funds for your children's education?	Yes	No	Don't Know
Is the education money held in the proper name?	Yes	No	Don't Know
Are there any grandchildren you want to help educate?	Yes	No	Don't Know
Have you gifted any money for their education?	Yes	No	Don't Know

(continues)

FIGURE 2-2   Financial Management Review™ Questionnaire (*continued*)

RETIREMENT PLANNING

Are you already retired?	Yes	No	Don't Know
If not, do you plan on retiring soon?	Yes	No	Don't Know
Do you know at what age you would like to retire?	Yes	No	Don't Know
Do you anticipate a rollover of company savings?	Yes	No	Don't Know
Do you anticipate a pension distribution?	Yes	No	Don't Know
Do you already have enough money for a secure retirement?	Yes	No	Don't Know
Will you have enough money for a secure retirement?	Yes	No	Don't Know

ESTATE PLANNING

Do you have wills?	Yes	No	Don't Know
Do you have financial and health care powers of attorney?	Yes	No	Don't Know
Do you have living wills?	Yes	No	Don't Know
Do you have trusts?	Yes	No	Don't Know
Have your estate documents been reviewed recently?	Yes	No	Don't Know
Are your beneficiary designations correct and current?	Yes	No	Don't Know
Are you the beneficiary of any trusts or wills?	Yes	No	Don't Know

COMPREHENSIVE FINANCIAL PLANNING

Do you know what a financial planning professional does?	Yes	No	Don't Know
Do you have a coordinated, integrated financial plan?	Yes	No	Don't Know
Do you spend careful time on planning your finances?	Yes	No	Don't Know
Have you set specific financial goals?	Yes	No	Don't Know
Are you concerned about your financial future?	Yes	No	Don't Know

What are your three most important financial management concerns, goals, or objectives?

1. _____

2. _____

3. _____

FIGURE 2-3   Cash Flow Planning Worksheet

In order to become the quiet millionaire®, you need to manage your money to produce a positive net cash flow. Use this worksheet to implement a cash management program that controls and monitors your current expenditures and to determine what amount of the positive net cash flow must be set aside to reach your specific future goals and objectives. It is important that your cash management system account for *all* expenditures because even **the morning visit to Starbucks can easily become a $1,000 per year unaccountable expense**.

(continues)

FIGURE 2-3   Cash Flow Planning Worksheet (*continued*)

Gross Income	Monthly	Annual
Your Income		
Spouse Income		
Other Income		
Total Gross Income		
Deductions		
Federal Taxes		
State Taxes		
Local Taxes		
Social Security/Medicare Taxes		
Group Employer Benefit Deductions		
401(k) Deduction		
Other Deductions		
Total Deductions		
Expenses		
Residence Mortgage(s)		
Property Taxes		
Rent (*if not homeowner*)		
Car/Lease Payments		
Personal Installment Loans		
Credit Cards		
(*amount if not paid off monthly*)		
Life Insurance		
Health Insurance		
Disability Insurance		
Automobile Insurance		
Homeowner Insurance		
Alimony/Child Support		
Day Care		
Tuition/Education Funding		
Groceries		
Meals Eaten Out		
Gas/Electric/Water		
Telephone/Cell Phone		

(continues)

FIGURE 2-3   Cash Flow Planning Worksheet (*continued*)

	Monthly	Annual
Cable/Internet		
Clothing Purchases/Dry Cleaning		
Medical/Rx/Dental/Eyecare		
Gas/Public Transportation/Parking		
Auto Repair/Maintenance		
Home Repair/Maintenance		
Computer Equipment/Software		
Furniture/Appliances		
Entertainment (*sports, shows, etc.*)		
Gifts for Family/Friends		
Charitable Donations		
Vacations/Travel		
Other		
Total Expenses		
Net Cash Flow		

(*Total gross income minus total deductions/expenses*)

FIGURE 2-4   Financial Statement Planning Worksheet

Your financial statement objective is to have a net worth (assets minus liabilities) of *at least* one million dollars.

ASSETS
Cash Equivalents
Cash _____
Checking and Savings _____
Money Market _____
Certificates of Deposit _____
Other _____

	Personal	Retirement Plans 401(k), IRA, 403(b), etc.
Investments		
Stocks		
Bonds		
Mutual Funds		

(continues)

FIGURE 2-4   Financial Statement Planning Worksheet (*continued*)

Annuities _____ _____
Life Insurance Cash Value _____ _____
Limited Partnerships _____ _____
Other _____ _____

Other Assets (*estimated value*)
Residence _____
Vacation/Second Home _____
Automobiles _____
Personal Property _____
Rental Real Estate _____

Total Assets _____

LIABILITIES
Secured Liabilities

Type	Current Balance	Term of Loan	Monthly Payment	Interest Rate %	Original Amount
Home Mortgage	_____	_____	_____	_____	_____
Second Mortgage	_____	_____	_____	_____	_____
Home Equity Line	_____	_____	_____	_____	_____
Rental Real Estate Mtg.	_____	_____	_____	_____	_____
Automobile Loan	_____	_____	_____	_____	_____
Automobile Loan	_____	_____	_____	_____	_____
Vacation/Second Home Mtg.	_____	_____	_____	_____	_____
Other Loans	_____	_____	_____	_____	_____

Unsecured Liabilities

Type	Current Balance	Monthly Payment	Interest Rate %	Credit Limit
Bank Credit Line	_____	_____	_____	_____
Overdraft Checking	_____	_____	_____	_____
Personal Loans	_____	_____	_____	_____
Credit Card Debt	_____	_____	_____	_____
Other Debt	_____	_____	_____	_____

Total Liabilities _____

NET WORTH _____
(*Total assets minus total liabilities*)

FIGURE 2-5   Insurance Planning Worksheet

The primary purpose of insurance is to protect you and your family from financial *loss* or hardship resulting from a catastrophic event. Your objective is to purchase insurance protection as cost effectively as possible. Most people overpay and/or have the wrong type of insurance. An independent insurance analysis can save you thousands of dollars in premiums and assure the protection you need.

Life Insurance	You	Spouse	Children
Total Group Death Benefit			
Total Individual Benefit			
Cash Value			
Annual Premiums			

Disability Insurance	You	Spouse
Group Coverage (Monthly Benefit)		
Individual Coverage (Monthly Benefit)		
Annual Premiums		

Auto, Homeowner, Personal Liability Umbrella Insurance
(Provide Most Recent Declaration Pages)

Health and Dental Insurance
(Provide Most Recent Benefit and Premium Information)

Long-Term-Care Insurance
(Provide Benefit and Premium Information)

FIGURE 2-6   College Planning Worksheet

(Complete Only If Applicable)

Paying for a college education is a challenging financial commitment that could take away from your savings program for funding a secure retirement. Starting a savings program for college early can mean the difference between having a worry-free retirement and no retirement. Planning on how to pay for college begins with knowing the amount of savings required for funding your commitment.

(continues)

FIGURE 2-6   College Planning Worksheet (*continued*)

Children:	Birth Date	# Yrs to Fund	Starting Age	Cost Per Year in Today's Dollars
Name _____	_____	_____	_____	_____
Name _____	_____	_____	_____	_____
Name _____	_____	_____	_____	_____

Current Annual Savings for College _____

Total Funds Saved to Date_____

Do you know your expected family contribution (EFC) toward the cost of college? Yes ❏   No ❏

FIGURE 2-7   Retirement Planning Worksheet

As with any savings program for funding a future financial objective, the sooner you start, the better. Because we now live longer during our retirement years, more money than ever needs to be accumulated for the security of not running out of money once you stop working. The retirement planning information requested below is used to prepare a retirement cash flow, which shows how much you need to accumulate in order to have a financially secure retirement.

Desired Retirement Age: You _____   Spouse _____

Monthly Retirement Income Desired
(after taxes—in today's dollars)   _____

Current Monthly *Tax-Deferred* Retirement Savings:

You _____   Employer match _____

Spouse _____   Employer match _____

Current Monthly *Non Tax-Deferred* Retirement Savings: _____

You _____

Spouse _____

FIGURE 2-8   Estate Planning Worksheet

If you accumulate significant financial assets, you are targeted for estate taxes besides income and capital gains taxes. Estate planning can protect your assets from lawsuits, unnecessary probate costs, and taxes.

Do you have a valid will for your current state of residence?	Yes ❑	No ❑
Has the will been reviewed and updated recently by an attorney?	Yes ❑	No ❑
Do you have durable financial and health care powers of attorney?	Yes ❑	No ❑
Do you have a living will?	Yes ❑	No ❑
Do you have a revocable living trust?	Yes ❑	No ❑
Do you have an irrevocable trust?	Yes ❑	No ❑
Do you know what the taxes and settlement costs of your estate will be?	Yes ❑	No ❑

Your Financial Management Review process will cover all of the planning topic areas that are specifically applicable to you. The review process should nail down specifically your determined concerns, goals, and objectives and should show where you are now relative to where you want to be and, most important, how to get there. As part of this review, you can make determinations for implementing and monitoring the best strategies to meet your financial goals and objectives.

In order for you to see what the outcome of the Financial Management Review process produces, a sample of a completed Financial Management Review is shown in the appendix at the back of the book and at *www.quietmillionaire.com*. While you should feel free to look at the sample now, it will have more meaning to you once you have completed your journey through the book. Also, keep in mind that everyone's review has different components included and that the illustrated review is just a sampling for you to get an understanding of how comprehensive the review is but yet how concise it is as a useful tool for following up on and monitoring your progress.

Your next step will then be to decide who will be responsible for getting things done and how: you alone or with the assistance from professionals such as a Certified Financial Planner™, Securities and Exchange Commission registered investment advisor, attorney, accountant, etc. Whatever the type of professional you seek, it is imperative that you proactively monitor your Financial Management Review status and progress. Also, it is important to update your financial management and investment portfolio requirements as needed when changes occur in your situation or objectives or as a result of shifting external factors such as changes in the tax laws, the economy, and the investment environment. If this is done properly, the Financial Management Review process will make your life simpler, give you more control of your finances, and help you to become and stay the quiet millionaire®.

Quiet Millionaire® Summary

■ **Always keep in mind the seven major obstacles to financial success.**

■ **Use the Financial Management Review process to overcome these obstacles.**

■ **Print out the Financial Management Review data input forms at *www.quietmillionaire.com* for your use while reading the chapters.**

■ **Keep all of your completed information organized in a hard-copy binder and/or a separate computer file for ongoing referral and monitoring.**

■ **Seek professional assistance for completing any portions of the Financial Management Review process that you are unable to complete on your own. (See Chapter Fifteen for how to find the best financial advisor for *you*.)**

CHAPTER THREE

How to Have a Positive Cash Flow

At times, do you feel overwhelmed by your daily financial commitments as well as the big-dollar obligations such as automobiles, college, and retirement? If so, you are probably not managing your personal finances wisely. Having an out-of-control financial situation can increase your debt and inhibit putting adequate amounts of money aside for future needs. In turn, this often leads to money anxiety, stress, and conflicts. The quiet millionaire® refuses to live this way of life.

Maintaining a positive cash flow is where intelligent personal finance begins. Just as a business needs to be profitable and maintain a healthy cash flow, so does the "business" of running a personal financial life. If successful companies have a financial business plan and cash management systems, then why shouldn't individuals develop a personal financial plan and manage their cash flow as well?

Know Where Your Money Goes

Many Americans earning high incomes are notoriously lax about managing their cash flow because they do not feel pressured financially to account for their spending. We have fallen prey to a disease that is spreading like crazy called "spendicitis." While many affluent family households may not build up a lot of debt to fund their materialistic lifestyles, they often fail to pay enough attention to the fact that they are not saving sufficiently for the big financial commitments, like funding college educations and retirements. Without being aware of it, they are creating a future cash flow problem because they do not evaluate, plan, and save accordingly for their future money requirements.

QUIET MILLIONAIRE® WISDOM
With two employed, there is twice as much chance that one of the earners will lose his or her job than in a single-income household.

The increased number of two-income households has fueled consumer spending. Because of the combined higher income levels, there is a false sense of financial security. Expensive houses, multiple luxury cars, technological gadgets, eating out, expensive vacations, impulsive spending, and borrowing to the hilt have become the norm. Two-income families often depend upon both incomes to pay the bills, and this results in more vulnerability for potential financial trouble. In particular, when an economic recession hits, many dual-income households can experience a devastating loss of earnings and become financially overcommitted.

Keeping more money than you spend and monitoring spending habits eliminates financial stress and struggles. Maintaining a positive cash flow is the only way you can prepare for the unexpected troubled times and accumulate for future needs such as college and retirement funding.

Why good people get into bad financial trouble, causing a stressful life full of anxiety

Impulsive and compulsive spending

With all of the advertising and media enticements for goods and services, it is more difficult than ever to control impulsive and compulsive spending. "Keeping up with the Joneses" has become a hallmark way of life. We are out for more and bigger: homes, stuff for the homes, new cars, another new car, clothes, jewelry, gifts, electronic gadgets—you name it, we want it, we *need* it! Unfortunately, it is easier than ever to get what we want. We do not even have to leave the house to buy things, with the convenience of cable and online shopping. Tempting deals are abound, many are even interest free (for a while), and you often do not have to start paying for it until the next year. You get the picture: the easy dollars spent can add up fast to become potentially devastating cash flow problems for tomorrow.

Poor cash management practices

We know from statistics that most family arguments develop around money issues, sometimes creating irreconcilable differences because an inability to control spending increases emotional conflict and causes further financial damage. Poor cash management practices, leading to financial anxiety and stress, are a major contributor to divorce. Moreover, reckless spending can even force a bankruptcy, an action for high-income earners that is more times than not a result of unintelligent financial management practices.

Poor communications

The quiet millionaire® recognizes that good communication and a sense of working together are the keys to harmonious and successful family financial management. In some families, one person may control how the family's money is spent. In other situations, family members may be spending money just as they please. For successful family financial management, planning meetings and cooperative discussions can be conducted for understanding and agreeing on the family's spending and savings plans. Just as successful companies have scheduled corporate board meetings, so should there be family planning meetings for financial peace and security.

Easy credit borrowing

Overspending often occurs because of today's easy credit borrowing. Even reputable banks behave as irresponsibly as loan sharks, tempting even the most un–credit worthy of households to borrow foolishly. High-interest-rate consumer debt, especially credit cards, is flat out bad for your financial health. Not only are the interest rates high and not tax deductible, but also the impact upon cash flow is horrendous.

For example, the interest cost for $12,000 of credit card debt charging a twenty-one percent interest rate represents a $210 per month or a $2,520 per year out-of-pocket cost, without reducing the debt. In a twenty-five percent income tax bracket, this means that $3,360 must be earned and $840 (25%) in taxes must be paid before the $2,520 in annual credit card interest can be paid. The result is that your hard-earned income is used to merely "rent" money from the credit card companies, valuable money that with controlled borrowing could be in your pocket for additional saving.

Very often high-income earners will not or cannot track where they spend their money, and the biggest dollar expense category on their cash flow worksheet is termed "miscellaneous" or "other." They do not consider that the failure to track their uncontrolled discretionary spending can cause a serious cash flow problem.

Most people are shocked when the totals for their spending categories are accurately accounted for. Especially surprising is how all of the little daily routines can add up so quickly to represent big expenditures. Impulse spending often is a contributing reason for unhealthy credit card borrowing and cash flow crunches.

Automatic Teller Machines (ATMs)

Using automatic teller machines (ATMs) allows ready access to cash that can be easily spent without any recording of the transactions. ATM usage is another reason why the biggest single expense category in a budget for many households is termed "miscellaneous" or "other."

Identity theft

With respect to cash flow monitoring and spending, there is a rapidly growing problem known as identity theft. Unfortunately, it may not be a matter of if but more like a high possibility of when this could happen to you. Therefore, you should obtain at least annually a copy of your credit report. This will help to monitor whether someone else is spending your money. At times, you may not be aware of identity theft because the transactions are in small amounts relative to your spending patterns and therefore may not trigger red-flag alerts. By reviewing credit reports on a regular basis, you can wisely monitor your credit reporting information for inappropriate transactions.

Another suggestion for partially protecting yourself from the threat of identity theft is to use a heavy-duty paper shredder to destroy all papers that contain *any* personal data. In addition, there is no reason to make your Social Security number and credit card information readily available to just any company or individual who requests it. You should be cautiously selective and suspicious about complying with such requests. Furthermore, you should be conscious about inadvertently displaying your Social Security number and credit card information. Your computer also makes you vulnerable and should have a firewall installed to block unauthorized access to your financial information. Check with a computer consultant or a local store for installing the most reliable computer protection, and remember that you must always update it to protect yourself from future threats.

Ways to Keep Cash Flow Positive, Avoid Costly Debt, Eliminate Financial Anxiety, and Save for Future Goals

Now is a good time to fill out your Cash Flow Planning Worksheet (Figure 2-3) shown in Chapter Two. See whether you can accurately complete the worksheet data as it applies to your situation. This reveals the heart and soul of your financial well-being. In completing the cash flow worksheet, oftentimes people are surprised to find out that they need to either make more money or spend less in order to assure a healthy cash flow required for meeting both current and future financial commitments. They come to realize specifically why they are in the circumstance of having "more month than the money."

Establish a financial budget or spending plan

By knowledgeably establishing a financial budget, or spending plan, you are able to monitor actual expenditures vs. budgeted amounts for each expense category. Importantly, this cash flow monitoring process will reveal the "big picture" of whether you are actually spending and saving money in accordance with what is important about money to you. This ongoing process can be a "chore" that becomes surprisingly easy if you use a personal finance computer software program such as Quicken or Microsoft Money, which makes for a more controlled cash management plan that is convenient and accurate in monitoring your financial transactions.

Use personal finance software

Not only is using personal finance software a valuable tool for keeping track of how much and where you spend your money, but it also enables you to stay up to date regarding your assets, liabilities, investments, tax preparation issues, and bank accounts. With respect to managing your bank accounts, by using a personal finance software program, you can reconcile your checkbook in minutes as well as print out your checks to pay bills.

Another advantage to using a personal finance software package is the ability to pay bills electronically through secure Web sites. By combining an electronic bill pay system with the use of a debit card, you can significantly reduce the number of checks you need to write manually. This saves a lot of time and lessens the chances for record entry mistakes.

Use automatic bill paying

You can set up your automatic bill paying either on a predetermined scheduled basis, such as for mortgage, insurance premiums, and other regular monthly bills, or on the usual as-needed basis for the nonregular transactions. All transactions are automatically recorded according to expense category for easy monitoring, and you do not have to be computer savvy to operate an electronic bill pay system. This will help your financial operating and planning system to become easier and more efficient.

QUIET MILLIONAIRE® WISDOM
If you spend before thinking, you will probably spend more than you think.

Another advantage to establishing and managing an informed spending plan is that it controls unhealthy debt, especially credit card debt, caused by impulse buying. It is far better to "pay as you go" instead of impulsively buying something without accountability and feeling remorseful about it later. You can accomplish the "pay as you go" approach with easy record keeping by paying for all purchases over some stipulated small dollar amount such as $10 with a check, a debit card, or by using a single credit card that is <u>diligently</u> paid off every month (it must be paid off each month to work).

Some people avoid purchasing something they have not planned for in advance by allowing a "cooling off" period to take effect. If you see something that is tempting, forcing yourself to walk away and *think* about it helps to avoid unthinking impulse spending. You can also reduce tempting and recreational purchases simply by making it a little more difficult to do so by, for example, paying for purchases with cash only. However, remember that if you pay with cash, you need to be diligent about keeping good records for tracking how much money was spent and where.

The following describes how Martha approached her impulsive spending:

> *Martha overcame her need to buy on the spot by writing down what it was she wanted at the time and waiting a week before buying the item. Then, every time she saw something else she wanted, she would add it to the list and do the same thing. However, the key was never to allow herself more than three items on the list at a time. To add the fourth, she had to remove one of the other items from the list. Martha found that she was constantly crossing off items to make room for the newest "must*

have" thing. She ended up making a lot of lists but fewer purchases. She also learned there is "always a deal and it's not a good deal if you really don't need it."

Determine how much cash flow is required to fund future goals and objectives

The quiet millionaire® knows the amount of money that is required to fund desired future commitments. This is important because it establishes the proper balance between your spending for today and your saving for tomorrow. Remember, as a high-income earner, that while you may not be having a current cash flow problem paying your bills, you may have a future cash flow problem without even knowing it by not saving enough for future financial obligations. By having

> QUIET MILLIONAIRE® WISDOM
> *Wealth is not accumulated by wanting many possessions but by having fewer wants.*

specific future goals to fund, knowing what is required to fund them, and putting aside enough, you will be less likely to unwisely purchase things today that jeopardize accomplishing those goals of tomorrow.

As unbelievable as it may seem, outside of the poverty-stricken third-world countries, Americans are notoriously the worst savers in the world, being more committed to paying on their loans than to a savings plan. We like to spend and believe that tomorrow will take care of itself. Wrong! Sadly, the overall savings rate for most Americans is zero percent, which is nothing more than a ticking financial time bomb that will seriously jeopardize being able to pay for challenging lifetime money commitments such as costly health care, educating children, and assuring a secure retirement.

The quiet millionaire® has a goal to save at least twenty-five percent of his or her gross income toward a variety of funding purposes, both near and long term. In order to accomplish savings goals, the quiet millionaire® skillfully sets up a cash management system in order to "pay himself/herself first," which is assured by having an automatic-deduction savings program.

Multiple accounts can be established, with automatic savings in place for different purposes. Some accounts can be for funding major long-term purposes such as college and retirement saving over and above your employer-sponsored retirement plan. Some accounts can be for some shorter-term purposes such as automobile replacement (instead of paying on an auto loan every month) and building a "kitty fund" for recreational and vacation spending.

Be an accumulator instead of a spender

In order to become the quiet millionaire®, be an accumulator instead of a spender, a lender instead of a borrower. In my professional practice, I have worked with "showy" affluent clients earning well over $100,000 a year who spend every dollar they earn and will never become financially independent enough to quit working. I have also worked with clients who earn much less money, yet they have become quiet millionaires® because they work at a patiently diligent accumulation program. Consider the story of Nancy, who is the quiet millionaire® extraordinaire:

> *Nancy is a single mother who* <u>*has never made more than*</u> <u>*$48,000 a year*</u>. *At age twenty she had two children and was struggling financially. Disgusted about her situation, it was then that Nancy vowed to take control of her life and her finances. So, she set a goal to become a millionaire. Today, at age fifty-five, Nancy has raised her two children entirely on her own and is a proud grandmother. She is also on the brink of reaching her planned goal to become a millionaire. How did she do it?*

One of the most significant things Nancy did was to diligently "pay herself first" and use the powerful benefit of compounding investment returns over time. When she planned her path to becoming a millionaire, she decided that <u>no matter what</u>, *she was going to live her life so that she could save and invest twenty percent of every dollar she earned every single year, year after year.*

Now, Nancy is planning to retire soon and intends to devote her "retired" life to motivating and teaching as many of today's struggling young women as possible that financial success is achievable even when there are heavy-duty life obstacles to overcome. Nancy is leaving lasting footprints for others to follow. She is also a sterling role model for how a commitment to intelligent financial management can enable you to become the quiet millionaire® and to live a meaningful, rewarding life.

Now you have learned that there are intelligent ways to control and monitor your spending and saving programs. You also learned that you first need to know where your money is going and what amounts of your cash flow must be set aside in order to fund your future goals and objectives. Then, you must commit to follow through in order to become and stay the quiet millionaire®.

Quiet Millionaire® Summary

- **Make more money than you spend.**
- **Keep track of where and how you spend money.**
- **Control impulse spending.**
- **Establish healthy family communication about money issues.**
- **Just say "no" to easy credit.**

(continues)

Quiet Millionaire® Summary (continued)

■ Walk on by ATMs.

■ Establish a financial budget.

■ Use personal finance software such as Quicken or Microsoft Money.

■ Develop a "pay as you go" attitude to replace a credit card mentality.

■ Purchase by check or debit card or by using a single credit card paid off monthly.

■ Pay yourself first with automatic savings deductions.

■ Plan your financial goals and objectives and save what is required to achieve them.

■ Determine cash flow requirements to fund future goals and objectives.

CHAPTER FOUR

Do You Own the Right Assets?

You have read about it in the newspapers and seen it on the nightly news: "unquiet" millionaires getting into financial trouble. With all that money, it seems unbelievable, and you might wonder, "How can that be?" One reason is that they did not wisely manage their cash flow as discussed in the previous chapter. Probably another reason is because they have a heavy load of costly debt from accumulating too many "things" that rapidly lose monetary value as well as usage value. The quiet millionaire® wisely knows that if you borrow heavily to live in a big showcase house, drive luxury cars, and own a bunch of showy possessions, while you might be "income" affluent, you are "asset" poor and merely a servant to the money changers.

Assets are what you own. They can be either a blessing or a curse. Your net worth is determined by calculating the difference between what you own (assets) and what you owe (liabilities).

Many outwardly appearing affluent people earn high incomes, but they have a negative net worth and are, in effect, bankrupt. They live precariously close to unanticipated financial disaster that can be caused by reduced or lost income.

QUIET MILLIONAIRE® WISDOM
Increase your net worth; you will increase your self-worth.

Your goal should be to make the value of what you own go up and the amount of what you owe go down. This discussion about intelligent asset management is not intended to tell you what to and what not to buy. That is for you to decide. Rather, the intent is to help you make more informed and wiser decisions about your purchases and management of assets and thereby increase your net worth.

The quiet millionaire® incurs only manageable, intelligent debt to accumulate possessions and therefore is asset affluent, with a high net worth, and is not just income affluent. The quiet millionaire® saves for emergencies and for funding preestablished goals and objectives. With today's readily available credit, many assets are made misleadingly affordable. This enables purchase decisions that are often impulsive and foolish. Thousands of precious dollars are wasted that could have been wisely invested to grow for meeting future desired lifetime goals and objectives such as funding college educations and retirement. The quiet millionaire® realizes that the actual possession of assets is often not as pleasurable as the expectation when *pursuing* them and therefore pays attention to the difference between what is foolish and intelligent spending.

Two Kinds of Assets

There are two kinds of assets, personal use and investment. Some assets are *pursued* for **personal use** with the intention of providing for necessity and/or enjoyment; some assets are *pur-*

sued mainly for **investment** with the intention of increasing wealth. Both are important and necessary as long as you have an intelligent and knowledgeable approach of when to or when not to purchase.

Personal Use Assets

Personal use assets include your residence, automobiles, home furnishings, clothing, computers, boats, electronic gadgets, and other personal "items"—those that are purchased for some combination of necessity and enjoyment. With the exception of your residence, most of these assets rapidly lose their dollar value and their usefulness.

Residence

Although your residence is primarily a personal use asset, it can also be considered an investment asset. Many homeowners have experienced financial bonanzas due to increases in the value of their homes. Buying a house can provide the combined financial benefits of owning an appreciating asset, financing it by using tax-advantaged mortgage debt, and paying no taxes on the gain when you sell it.

Owning a home can be your most expensive personal use asset as well as one of your best investment assets

That being said, it may also be the most costly personal use asset you will ever purchase. The house purchaser must not overlook the fact that it costs a lot of money to own a home beyond the initial purchase price. There are the costs of mortgage interest and property taxes (even though tax deductible), homeowner insurance, and personal liability insurance. In addition, there can be sizable amounts of money required to be spent on maintenance, improvements, decorating, and home furnishings.

The result is that homeowners can find themselves stressfully "house poor" because they bought their dream home with emotional influence and did not thoroughly think through all of the financial ramifications of their purchase. They did not factor in all of the combined expenses associated with owning a house that can consume a disproportionate amount of their income. Their house then becomes not a home to enjoy but more of a burdensome financial drain. What was deemed affordable is actually severely affecting their accumulation requirements for handling the unexpected and is harming their funding of future financial commitments.

In most instances, it is preferable to own your home rather than to rent because of the benefits you gain through market value appreciation, favorable tax advantages, and basic pride of ownership. However, there are circumstances when renting makes more sense, such as if you plan to move within three or four years, and you have to overcome the costs incurred when buying and selling a house. When you rent, you are just paying for a place to live with more flexibility to move someplace new whenever you want. Furthermore, if the time is not right to purchase, by removing all of the responsibilities for maintaining a house, you will have more time for doing other prioritized things that you might value and enjoy more.

When you buy a house, you are paying for more than just a place to live. You are also paying for the responsibility that comes with home ownership: fixing problems, and improving and maintaining the home and property in order to enjoy and increase the value of your investment. Then, when it comes time to sell, you will reap the financial rewards of any built-up equity (tax free) or, regrettably, experience any loss in value (yes, this can happen). Also, keep in mind the reality that the actual rate of return (the difference between the purchase price and the sale price) on the investment in your home is the net of all the costs associated with buying, owning, and selling the home, which include:

- Real estate agent commissions
- Mortgage interest
- Property taxes
- Title company settlement costs
- Maintenance and improvement costs

The decision to purchase a house involves making many choices, and if you allow your emotions to rule, they can override your actual living requirements and what truly makes sense within the context of your long-term comprehensive financial planning scheme. Very often the mental picture of your "dream home" costs more than what is appropriately affordable. What might be affordable in terms of your current cash flow may not actually be affordable in the long term because it is jeopardizing your ability to accumulate enough money for other financial goals and objectives. Again, this is why you need to have a solid base of knowing what is important about money to you. Even high-income earners do not have the luxury of living a "having it all" approach to life. Priorities still have to be set and comprehensive planning needs to be done accordingly.

Research reveals the way the quiet millionaire® buys a residence

The quiet millionaire® has figured all of this out and is an astute and savvy home buyer. While millionaires can choose to live pretty much anywhere, research by Thomas J. Stanley, Ph.D., author of *The Millionaire Mind,* reveals that they have a common, distinctive approach to house selection and purchase.

Quiet millionaires® buy homes that are:

- **Older:** The quiet millionaire® typically buys a house between thirty and fifty years old, with a proven track record of having appreciated significantly. The houses are located in established neighborhoods with top-flight school systems.

They avoid buying modern homes in new developments loaded with showy amenities. Their older, established homes do not have the same downside risk associated with owning a brand-new home in a subdivision filled with similarly priced houses that have not produced any history of price trend data.

■ **Solidly constructed:** The quiet millionaire® favors houses that are well constructed, more commonly brick or stone, some with slate roofs, usually with hardwood floors, and they have predictable cash flow requirements for maintenance and upkeep expenses.

■ **Smaller:** The quiet millionaire® prefers homes having four or fewer bedrooms and without much surrounding property to maintain, as opposed to newer homes with between five to eight bedrooms and a lot of grounds-keeping maintenance.

■ **Bargains:** The quiet millionaire® looks for homes resulting from a foreclosure, a divorce settlement, or an estate sale. The home buying process is part of an overall comprehensive financial plan. In negotiating for the purchase of a house, he or she is not hesitant to say no to the seller and is willing to walk away from any house of interest at any time. Emotions or ego does not come into play with the purchase decision. He or she never pays the initial asking price for a house unless research indicates it is a true bargain. This patient and disciplined approach allows for a smart business decision as well as for meeting living requirements and is why the quiet millionaire® never rushes to purchase a residence within a short span of time.

Automobiles

The quiet millionaire® considers automobiles as being necessary for transportation only and that owning them for pleasure is a discretionary added benefit usually too costly to justify. A luxury automobile today costs almost as much as some houses did not too many years ago. In fact, the quiet millionaire® purchases automobiles similar to the way he or she buys a house. Because automobiles are a very poor investment with diminishing monetary value, the quiet millionaire's® purchase decision is not influenced by costly emotion. Instead, it is a practical decision based more upon actual transportation need.

Automobiles are expensive to buy and operate and rapidly lose their value

Most families today require having at least two cars as a minimum, with the added possibly of one or two additional cars for the teenage drivers. As a result, if not careful, they can become automobile and car insurance poor. Today, it is commonplace for families to purchase three to four cars costing a total of $75,000 to $100,000. On top of the initial purchase costs are the ongoing expenses for fuel, maintenance, and insurance, which can amount to as much as another $20,000 to $25,000 annually. In addition, if the automobiles are acquired with a loan or a lease, the cost of using the lender's money also has to be factored in, which can be an additional $5,000 a year.

When all factors are considered for a multi-car family, it is possible that the combined costs of acquiring and operating automobiles could total as much as $50,000 a year. These are staggering numbers, ones that hopefully motivate you to take a closer look at your own automobile situation. Whether you purchase or lease an automobile, there are some general rules and guidelines to follow, yet as is often the case in the financial world, there can be exceptions.

First, given the fact that new cars lose sizable value the minute they are driven off the dealer's lot, it is more economical to buy a recent model year used car with low mileage to avoid the immediate off-the-lot discount. If the quiet millionaire® does purchase a new car, he or she often looks for the attractively priced deals that can result from overstocked cars at the end of each model year. Overstocked cars represent leftover car inventory, which the dealers are anxious to move with discounts.

Do as the quiet millionaire® does: plan in advance, do your research, shop around at dealerships that sell the makes of cars you are considering, visit and make yourself and your specific car interest known to a salesperson with whom you feel comfortable, and have the salesperson keep an eye out for your interest. Become familiar with book values so you can intelligently negotiate from strength and knowledge and most importantly so you can be prepared to walk away if you are not getting the deal you want.

Personal property

Personal property as a category consists of the many possessions you use, sometimes use, or never use and includes such things as furnishings, clothes, jewelry, electronic gadgets, exercise equipment, etc. Depending upon how the items are paid for, you may or may not actually "own" them. Personal property items have different values, which include the purchase price, actual current market value, usage value, replacement value, sentimental value, and ego value.

Personal property can be useful and worthwhile or useless and worthless

The real worth of most of our personal property is in the usage, yet the usage value can be questionable. Frequently, after the excitement of the initial use is gone, our impulsive purchases just sit around unused, often hidden from sight in drawers, closets, attics, basements, or garages so full that the automobiles have to sit outside in driveways. Fundamentally, if you do not use "it," then your personal property has no value. Monetarily, unless it is a collectible or antique, your extra "stuff" is usually not worth much compared to the price you paid for it. This fact is proven at every garage, rummage, or yard sale and every delivery made to a local charity or the worst fate of all, a trip to the trash pile and dump.

> **QUIET MILLIONAIRE® WISDOM**
> *Control spending for today's wants in order to save and invest for tomorrow's needs.*

Because our wants for personal items often exceed our requirements for necessities, we can consume a lot of *wanted*, but not necessarily *needed*, things. Uncontrolled and unmonitored spending for personal property, or all the extra *stuff*, can excessively consume cash flow and insidiously affect your *monetary* net worth. Birthday and Christmas gifts can be particularly notorious for limited usefulness and fading enjoyment. We need to remember that we can love our family and friends, but it should be done without incurring burdensome debt. We can also help teach our children the true value of caring and love without indulging their every want and raising their expectations for getting more and more things as the only way to show affection. Furthermore, parents must learn how to manage peer pressure, their own as well as their children's. This means thinking independently from other parents who may be foolish about their spending and not giving in to your children's peer pressures of "needing" this or that unnecessary item to "fit in."

The quiet millionaire® avoids the tempting allure of purchases fueled by the entertainment and advertising media. He or she does not have a "buy now, pay later" mentality and is not enticed by easy credit. Instead, cash flow management is always in the forefront, thus keeping cash flow positive, avoiding costly debt, eliminating financial anxiety, and saving for future goals. As much as possible, the quiet millionaire® plans for purchases of personal property and makes it a good financial management decision, as well as a purchase that will be used and enjoyed for a long time. When deciding to buy, the quiet millionaire® compares whether the real usage value is worth the monetary price of the contemplated purchase. He or she makes sure that the purchase price is worthwhile, remembering that it is not a good deal if the usage does not endure.

While you certainly should enjoy your daily life, you need to also understand and prioritize the purchase of items as to how they relate to and affect your overall goals and objectives in life. The quiet millionaire® strives to save at least twenty-five percent of his or her gross income in order to fund short- and long-term financial requirements and avoid causing excessive debt. He or she controls current spending by being aware of what savings amounts are required to fund determined lifetime goals and objectives.

Vacation or second homes

Most of us at one time or another dream of owning a home at the beach, on a lake, or in the mountains, most likely at a place we love being. The decision to purchase a second home is often an emotional one, with a rationalization that a home is a good investment rather than a good financial decision.

Vacation or second homes require making a commitment of time and money

While buying a second home can be a good investment, there is one real estate rule to remember: *location, location, location.* This means that you should choose a location where further development is limited or at least maturely established, the same basic concepts as when buying a primary residence. As a result, the venture may be pretty pricey relative to less desirable alternatives. Be wary about places where the increases in prices are hyped to be a sure thing or where they have already become speculatively high. They could fall just as quickly to turn your dream house into a losing proposition, and it can take years to recover while your money is tied up and unavailable for more productive uses.

Most certainly, the infrastructure for a second home location must be considered. While you may want to be tucked away from your neighbors, too much isolation can limit the investment value. The location's infrastructure has to be accessible, attractive, and appealing recreationally and culturally. In order for it to be a good investment decision, the second house's locale should be in a compelling place for people to enjoy beyond just that of satisfying your desire for an idealized hideaway.

Even more risky and uneconomical is buying raw land for future building of a home. Be prepared for it to be a disappointing investment that will not return what you paid for it. Is it possible for raw land to give you a bonanza-sized investment return? Yes, but it is not likely to. More likely, it will play out to be an ill-fated investment that provides no appreciation, no income, no enjoyment, and it will cost you financially with loan payments, property taxes, and other assessments.

Furthermore, if you are buying with the intention of later building a home on the land, you are also speculating about your own future for actually doing so. Your desired lifestyle objectives, geographic preferences, or the then-located residences of your loved ones may cause you to change your mind. Or, it could be that your financial circumstances at the time will not allow building a desired home for you that is affordable, either because you did not plan properly or because the building costs for the required house relative to the land's value may make it an option that is economically viable.

Financing, maintaining, improving, and furnishing a second home all cost you in the same ways that your primary residence does, and the value of your actual usage vs. the costs to own needs to be realistically assessed. In addition, you need to consider the expenses associated with your time and money spent getting to and from the second home location. With some good planning, you may find that you are actually better off renting as needed to enjoy the area and not having an ongoing commitment associated with ownership.

If you own a vacation home with the idea of renting it out for income to assist in the ownership commitment and make it a good investment, you need to understand all of the tricky tax rules, as well as the disadvantages of owning a rental property. Also, realize that it is very likely that the most opportune time for you to generate rental income is just about the same time you yourself would most want to enjoy the use of it.

Importantly, when considering a second home purchase, you must address how the commitment affects your other financial commitments and objectives such as caring for an ailing family member, paying for college, and saving enough for actually being able to retire. In the end, you need to ask yourself, is it really worth it?

Timeshares

The true value of buying a timeshare is that it gives you the ability to purchase in advance future vacations at today's prices. A timeshare is a personal future use asset, which has worthwhile value only if it is, in fact, used. Therefore, **timeshares are poor investments and have value only if you use them**. Timeshares certainly should not be considered an attractive investment asset because they are difficult to sell and are typically sold at a loss in dollar value. If you do decide to buy a timeshare, you are most likely better off taking advantage of the purchase discounts available in the secondary timeshare market, which is loaded with owners trying to shed their purchase mistake. Here again, this purchase decision is typically an emotional one and probably not a good business decision.

Investment Assets

Investment assets are acquired in order to create wealth, increase your net worth, fund your future goals and objectives, and gain your financial independence and security. However, a socioeconomic time bomb is ticking because most Americans are insufficiently accumulating money and investing it for future usage and financial security. Intelligent investing can make you wealthy; foolish investing can disappoint you and cause financial hardship. Many investments go bad because of investor greediness whereby "greed turns to grief."

This section is intended to give you an *overview* about the more common types of investment assets such as individual stocks and bonds, mutual funds, employee stock options, self-employment business ownership, and rental properties. Other chapters go into more depth as to the advantages and disadvantages as well as the risks and rewards of the various forms of investment assets.

Some investments are situated in a taxable environment such as those within a bank or brokerage account. Unless these investments are designed to be tax free, as is the case with tax-free municipal bonds, you pay taxes on the earnings and

QUIET MILLIONAIRE® WISDOM
Investing pretax dollars in tax-deferred retirement accounts may not always be in your best financial interest.

gains each year as they occur. Other investments are inside a tax-deferred environment whereby no taxes are paid until the investments are withdrawn. The most commonly used tax-deferred accumulation vehicles for investments are 401(k) and 403(b) retirement plans, IRAs, annuities, and 529 college savings plans.

Many people believe that they will pay a lesser amount of taxes during retirement because they will no longer be earning an income. This can be a serious and harmful retirement planning mistake because, first of all, it is very possible that future legislated tax laws will increase the income tax rates to previous higher levels and result in your paying a greater amount of taxes with less money available to spend.

Moreover, even if the income tax rates are not increased, it is very probable that you will still pay more in taxes, especially if most of your retirement savings have been invested in tax-deferred retirement accounts. This is because in order to keep up with increases in the cost of living (inflation) and maintain your accustomed standard of living, you will need to withdraw more money each year from the tax-deferred retirement accounts. And, the more you take out of the tax-deferred retirement accounts, the more taxes you will have to pay on the money that has never been taxed. You are experiencing the very costly double-whammy of inflation and higher taxes, which can financially devastate your retirement portfolio and how long it will last. This is one of the reasons why, if you are eligible, contributing to a totally tax-free Roth IRA or Roth 401(k) or 403(b) is such a good deal because not only do investments inside of those accounts grow tax-deferred but also the withdrawals are tax free if you abide by IRS rules.

Liquid assets

Liquid investment assets consist mainly of cash located in checking and savings accounts, certificates of deposit, and money market accounts. Money in these accounts should be there only to meet emergency and current cash requirements and should not be intended to fund long-term goals and objectives that require growth to protect against inflation and taxes.

Although the money in these accounts may be "guaranteed" against loss for the amount deposited and earns interest, the interest rates paid do not keep up with inflation, causing a sure loss of purchasing power, and the interest income earned is usually subject to current or future income taxes as well. This harmful combination of losing purchasing power as a result of inflation and paying taxes on the interest means that, in reality, you have guaranteed yourself an investment loss.

Liquid assets are guaranteed to lose money

Consider this example: You are in a twenty-five percent income tax bracket and purchase a $100,000 certificate of deposit (CD) that pays a four percent interest rate. Further assume that the inflation rate is five percent (this is a more actual and realistic inflation percentage increase than the government's published Consumer Price Index [CPI], which states that inflation has historically increased an average of only three to four percent). Here is how you end up having a guaranteed two percent ($2,000) annual loss on your "*riskless*" investment:

4%	$100,000 annual CD interest	**$4,000**
−1%	Annual taxes (25% tax rate)	**−1,000**
3%	Net after-tax annual interest rate	**3,000**
−5%	Annual inflation	**−5,000**
−2%	Guaranteed annual loss	**−$2,000**

The net result is that annually your $100,000 CD produces a minus two percent (-$2,000) negative real return, which means that you lose that dollar amount in purchasing power each year. This is not an intelligent way to invest your money. The quiet millionaire® realizes that with this investment approach, you are actually lending your money to the bank at a loss so it can lend your money to someone else at a much higher interest rate, such as at twenty-one percent on credit cards, for big gains. This is an appealing financial transaction for the banks in which you lose and they win!

Today, there are innovative working capital tools such as home equity lines of credit and brokerage margin loan accounts as alternatives for providing immediate liquidity and replacing the traditional need to maintain high cash balances. Therefore, you should limit the amount of unwarranted sums of cash being maintained for liquidity purposes, and definitely you should not use liquid-type assets for long-term investing in order to make certain that you can overcome the ravages of inflation and taxes.

Stock (*equity*) and bond (*fixed income*)

When you buy a stock, you are a partial <u>owner</u> of *equity* in a company. When you buy a bond, you are a <u>lender</u> to either a company or a government body that pays you a *fixed income* (interest) for the use of your money. You can purchase stocks and bonds either individually on your own or mutually with other investors through a mutual fund.

Stock investments are purchased with the intention of making your money accumulations grow and keep up with inflation. The whole idea behind investing in stocks is to "buy low and sell high" for a profit. Many investors in stocks actually do just the opposite, and often their "greed turns to grief."

Bond investments are less risky than stocks and are intended to provide more income than growth. Bonds can also serve as an anchor for reducing volatility in your overall investment portfolio. By combining the use of both stocks and bonds, you can diversify your investments to achieve growth while reducing the magnitude of the fluctuations in value affecting your total portfolio.

Stock (*equity*) and bond (*fixed income*) investments are the primary investment assets used to achieve your financial security

Investing is a loser's game for most do-it-yourself investors. They tend to invest more with their emotions than with a proven systematic, intelligent approach. In fact, it can be a loser's game even for the so-called "pros." Investment research shows that even most of the professional stock pickers and the market timers (those who profess knowing when to time getting in and out of the stock market) underperform a well-structured, diversified investment portfolio that stays fully invested at all times. You will learn in Chapter Seven about Nobel Prize–winning economic research that produces an investment approach that provides highly predictable performance results, both short and long term and in accordance with your individually determined tolerance for risk. This academically sound research, which has been proven by real-life investment management experience, reveals overwhelmingly that a well-structured, diversified portfolio can win the loser's game of investing.

Employee stock options

Many companies offer their top executives and key employees stock options as part of their compensation package. Very simplistically, the company provides certain selected employees the option to purchase, or exercise the right to purchase, their company's stock for a very low price relative to the price at which the shares are expected to be trading in the marketplace. The whole idea is to have the employees with stock options work really hard to make profits for the company so that the market value of the share prices goes up. When that happens, they exercise their option to buy shares at the low option price relative to the higher-priced shares being purchased by outside investors. The employee then sells the exercised shares at the higher publicly traded price.

Employee stock options can make or break you being the quiet millionaire®

Although it seems like a simple enough way to make some big bucks, the whole stock option exercise process is actually complex and can be very risky. If managed intelligently, stock options can make quiet millionaires®; if managed improperly, they can cause financial disappointment and even personal bankruptcy. Chapter Eight explains stock options, how they work, and how to manage them for maximum gains in value.

Business ownership

A large number of quiet millionaires® are business owners. However, they know that the road to building a successful, richly rewarding business can be risky and rough. They are willing to make a steadfast commitment to whatever amounts of energy, time, and money are required to succeed. I know this firsthand from my own business ownership experience. When I founded the Financial Management Group, Inc., in 1989, my business objective was to offer financial and investment advice that was intelligent, innovative, and relevant to the client's best interest. I had the professional credentials and the learned experience to provide objectively honest advice and valuable financial and investment management services. By offering advice and services on a fee-only basis, and without any hidden agenda to sell commission products, I naively thought, "Build it and they will come."

Business ownership can make you the quiet millionaire®

I quickly learned that gaining the number of clients needed for achieving business success did not happen that easily. Instead, I had to go through the four "under" stages of business transition that most entrepreneurs have to effectively manage to reach what is laughingly often termed "overnight" success. These four "under" stages—**W**under, **Bl**under, **Th**under, **Pl**under—are subsequently fully explained in Chapter Eleven, which explains the ways you can become the quiet millionaire® through owning a profitable business.

Rental properties

Owning rental properties can be very lucrative, provided you know what you are doing and you are willing to put up with a lot of potential aggravation. Television infomercials hyping how easy it is to make money in rental real estate are a lot of hooey for most real estate investors. In fact, most owners of rental properties do not know the real rate of return on their investment. They mistakenly believe that they are making a reasonable return on their investment and are benefiting from tax advantages. More times than not, the fact is that they are deriving an investment return that is less than what they would gain by having their money invested in a diversified portfolio consisting of stock and bond mutual funds and with a lot less hassle and risk.

Rental properties can be a headache to manage and can provide you with a surprisingly poor investment rate of return

The real rate of investment return for rental properties is determined by calculating the property's net operating profit, the appreciation in market value, and the tax benefits derived. You should earn a rate of return on rental property that, after all expenses to operate and maintain, is worthwhile relative to the risk and responsibility assumed. Managing a rental property is riskier and is more of a hassle than managing an investment portfolio of marketable securities.

The *least* acceptable rate of return for your out-of-pocket investment money that is tied up in the rental property should be at least 1.5 percent per month, or eighteen percent per year on your equity investment. For example, if you buy a rental property for $200,000 by investing $60,000 out of pocket as a thirty percent down payment and finance the balance with a $140,000 mortgage, you should realize a total dollar investment rate of return of $10,800 annually ($60,000 x 18%) <u>after</u> paying all expenses incurred for maintenance and improvement, mortgage loan interest, and taxes. Otherwise, owning a rental property is probably not acceptable as an investment asset to retain.

How well you manage your assets and liabilities determines your financial well-being

The quiet millionaire® knows that how you manage your assets, as well as the debt used to purchase them, is the catalyst for living a lifestyle you want and for achieving financial freedom and security. In the next chapter, you will learn about the savvy and prudent ways for using debt to leverage your assets in order to maximize increasing your net worth.

This would be a perfect time to go to the Financial Statement Planning Worksheet (Figure 2-4) in Chapter Two and fill in the asset information for your own situation. You can go to the Web site *www.quietmillionaire.com* and print out the worksheet. By completing the asset information portion of your financial statement, you will be at the halfway point for determining your financial net worth, the difference between your assets and liabilities.

Quiet Millionaire® *Summary*

■ Understand the distinction between *personal use assets* and *investment assets*, and be intelligent and knowledgeable about when to or when not to purchase them.

■ Make purchasing assets a good business decision rather than an emotional or impulse decision.

■ Realize that the quantity of what you own does not necessarily enhance the quality of your life.

■ Understand how spending foolishly today negatively affects your life tomorrow.

■ Complete the assets section of the Financial Statement Planning Worksheet, and update it at least annually.

CHAPTER FIVE

Are You an Intelligent Borrower?

The quiet millionaire® realizes that the intelligent management of **liabilities** (what you owe) is just as important as the intelligent management of **assets** (what you own). He or she does not like unintelligent, unnecessary debt. Moreover, any debt that he or she does have is used to contribute toward an increase in net worth rather than being *troublesome* bad debt that causes financial problems.

> *"Getting into troublesome debt is getting into a tanglesome net."*
>
> **—Ben Franklin**

In order to assure having a financially healthy personal financial statement, the quiet millionaire® lives an enjoyable lifestyle without being flashy. He or she cannot relate to people whose financial philosophy is "Live for today, even if you have to borrow money to do it." The following is a contrast of financial philosophies based upon the facts of two actual situations. Think about which of the circumstances described more closely relates to you. You only need to answer to yourself, so be honest.

Their names are Joe and Bill. Joe has an affluent-appearing lifestyle (which is all too prevalent today) and lives in the exact opposite of the manner in which Bill, the quiet millionaire®, lives. Joe is a popular radio show personality, and Bill is the owner of an equipment rental company. They similarly earn about $200,000 a year, putting them in the top one percent of all income-producing individuals. Both are in their late forties and have two children heading for college and their families vacationed in Europe. This is where the similarities end.

Joe bought a $500,000 house with all the expensive amenities in a new development. He is financed to the hilt—a $400,000 jumbo-size first mortgage with a relatively high interest rate and a $50,000 second mortgage with a still higher interest rate. He also has a $50,000 home equity line of credit that is almost topped out with $48,000 outstanding because of paying down credit card balances. In contrast, Bill bought a $350,000 house in an established neighborhood and financed it with a $210,000 non-jumbo-size lower interest rate first mortgage; he also has a $35,000 home equity line of credit with no outstanding balance, which means the money is fully available for appropriate short-term borrowing usage.

Joe leases both a brand-new BMW for himself and a one-year-old Range Rover for his wife. His combined lease payments total $1,500 per month. Bill instead drives a five-year-old Volvo, and his wife drives a three-year-old minivan, both of which he bought slightly used, and has no automobile loan payments.

Joe is a hyperactive spender who borrows money for buying personal use items, including all the latest gadgets, in order to enjoy life and be happy. As a result, he constantly maintains outstanding credit card debt that costs him more than $7,500 in annual interest payments; Bill in turn spends well below his means and pays off his credit card balances every month so that his annual credit card interest is zero.

Joe's job situation is loaded with pressure for him to keep his listening audience and his radio advertisers happy. Slipping listener ratings could cause his show to be canceled and him to be without a job. He feels extra anxiety because he needs to earn even more money not only to pay his necessary bills but also to keep up with all the debt payments he has accumulated. He could not last one month without having a salary. Bill, on the other hand, has a business that is well managed and thriving. He loves his work and feels secure with no one to answer to but himself: he is the boss. Even though he had gone through the pressure years of starting his own business, he remained focused and true to his financial goals, which led him to financial security.

Joe's personal financial statement shows more dollars in debt than his assets are worth. Making matters worse, he even leveraged himself for money to buy individual stocks he picked on his own, which he hoped would bail him out of debt. But unfortunately, the stocks he picked lost more than fifty percent, and he had to sell at a loss. In effect, he is affluently broke with a negative net worth and is a hairbreadth away from personal bankruptcy. Bill's cash flow and net worth are positive; he has enough money saved for weathering a financial adversity should it occur and has a well-planned accumulation program for funding college and for other future goals and objectives.

QUIET MILLIONAIRE® WISDOM
If you are borrowed to
the hilt, then you really
do not own anything—
the lenders do.

The good news about Joe is that he sought professional financial counseling and is now starting to get financially healthy. His earned high income is now being directed and prioritized by an intelligent financial and cash management program. He feels relieved and is a lot happier with having a more controlled spending plan. After having made some downsizing lifestyle adjustments, he is getting rid of his troublesome bad debt, and his net worth has now turned positive. Best of all, he is motivated and excited about heading toward becoming a quiet millionaire®.

How Joe got to where he was, so loaded down with debt in order to fund his affluent lifestyle, is another story unto itself. Although he went to an extreme, to the brink of financial disaster, his story is one that can and does happen in varying degrees to many people who are not managing their finances intelligently. Joe's accumulation of debt was financially dangerous and started in his youth when he first got out of college. He saw what his parents had and wanted to replicate a lifestyle that he was accustomed to. *Joe's parents achieved their lifestyle patiently and wisely; Joe got his impatiently and foolishly.*

Unfortunately, we learn more about accumulating debt before we learn about accumulating money for investments. Some debt is happenstance dictated by the natural progression of our financial stages in life. However, increasingly, debt is the result of our cultural progression toward an attitude of having instant gratification, living for today, and letting tomorrow take care of itself.

The Cardinal Rules for Debt Management

The quiet millionaire® knows that debt management is just as important as investment management for increasing wealth. Debt managed intelligently can help create wealth; managed foolishly, debt drains the financial energy from any wealth accumulation program. Before getting into the specifics about what constitutes intelligent debt management, the following are a couple of cardinal rules that serve as the foundation for the entire discussion.

The first cardinal rule

Always spend less than you make, not the opposite, to maintain a positive cash flow, and avoid troublesome high-interest-rate, non-tax-deductible borrowing such as credit card debt. Commit to not being a slave to the lenders.

The second cardinal rule

Always match the term of your debt to the purpose. It is not intelligent to borrow long term to purchase items having a relatively short-term useful life. For example, you should not become so overloaded with credit card debt from purchases made for such items as clothing, electronics, vacations, etc., that you need to refinance your home mortgage in order to pay off the credit card debt. Be aware that the *lending establishments* can cause you to be irresponsible about your financial well-being because they offer borrowing enticements that cause violations of this rule.

Types of Debt and How to Manage Them
First Mortgage Debt

First of all, understand that a mortgage is not the actual debt instrument itself. Rather, it is the legal document that transfers full ownership of the property to you, the mortgagor (the buyer), by the mortgagee (the lender) upon payment of the debt and cancellation of the mortgage note. In the meantime, the lender essentially owns the property, and if you do not pay, the lender will take your house. So, you need to be serious and intelligent about taking on a mortgage borrowing arrangement that is for certain affordable and has the best borrowing terms available for meeting your needs.

In terms of what is affordable and intelligent debt, the quiet millionaire® has a different viewpoint than that of the lenders. The lender wants to lend as much money as you can afford, at the highest interest rate possible. On the other hand, the quiet millionaire® prefers to intelligently borrow at the lowest interest rate possible and have enough additional money available to accumulate for funding other important goals and objectives.

The following is a comparative example that shows how an **intelligent mortgage borrowing approach** vs. an **affordable mortgage borrowing approach** can make a difference for becoming a quiet millionaire®.

	Intelligent Mortgage Debt	Affordable Mortgage Debt
Borrower Gross Monthly Income	$12,500	$12,500
House Market Value	350,000	425,000
House Down Payment	70,000 (20%)	85,000 (20%)
Mortgage Loan Amount	280,000	340,000
Length of Mortgage Loan	30 Years	30 Years
Mortgage Interest Rate	8% (Conventional Mortgage Rate)	9% (Jumbo Mortgage Rate)
Mortgage Payment (Monthly)	$2,055	$2,859
Property Taxes and HO Insurance (Monthly)	583	708
Total Payments (Monthly)	**$2,638**	**$3,567**
Mortgage, Taxes, Insurance Debt Ratio	21% of Monthly Income	28% of Monthly Income

According to mortgage approval guidelines, the twenty-eight percent of gross monthly income *from all sources* for the combined payment of mortgage, property taxes, and homeowner insurance is affordable. In fact, some mortgage lenders allow as much as thirty-three percent of gross monthly income, which is still considered affordable. While taking advantage of the affordable mortgage may not seem harmful, consider the following analysis of the above intelligent vs. affordable mortgage debt illustration.

The intelligent mortgage borrower's total monthly payment for the mortgage, property taxes, and homeowner (HO) insurance is $2,638 per month vs. $3,567 per month for the affordable borrower. This $929 per month lower monthly payment is available for an investment program, which can make becoming the quiet millionaire® a reality for the intelligent borrower.

Here is how: Refer to Figure 5-1 and assume that the extra available $929 is saved monthly. At the end of the first year, the monthly savings accumulation totals $11,148. Next, assume for the second year that the monthly savings amount invested is increased by five percent ($929 + $46) to $975. Then, assume the same five percent increases for the savings amount are again implemented in the third year and each year thereafter. Last, further assume that the annual savings are placed in an investment program that grows at a ten percent average annual rate of return. It would look like the chart on the following page.

Notice that the result is that in just twenty-one years, the intelligent mortgage borrower has saved a cumulative total of $397,937, which if invested and averaging a ten percent annual rate of return, the investment program grows to $1,131,022, making the intelligent mortgage borrower become the quiet millionaire®. In fact, just nine years later at the end of the thirty-year mortgage period, the investment program has nearly tripled in size during that remaining period to make the intelligent borrower a multi-millionaire, with the total cumulative savings of $740,141 having grown at ten percent annually to $3,217,613. This $2,477,472 investment growth (the difference between cumulative annual

FIGURE 5-1   Monthly $929 Savings Increased 5% Per Year

Year	*Monthly* Savings Increased 5% per Year	Total *Annual* Savings	Cumulative Total Annual Savings	Cumulative Total Annual 10% Return
1	$929	$11,148	$11,148	$12,263
2	975	11,700	22,848	26,359
3	1,024	12,285	35,133	42,508
4	1,075	12,902	48,035	60,951
5	1,129	13,545	61,580	81,946
6	1,185	14,225	75,805	105,788
7	1,244	14,931	90,736	132,791
8	1,306	15,674	106,410	163,311
9	1,371	16,456	122,866	197,744
10	1,440	17,275	140,141	236,521
11	1,512	18,144	158,285	280,131
12	1,588	19,051	177,336	329,100
13	1,667	20,009	197,345	384,020
14	1,750	21,004	218,349	445,526
15	1,838	22,050	240,399	514,334
16	1,930	23,159	263,558	591,242
17	2,027	24,318	287,876	677,116
18	2,128	25,540	313,416	772,922
19	2,234	26,813	340,229	879,708
20	2,346	28,148	368,377	998,642
21	2,463	29,560	397,937	1,131,022
22	2,586	31,034	428,971	1,278,262
23	2,715	32,584	461,555	1,441,931
24	2,851	34,209	495,764	1,623,754
25	2,994	35,923	531,687	1,825,645
26	3,144	37,724	569,411	2,049,706
27	3,301	39,614	609,025	2,298,252
28	3,466	41,593	650,618	2,573,830
29	3,639	43,672	694,290	2,879,252
30	3,821	45,851	740,141	3,217,613

savings and the ten percent investment program) shows the power of investment compounding.

Note: In order for the intelligent mortgage approach to work successfully, the additional money made available must in fact be wisely invested and not spent foolishly elsewhere.

The lesson to be learned is that while the mortgage lenders may afford you a bigger house and mortgage loan, it may not be in your best interest if you want to accumulate money for your financial freedom and security. Accordingly, you should allocate no more than twenty-five percent of your monthly gross income to pay the combined total monthly amount of your mortgage, property taxes, and homeowner insurance. Committing an even lesser percentage of your monthly gross income is more beneficial as the above illustration shows.

QUIET MILLIONAIRE® WISDOM
Prepaying your mortgage may feel right emotionally but be wrong financially.

Another financial management consideration is whether to prepay your mortgage in order to pay it off early. Paying off a mortgage loan as soon as possible is often an emotional decision by some homeowners, especially older ones closing in on retirement. However, this emotional decision may not be an intelligent financial management decision if the mortgage interest rate is low or if the mortgage loan maturity is relatively close, with most of the interest costs having been previously paid.

The quiet millionaire® will not prepay a mortgage loan if there is a reasonable expectation for earning a better rate of return by investing that money elsewhere. For example, if there is an opportunity to earn ten percent on invested money, it is not intelligent to make extra payments on a mortgage loan with an interest rate of, say, six percent. Better to invest the extra payment to increase your net worth more rapidly. Of course, if the mortgage rate is higher than the return on an investment alternative, it makes sense to prepay the mortgage loan.

The same intelligent leveraging concept applies when deciding upon what length of time to take for a mortgage loan. If mortgage interest rates are relatively low and you plan to remain in the same house, it might be more intelligent to choose a thirty-year mortgage term instead of a shorter-term mortgage period, even though the interest rate is slightly higher for the thirty-year. This would keep your monthly mortgage payment lower, and the difference in the payment amount between thirty-year mortgage (lower payment) and the shorter-period mortgage (higher payment) could be invested for growth.

Refer to Figure 5-2 for a comparison between a thirty-year and a fifteen-year fixed-rate mortgage loan program. It serves as an example of how investing the difference between the two monthly mortgage payment amounts can pay off. Assume that the difference is invested for growth at a ten percent average

FIGURE 5-2   Monthly Savings from 30-Yr vs. 15-Yr Mortgage Payment

Year	*Monthly* Savings	Total *Annual* Savings	Cumulative Total Annual Savings	Cumulative Total Annual 10% Return	30-Yr Mortgage Balance (6.5%)
1	$593	$7,116	$7,116	$7,828	$276,870
2	593	7,116	14,232	16,438	273,531
3	593	7,116	21,348	25,909	269,968
4	593	7,116	28,464	36,328	266,167
5	593	7,116	35,580	47,788	262,111
6	593	7,116	42,696	60,394	257,783
7	593	7,116	49,812	74,261	253,165
8	593	7,116	56,928	89,515	248,239
9	593	7,116	64,044	106,294	242,982
10	593	7,116	71,160	124,751	237,373
11	593	7,116	78,276	145,054	231,389
12	593	7,116	85,392	167,387	225,004
13	593	7,116	92,508	191,953	218,191
14	593	7,116	99,624	218,976	210,922
15	593	7,116	106,740	248,701	203,166

annual rate of return, which is a reasonable *average* rate of return expectation for a well-diversified portfolio. Further assume that no capital gains taxes are paid until the investment account is liquidated. The following is the result:

	30 Years	**15 Years**
Mortgage Loan Amount	$280,000	$280,000
Interest Rate	6.5%	6.0%
Monthly Payment	$1,770	$2,363
Difference in Monthly Mortgage Payment	**$593**	

To clarify further, the $593 per month additional cash flow available with the lower-payment thirty-year mortgage can be invested each month for fifteen years. The total amount invested is $106,740. Invested with a ten percent rate of return, the investment account balance at the end of fifteen years is $248,701, which represents a $141,961 investment gain ($248,701–$106,740). Assume that the $141,961 investment gain is taxed at the fifteen percent capital gains tax rate, which results in a $21,294 capital gains tax. The net result is that the investment account at the end of fifteen years has a $227,407 net after-tax balance. Meanwhile, the $280,000 thirty-year mortgage balance at the end of fifteen years has been reduced to $203,166, and the $227,407 *net* after-tax investment balance is available to pay the mortgage, with a $24,241 investment balance still remaining. The following is a summary:

Cumulative Savings Invested	$106,740
Investment Account Balance (After 15 years @ 10%)	248,701
Less: Capital Gains Tax (15%)	−21,294
Net After-Tax Investment Account Balance	227,407
Payoff 30-Yr. Mortgage Balance (After 15 years @ 6.5%)	−203,166
Net Investment Account Balance (After-Tax and Mortgage Payoff)	$ 24,241

However, if you want to be really intelligent, you would not choose to prepay the thirty-year mortgage loan at the end of fifteen years. Remember that from that point on, you could still pay off the mortgage balance at any time with the investment account proceeds if circumstances warrant or if your emotions dictate that you just want to have a free and clear house. A smarter choice is not to liquidate the investment account and to just let the full $248,701 (pre-capital-gains tax) investment account balance continue to grow for the remaining fifteen years of the thirty-year mortgage without having to add any further savings to the investment account.

By doing that, notice on Figure 5-3 (a continuation of Figure 5-2) how rapidly the investment account builds up in value as a result of the power of compounding investment returns and meanwhile how rapidly the mortgage loan balance reduces as a result of an increasing amount of your mortgage payment going to principal reduction rather than to interest costs each year. By the end of the remaining fifteen years, the thirty-year mortgage balance has been reduced to zero, the investment account has grown to $1,038,886, and you have become the quiet millionaire®, with your home being free and clear of any mortgage. This is intelligent debt leveraging and investment compounding for building your net worth.

Another mortgage consideration is whether to have your house mortgaged during retirement. This can be a very emotional decision that often overrides making an intelligent financial management decision. As shown on Figure 5-3, if your mortgage interest rate is lower than what you can reasonably expect to earn on your investment money, this can be a form of good debt during retirement. Furthermore, the income tax deduction for the mortgage loan interest can be beneficial in offsetting some of the tax sting resulting from making withdrawals from IRA

QUIET MILLIONAIRE® WISDOM
Seductively attractive mortgage loans can lure you into a harmful financial situation.

FIGURE 5-3   Monthly Savings from 30-Yr vs. 15-Yr Mortgage Payment
             (continuation of Figure 5-2)

Year	Monthly Savings	Total Annual Savings	Cumulative Total Annual Savings	Cumulative Total Annual 10% Return	30-Yr Mortgage Balance (6.5%)
15	593	7,116	106,740	248,701	203,166
16	0	0	106,740	273,571	194,890
17	0	0	106,740	300,928	186,061
18	0	0	106,740	331,021	176,640
19	0	0	106,740	364,123	166,588
20	0	0	106,740	400,535	155,863
21	0	0	106,740	440,589	144,419
22	0	0	106,740	484,648	132,210
23	0	0	106,740	533,113	119,182
24	0	0	106,740	586,424	105,282
25	0	0	106,740	645,066	90,452
26	0	0	106,740	709,573	74,628
27	0	0	106,740	780,530	57,744
28	0	0	106,740	858,583	39,729
29	0	0	106,740	944,442	20,508
30	0	0	106,740	1,038,886	0

accounts. The result is more money upon which to earn an investment return and with a lessened overall tax liability. This adds to your retirement wealth. However, while this approach for leveraging may be intelligent and prudent, it sometimes is not a suitable, comfortable option for certain senior clients. In each instance, realistic input assumptions must be made, with informed calculations prepared for review and analysis.

Not all mortgage options are beneficial, and any decision about which mortgage loan is the right choice needs to be carefully evaluated. You have to be especially cautious about mortgage loan offers that lure you with enticing, but potentially harmful, options.

Examples of these types of mortgage loans include interest-only loans and low-interest-rate loans that change to less favorable terms after a certain time period has passed, usually three, five, seven, or ten years. At the end of the stipulated period, the interest-only or low-interest-rate "honeymoon" is over, and the interest rate and mortgage payment amounts can increase drastically.

There are too many variations of these seductive loans to cover, but the main message to be gained here is that they are financially dangerous because of all of the uncertainties that can arise regarding your personal situation and because of the relative unattractiveness of your loan options that occur at the end of the term. Unless you plan to be out of the house by the end of the stipulated term, it is usually safer to lock in the interest rate with a fixed-rate mortgage in order to avoid having a cash flow surprise at the end of the initial favorable loan period.

Second Mortgage Debt

As implied, a second mortgage lender assumes a secured second position behind a first mortgage lender's home equity security. Because the second mortgage lender is taking a greater risk for getting repaid, the interest rate is typically higher than that charged by the first mortgage lender. Some mortgage lenders lend you as much as one hundred twenty-five percent of your house equity. It is financially dangerous to leverage your residence so heavily unless it is necessary because of unfortunate reasons beyond your control. Second mortgage debt is especially dangerous if it is used to pay off credit card debt and then additional credit card debt is subsequently built up on top of it. This financial burden and stress is one of the major reasons that homes are foreclosed upon, so manage your home equity debt responsibly and be cautious.

Home Equity Line of Credit

This form of debt is prearranged prior to the need for a certain dollar amount that is available to borrow immediately at any time for any reason. It is a stated dollar credit line collateralized by your home equity. The interest rate charged is tied to a particular index such as the bank's prime lending rate or a government Treasury bill index. Therefore, the cost to borrow changes up and down as the index moves; however, the interest rate charged is usually the lowest that lenders offer and is tax deductible.

A checkbook is provided to borrow for any purpose, worthwhile or not. Repayment options are flexible according to cash flow, and the line availability can be used over and over again. The credit line can be used as intelligent borrowing for short-term cash needs and even to finance a car purchase in lieu of using a non-tax-deductible, higher-rate automobile loan. It becomes troublesome borrowing if the line is used to pay off ongoing credit card debt created by frivolous spending, especially if you run the credit card debt back up again.

Automobile Loans

The purchase price for an automobile is expensive, with some cars today costing what an entire house did not that long ago. Many families require two or more automobiles and therefore have to borrow to buy them. As a result, the loan amounts, interest costs, and monthly payments can be financially draining.

The good news about automobiles is that they are built today with better quality to last a long time if properly serviced and maintained. The bad news is that they depreciate in value, some much more rapidly than others. You need to know how fast your particular car loses value in order to make sure that the outstanding loan amount never exceeds the value of the car. The structuring of the size and the term of the loan must assure that you do not get yourself into an "underwater" or "upside down" situation. This occurs when the automobile loan balance outstanding is larger than the value of the car upon selling it or in the event of an accident in which it is considered a total loss.

As a general rule, it is intelligent to make at least a twenty-five percent down payment and to limit the length of time for the borrowing to thirty-six months. Exceptions to this may be appropriate if the auto financing involves a zero or very low percentage interest rate that is offered as an incentive to purchase. However, you must still make certain that the value of the automobile always exceeds the loan amount outstanding at any given time, unless you have other resources to pay off the loan balance if required. This same loan-to-value thinking applies if you decide to use a tax-deductible, low-interest-rate home equity line to finance the automobile purchase. You need to make sure that the reduction of the amount under the credit line matches the decrease in the car's value.

Instead of borrowing to purchase a car, some people get caught in the leasing treadmill, which can be a very expensive proposition. Leasing enables you to drive a more expensive car with a negligible down payment and lower monthly payments than those made when purchasing with a loan. However, unless the true cost and terms of lease are carefully reviewed and understood, you could be in for a very unpleasant financial surprise when the lease term is up. In effect, leasing is never-ending borrowing, and the true cost for a lease can be complicated and difficult to understand. General rules for leasing are to lease only a new car, never lease used, and be sure not to exceed the annual mile limits specified in the lease. The financial penalties for excess mileage and wear and tear are too costly.

Retirement Plan Loans

Be aware that there are no allowable loan provisions for borrowing against a traditional IRA, Roth IRA, SEP-IRA, or SIMPLE IRA. What is being discussed here are *allowable* retirement plan loans made against a qualified 401(k) plan, 403(b) plan, or defined benefit pension plan, when permitted by the employer. Depending upon the plan's summary description, which specifies the availability and eligibility for retirement loans, you may be permitted to borrow as much as fifty percent of your vested interest in the plan, up to $50,000. Retirement plan loans typically must be repaid within five years.

However, you should be aware that retirement plan loans have two potentially devastating pitfalls. The first pitfall is the fact that when you borrow against the plan, the amount borrowed is set aside separately from the investment funds in order to secure the loan. Instead of growth, you earn an interest rate of return that is equivalent to what your borrowing rate is on the loan. Basically, you are paying yourself interest, which is *not* tax deductible except in very limited instances involving a defined benefit pension plan as permitted by tax laws.

The second pitfall is the biggest disadvantage by far and can occur if you leave your employer for any reason, including termination, with a loan balance against your retirement plan. This is because upon leaving, the loan must be repaid in full or else the loan is considered in default and is then deemed by the IRS to be a "retirement distribution" for the entire amount of the unpaid loan balance. Accordingly, the distribution is considered additional taxable income in the year that the loan defaulted, and the IRS expects you to pay income taxes on the remaining loan balance.

Furthermore, it gets even worse if you are under age 59½ because the "deemed distribution" is also considered an "early distribution," which is subject to a ten percent penalty. This penalty combined with federal and state income taxes could make your total liability as high as fifty percent of the outstanding loan balance. This is a heavy price to pay, so make sure that you keep all of this in mind before you decide to borrow against your retirement plan.

Timeshare Debt

The purchase of a timeshare is difficult to justify economically unless it is used extensively over the years for vacationing. Furthermore, it usually makes more financial sense to purchase your timeshare at a substantial discount from someone who is trying to sell the timeshare on the secondary market. You should also be careful about borrowing to own a timeshare and thereby making the purchase even more costly and uneconomical. In fact, if you have to borrow to make the purchase, you really cannot afford the timeshare and should probably avoid the transaction.

Some timeshare buyers use their home equity credit line to make their purchase. This can be a huge mistake unless the line usage is for a relatively short amount of time until other sources of cash become readily available. Otherwise, the line usage could turn into inappropriate long-term borrowing. Any borrowings under a home equity line of credit should be limited to financing short-term needs and should not tie up the credit line's availability on a long-term basis.

Student Debt

College is very expensive, and most parents are not sufficiently prepared to pay for it. As a result, families often have to resort to borrowing large amounts of money. When borrowing to pay for college, do not do so in the parents' name. Instead, borrow in the student's name. Student loans have more favorable interest rates and repayment terms and, if intelligently structured, can be useful to fund college.

Consumer Credit Loans

Prior to the advent of credit cards, unsecured consumer credit loans were the prevalent means to finance the purchases of appliances, furniture, vacations, etc. Consumer credit loans are not as convenient as credit cards because for every purchase, you have to apply for a loan and be approved. The lender can turn down the borrower if there is too much other debt already outstanding or if the purpose is deemed unworthy. However, the use of credit cards has made consumer credit loans nearly obsolete.

Credit Cards

Enough *bad* cannot be said about the worst debt of all: **high-interest-rate credit cards**! They should have no role in your financial life unless they are used intelligently and paid off every month without incurring any interest charges. Otherwise, it is the most troublesome of all borrowing, and here are two primary reasons.

Two Reasons Why Credit Cards Are So Troublesome

Reason One

The repayment schedule for credit card borrowing often does not appropriately match the expected life of the item purchased.

This is a violation of the second cardinal rule for borrowing, whereby you should always match the term of your debt to the purpose, as discussed at the beginning of this chapter. In fact, the only thing more foolish than investing in things that lose value is paying interest on money invested in things that no longer have <u>any</u> value. The following computer purchase scenario illustrates this.

Let's assume that you buy a computer costing $2,000 and finance it with a credit card. From the minute you take the new computer out of the store, it loses value very fast because of the rapidly changing technology. What will be the monetary value of the computer at the end of, say, three years? At best, it is probably worth a miniscule charitable income tax deduction even before the end of three years. Therefore, when the monetary value of the computer becomes less than the outstanding balance on the credit card resulting from the computer purchase, the borrowing is foolish.

However, the foolishness may not end there. Let's say that after two or three years, you decide to upgrade to a new computer while you are still paying the balance on the now functionally useless computer. Now, you have a forever revolving credit balance not recognized for what it really is: a very costly debt for purchases that are either no longer around or hidden away and no longer used.

Reason Two

The interest rates charged on credit cards are usually the highest of any type of debt.

Typically, the rates are extremely high and rob wealth. Let's suppose you use a credit card with a 17.8 percent interest rate to buy the previously illustrated $2,000 computer, and you pay the minimum required monthly payment on the outstanding balance. The result is that it will take you almost fourteen years to repay a total of $3,759 ($2,000 for computer purchase plus $1,759 in interest paid). In actuality, you pay nearly two times the original purchase price for an asset that is long gone.

QUIET MILLIONAIRE® WISDOM
Live within your means and do not borrow money to live beyond them.

Let's take the above foolish computer purchase scenario one step further by assuming that you start using your credit cards to pay for groceries, entertainment, gasoline, vacations, gifts, utilities, etc., and you pay only the minimum required monthly payments. As the computer purchase illustration shows, the borrowing at high interest rates can effectively double the original costs for everything put on the credit cards, which is an ugly scenario and the reason why credit card debt is such bad news!

In recent years, a significant amount of credit card debt and other high-interest loans was paid off by borrowers refinancing their home mortgages that fell to record low interest rates. This enabled homeowners to extract home equity dollars to pay off choking high-interest credit card debt and to alleviate a lot of the cash flow pressure. However, refinancing credit card debt can be financially dangerous if you once again continue to run up new credit card debt that is added on top of that which was paid off by the mortgage refinancing. With the added credit card debt, as interest rates head back up, more bankruptcies will occur as positive cash flows turn negative. Only this time, there might not be any home equity built up, and because of the recent changes in the bankruptcy laws, and going forward, it will be much more difficult for overextended borrowers to get off the hook from paying back money owed.

Remember that if you decide to refinance your house in order to pay off credit cards and start the credit card borrowing process all over again, you will never become the quiet millionaire®, and for sure the credit card companies are the ones getting rich and depriving you of your wealth.

Now go to the Financial Statement Planning Worksheet in Chapter Two, Figure 2-4. (This can also be printed from the Web site *www.quietmillionaire.com*.) Complete the liability portion of your financial statement, and then determine your current financial net worth. With this knowledge, you will know specifically how much money is required in order become and stay the quiet millionaire®.

Quiet Millionaire® Summary

■ Remember the two cardinal rules for debt management: Spend less than you make to avoid a troublesome debt situation and always match the repayment term of your debt to the expected usage life of the item purchased.

■ Understand the different types of debt and how to manage them.

■ Only borrow in order to intelligently leverage the purchase of your assets.

■ Realize why credit cards are troublesome and why you should not pay a single penny in credit card interest.

■ Intelligently leverage low interest rates with higher investment returns.

■ Research your options for intelligent borrowing before incurring debt.

■ Know the true cost of your debt and how it affects your wealth accumulation.

■ Be an intelligent borrower in order to become and stay a quiet millionaire®.

CHAPTER SIX

Are You Paying Too Much Tax?

The quiet millionaire® knows the difference between taking tax <u>de</u>ductions and planning tax <u>re</u>ductions. While intelligent tax *preparation* can maximize your deductions, it is intelligent tax *planning* that provides the most tax reduction. In order to gain the highest possible tax reduction, it requires ongoing planning and research about how to apply the changing tax laws as they relate specifically to your situation. Consistent tax planning throughout the entire calendar year reduces taxes more than by waiting to take advantage of all the allowable tax deductions when preparing your tax return. Even the most competent CPAs are too busy to do meaningful tax reduction planning for you during the height of the tax-filing season, so you need to constantly manage your tax situation as part of an ongoing comprehensive financial management program.

Understand the difference between taking
tax deductions vs. planning tax reductions

This information about taxes is *not* to educate you about all of the tax deductions you can take on your tax return; any competent tax preparer should do that. Instead, the focus is on beneficial tax *reduction* techniques and how they can be applied to your financial situation. Keep in mind that the tax laws are always changing, and this requires that tax reduction strategies be constantly reviewed and adjusted in response to these changes. Also, applying "rules of thumb" strategies to your situation can be inappropriate and very harmful. Strategies that might benefit one taxpayer could be worthless, even costly, to another, and they need to be individually implemented throughout the year.

It is not unpatriotic to reduce paying your taxes

"Anyone may so arrange his affairs so that his taxes shall be as low as possible. He is not bound to choose that pattern which best pays the treasury. There is not a patriotic duty to increase one's taxes."
—U.S. Federal Court Judge Learned Hand

Taxes have to be paid, and they should be. However, it is not your patriotic duty to pay more than your fair share, and this should be legitimately *avoided*, but not illegally *evaded*, to the maximum extent possible. But, avoiding taxes should not be done at the expense of jeopardizing intelligent financial decision making. For example, not selling an investment because it has a large capital gain may not be in your best interest if the expected future appreciation of the retained investment is not as opportunistic as a substitute alternative.

Federal tax policy robs a few *Peters* to pay a lot of *Pauls*

The quiet millionaire® bears the brunt of the tax burden, and the next time you hear the political cry that "tax cuts benefit only the rich," consider this. According to the most recent IRS statistics as of 2005, the top five percent of all income earners pays fifty-four percent of all federal personal income taxes paid, while the bottom fifty percent of all income earners pays only 3.5 percent of the total federal personal income taxes paid. You may be surprised to know that if your annual gross income level is $127,000, you are considered to be in the top five percent of all income earners, and hopefully this will motivate you to do serious tax reduction planning beyond the ritualistic last-minute rigmarole at tax time.

> QUIET MILLIONAIRE® WISDOM
> *Taxes affect every financial decision but should not determine every decision.*

Most "normal" people think that the subject of taxes is an absolute bore and would much rather spend their free time thinking about more interesting, stimulating, and happier aspects of life. However, paying taxes is something that everyone wants to avoid, and like it or not, the subject of taxes is something that influences almost every financial decision.

Often, people can be so concerned about paying taxes that they make personal and business financial decisions in order to avoid payment, which in turn costs them more than the amount of taxes they sought to avoid in the first place. For example, an investor decides not to sell an investment because of the taxes to be incurred on the gains, and then the investment declines in value far greater than the tax bite required to "lock in" the previous gain. While you need to plan to minimize tax consequences of a transaction, be careful about allowing taxes to drive your financial decision making.

The basic structure of the federal income tax system is simple, but the application of it has become complex

Underneath all of the complicated tax laws is a relatively simple income tax structure. Taxpayers add up their ***income*** from all taxable sources, subtract certain allowable **deductions** and **exemptions**, then apply the appropriate **tax rates** to the remainder, and finally reduce their calculated tax liability dollar for dollar with any eligible tax **credits**. Pretty simple until the government made the application complex and loaded the structure with costly pitfalls for the taxpayer.

The content of this chapter is intended to provide you, as simply as possible, with the main features of the federal income tax structure for your better understanding and reasoning behind the tax reduction planning strategies presented throughout the book. However, because of the very complex nature of the evolved tax beast, even my best effort to simplify is a challenge. **It will help your understanding to have a copy of your Form 1040 (the first two pages of your U.S. Individual Tax Return) to refer to while reading this chapter.**

Basic Federal Tax Structure and How to Manage It

The following outlines how the federal income tax system determines your net taxable income:

Gross Income

Gross income is the total amount of taxable earned and investment income from all sources. However, there are certain tax adjustments and deductions from your gross income that are allowable and that you should legally maximize in order to reduce your taxable income and resulting tax liability.

Tax Adjustments

Deductible from the gross income are certain allowable *adjustments* pertaining to education, self-employment, individual retirement account (IRA) contributions, and alimony, which result in your adjusted gross income (AGI).

Adjusted Gross Income (AGI)

Adjusted gross income (AGI) is the resulting taxable income after deducting the allowable adjustments. Deductible from the AGI are certain **deductions** for personal *expenses* (standard or itemized) and *exemptions*.

Tax Deductions

The first type of deduction is for certain personal *expenses*, which can be taken either as a standard deduction or as an itemized deduction if the total itemized deductions exceed the standard deduction amount. Everyone is allowed to take a standard deduction, which is adjusted upward annually for inflation. In 2006, the standard deduction amounts are as follows:

- Single persons and married persons filing separately: **$5,150** plus $1,250 for persons age sixty-five or older.

- Married persons filing jointly and surviving spouses: **$10,300** plus $1,000 for each spouse age sixty-five or older.

- Heads of household (single persons with dependents): **$7,550** plus $1,250 if over age sixty-five.

If you have more personal expenses to deduct than the allowed standard deduction amount, you can itemize the expenses and total them for maximum benefit. The primary expenses allowable for deduction, *within certain limitations*, are mortgage interest, property taxes, state and local taxes, medical and dental expenses, property casualty or theft losses, un-reimbursed employee business expenses, charitable contributions, professional fees, and investment-related expenses.

> QUIET MILLIONAIRE® WISDOM
> *Tax avoidance is legal; tax evasion is illegal and a criminal offense.*

Caution: Be honest when itemizing personal expenses for the purpose of taking tax deductions in order to reduce your tax liability. Plan your tax reduction strategies to legitimately maximize tax deductions rather than to imaginatively inflate them. It is not worth the risk of attracting IRS scrutiny, especially when good planning can produce worthwhile tax reduction results.

The second type of deduction automatically provides for a personal *exemption*, which as of 2006 is $3,300 per person and is annually adjusted upward for inflation.

Be aware that the tax laws phase out the allowance of both the personal-expense and personal-exemption deductions for high-income earners. As a result, high-income taxpayers experience an increased income tax liability, and intelligent advance tax planning is required in order to avoid being penalized by the income limitations for these deductions.

Taxable Income

Taxable income is the resulting income used to calculate your federal income tax liability after taking all allowable adjustments and deductions. The tax rate system is divided into increasing tax rate brackets (see Figure 6-1). This means that as your taxable income increases, you move up higher in the tax brackets, which results in an increasingly higher tax rate percentage being applied to your income. How much of your income falls into each bracket depends upon your taxpayer status, which can be one of the following five income tax filing categories:

- Married filing jointly
- Qualified widow(er)
- Single
- Head of household
- Married filing separately

The income amounts within the tax rate brackets are annually adjusted upward for inflation, and as of 2006, the IRS tax rate brackets are as follows:

FIGURE 6-1   Tax Rate Bracket Schedules for 2006

Tax Rate Bracket	Married Filing Jointly or Qualified Widow(er)	Single	Head of Household	Married Filing Separately
10%	$0–15,100	$0–7,550	$0–$10,750	$0–7,550
15%	$15,101–61,300	$7,551–30,650	$10,751–41,050	$7,551–30,650
25%	$61,301–123,700	$30,65 –74,200	$41,051–106,000	$30,651–61,850
28%	$123,701–188,450	$74,201-154,800	$106,001–171,650	$61,851–94,225
33%	$188,451–336,550	$154,801–336,550	$171,651–336,550	$94,226–168,275
35%	Over $336,550	Over $336,550	Over $336,550	Over $168,275

The highest tax rate bracket to which your taxable income level increases to is your *marginal* tax rate. For example, referring to the shaded box in Figure 6-1, if you are married filing jointly and your taxable income is $140,000, every taxable dollar from $123,701 to $140,000 is taxed at twenty-eight percent, and that is considered your marginal tax rate. By knowing the income breakpoints for the tax rate brackets, you can intelligently plan strategies to reduce your taxable income and thereby lower your graduated exposure to the tax rate brackets and lower your marginal tax rate.

For example, if you are married filing jointly with a gross income of $165,000 and after taking advantage of all your tax deductions, exemptions, and credits, your taxable income is $140,000, your planning goal throughout the year should be to find ways to reduce as much as possible the amount of your taxable income being taxed in the twenty-eight percent tax bracket. So, if you could reduce your taxable income to less than $123,701, your marginal income tax rate would be reduced from twenty-eight percent to twenty-five percent, and none of your income would be taxed at the twenty-eight percent rate.

By reducing your marginal tax rate, you are also reducing your *effective* tax rate. Using the same example as above, if you are married filing jointly with a gross income of $165,000 and after taking advantage of all your tax deductions, exemptions, and credits, your taxable income is $140,000, and you learned that your marginal tax rate is twenty-eight percent. However, your *effective* tax rate, which is the blended average of all the tax rate brackets that apply to your taxable income, is seventeen percent, and referring to Figure 6-1, the effective rate is calculated as follows:

Taxable Income	×	Tax Rate Bracket	=	Income Tax
$15,100	×	10%	=	$1,510
46,200	×	15%	=	6,930
62,400	×	25%	=	15,600
16,300	×	28%	=	4,564
Total $140,000				$28,604

The result is that you effectively paid $28,604 in income taxes on $165,000 of gross income, which makes your effective (blended) tax rate seventeen percent ($28,604 divided by $165,000). As you can see, by reducing your *marginal* tax rate, you are also reducing your *effective* tax rate, which should be your tax reduction planning objective throughout the *entire* tax year.

Inflation causes your tax rate bracket exposure to creep upward and causes you to pay more taxes.

The upward creeping of the tax rate brackets quietly subjects you to paying higher taxes. Creeping occurs because personal incomes are increasing each year more rapidly than the inflation-adjusted dollar amounts are increasing for the various tax brackets.

For example, referring to Figure 6-1, IRS tax rate bracket schedule for 2006, look at the shaded box for the twenty-eight percent tax bracket for married individuals filing jointly. Note that the lowest dollar amount in the tax bracket is $123,701 and the highest is $188,450. In 2005, for this same twenty-eight percent tax bracket, the lowest dollar amount in the bracket was $119,951, and the highest was $182,800. The upward inflation adjustment for these numbers from 2005 to 2006 represented only a 3.15 percent increase.

Therefore, if your income (salary, IRA withdrawals, investment income, etc.) increased from 2005 to 2006 at a percentage rate greater than 3.15 percent, and if this situation continues to occur during each tax year, you are automatically creeping toward a higher tax rate bracket, and you are exposed to paying more taxes. While having an increasing income level is desirable, each year you need to project and monitor your taxable income in order to plan throughout the year on how to keep your taxable income from creeping into a higher tax bracket.

Tax Liability

The calculated tax liability on your taxable income is the amount you are obligated to pay the IRS unless you are eligible for certain tax credits, which provide dollar-for-dollar reductions from the tax liability.

Tax Credits

Tax credits are allowed for the elderly and disabled, education expenses, child and dependent care expenses, adoption costs, foreign taxes paid, certain retirement saving contributions, and affordable housing investments. For tax planning purposes, you should understand that a tax *credit* is a dollar-for-dollar tax *reduction* in taxes paid and is much more beneficial to you than a tax *deduction*, which reduces only the amount of income upon which your taxes are calculated.

For example, if you have tax deductions totaling $10,000 and you are taxed at a twenty-eight percent rate, your taxable income is reduced by the $10,000 in deductions, and your tax savings amounts to only $2,800. In turn, if you have tax credits totaling $10,000 and you owe $10,000 in taxes, your tax liability is reduced dollar-for-dollar to zero. So you can see that $10,000 in tax credits is a lot more valuable than $10,000 in tax deductions. However, here again the tax laws discriminate in many instances against the high-income earners, with the eligibility to use many of the tax credits being phased out as your income increases to higher levels.

Net Tax Liability (After Credits)

Your net tax liability is the final destination for the federal income tax system unless you are determined to be subject to the alternative minimum tax (AMT).

Alternative Minimum Tax (AMT)

Ironically, if you earn a relatively high income and do too good of a job of reducing your tax liability, the IRS can force you to pay a higher alternative minimum tax, or AMT. This complex and unfair tax is affecting more and more taxpayers as their incomes increase. In essence, the IRS is saying, "Your computed tax bill is too low, and we have an alternative minimum amount of taxes that you should pay." The computation for AMT is *very* complicated and is triggered by a number of combined variables beyond the scope of this discussion. Just be aware that as your income increases, there are certain triggers that may automatically cause you to become subjected to AMT. The following are the AMT triggers that, while fully tax deductible to reduce your regular tax liability as a high-income earner, do not fully reduce your AMT tax liability if, as an income tax deduction, they become disproportionately too high:

- State and local taxes
- Real estate taxes
- Home equity debt not used to buy, build, or improve your home
- Miscellaneous itemized deductions, such as accounting and legal fees as well as unreimbursed employee business expenses
- Personal exemptions
- Medical expense deductions
- Incentive stock options

AMT is costly, so it warrants doing a tax projection for your situation each year to determine whether you are wandering into AMT territory and to plan accordingly to avoid it. However, if you look at the above listed AMT triggers, there is a very limited ability to maneuver the dollar amounts for those tax deduction items, and each year more taxpayers, as their incomes increase, are being caught in the AMT web and cannot escape it. In essence, as a high-income taxpayer, you are automatically experiencing a tax increase without the government having to legislate it.

The *Two* Cardinal Rules for Reducing Taxes and Managing Cash Flow

The existing tax laws are always subject to change at the whim of the politicians. This means that what works effectively today may become obsolete tomorrow. However, there are two cardinal rules that never change, regardless of the political environment or what changes occur in the tax laws.

Cardinal Rule One

Proactively, throughout the *entire* year, perform intelligent tax reduction management in order to maximize your after-tax dollars for wealth accumulation and financial security.

Cardinal Rule Two

In managing your cash flow, think in terms of what you must earn in pretax dollars in order to make purchases with after-tax dollars.

The following describes how Todd and Audrey abided by the two cardinal rules in order to reduce their taxes and manage their cash flow.

Todd, age fifty-five, and Audrey, age fifty-two, have two college-bound children, Jack, age eighteen, and Sally, age fourteen. They want to retire in eight years at Todd's age of sixty-three, when both children will be out of college. Todd owns a construction company that builds high-priced custom-built homes, and Audrey is a part-time self-employed interior designer working out of her home office.

Neither Todd nor Audrey has a retirement plan for either of their businesses. Instead, they use a taxable brokerage account to save for funding both college and retirement, which currently is worth $600,000, with mostly holdings that produce a high amount of interest, dividends, and capital gains that they have to pay taxes on every year.

Before they used the cardinal rules, Todd and Audrey were very busy earning a high amount of income and did not concern themselves with monitoring their cash flow and the total amount of taxes paid. They pretty much spent money for whatever they wanted, whenever they wanted.

However, at the end of every year, they never seemed to have much money left over and complained about all the taxes they had to pay. That was a concern, and so was how they were going to afford paying for college without using a large portion of the money that they had set aside for retirement in their $600,000 taxable brokerage account.

They have a CPA who prepares their business and personal tax returns, but unfortunately, while the CPA competently prepares their tax returns, they receive no tax reduction planning, which was costing them dearly. They decided to prepare a breakdown of all of the taxes they pay (excluding sales taxes on items purchased) in order to see the total they pay and where they can plan to reduce their tax liability.

This is how Todd and Audrey abided by Cardinal Rule One

Figure 6-2 summarizes how Todd and Audrey's total tax situation changed from before to after they started abiding by Cardinal Rule One for managing their taxes:

First, notice in Figure 6-2 that Todd and Audrey were able to reduce their total gross income by **$72,000** ($285,000 − $213,000 = $72,000). This was accomplished by doing the following:

- Establishing a new retirement plan for Todd's construction company and making a $42,000 pretax contribution to it instead of to their taxable brokerage account on an after-tax basis, which reduced the amount of their gross earned income that is subject to taxation.

- Replacing certain investment holdings in their $600,000 taxable brokerage investment account to make the investments produce less dividends, interest, and capital gains (more tax efficient), thereby reducing their gross investment income by **$30,000** ($60,000 − $30,000 = $30,000).

FIGURE 6-2   Todd and Audrey's Cardinal Rule One Comparison

	Before Cardinal Rule One	After Cardinal Rule One	Difference
Gross Earned Income:	$225,000	$225,000	
MINUS: Pretax Contributions to Retirement Plan:	0	42,000	
NET Gross Earned Income:	225,000	183,000	$42,000
Gross Investment Income:	60,000	30,000	$30,000
(Dividends, interest, and capital gains)			
TOTAL Gross Income:	**$285,000**	**$213,000**	**$72,000**
MINUS: Income Taxes & SS/Medicare			
Federal Income Tax:	($57,000)	($42,600)	($14,400)
State Income Tax:	(17,100)	(10,650)	(6,450)
Local Income Tax:	(5,700)	(4,250)	(1,450)
SS/Medicare:	(8,650)	(8,150)	(500)
TOTAL Income Taxes & SS/Medicare:	**($88,450)**	**($65,650)**	**($22,800)**
MINUS: Property Taxes	(6,000)	(4,000)	($2,000)
TOTAL All Taxes:	**($94,450)**	**($69,650)**	**($24,800)**
(33% of Total Gross income)			

Second, notice how by doing the above in order to reduce their total gross income by **$72,000** ($285,000 − $213,000 = $72,000), they were able to reduce their total income taxes and Social Security/Medicare paid annually by **$22,800** ($88,450 − $65,650 = $22,800).

Third, Todd and Audrey were able to reduce their property taxes by **$2,000** ($6,000 − $4,000 = $2,000) annually because they appealed their property tax situation upon receiving a reassessment notice. The property tax is an imprecise tax that depends upon an assessor's subjective value determination. Many homeowners do not monitor their property value assessments, which can be a costly mistake because the assessment may be overin-flated and can be challenged through a structured appeal process that starts with the assessor's office.

The payoff for Todd and Audrey abiding by Cardinal Rule One was that they were able to reduce the total amount of annual taxes paid by **$24,800** ($22,800 income and Social Security/Medicare + $2,000 property), which was enough to nearly pay the annual cost for the college education of both of their children, who would be attending college fours years apart without an overlap. Furthermore, they were able to preserve the money invested for retirement in their taxable brokerage account and invest $42,000 a year in a company retirement plan, which they had not been doing before.

However, Todd and Audrey did not stop at Cardinal Rule One: to proactively, throughout the *entire* tax year, perform intelligent tax reduction management in order to maximize their after-tax dollars for wealth accumulation and financial security. Next, they addressed their violation of Cardinal Rule Two: to manage their cash flow thinking in terms of what they must earn in pretax dollars in order to make purchases with after-tax dollars.

This is how Todd and Audrey abided by Cardinal Rule Two

With Cardinal Rule Two, they began by reprogramming their spending mentality to think in terms of what they must earn in pretax dollars in order to purchase items with after-tax dollars. Once Todd and Audrey assimilated the fact that thirty-three per-cent of their total taxable income went to pay taxes, they realized that they have to earn $1.33 pretax in order to spend $1 after tax, which was a wake-up call to pay more attention to their spending.

For example, they realized that in order to purchase a $25,000 auto-mobile, they must earn $37,000 before paying $8,000 in taxes ($37,000 x 33% marginal rate income tax rate), and this is assuming that they pay cash for the purchase. If instead of paying cash, they financed the car purchase with a $25,000 five-year, eight percent auto loan, they would pay $6,500 in non-tax-deductible interest, which makes the total purchase of a $25,000 automobile cost $39,500 ($25,000 purchase + $8,000 taxes + $6,500 interest).

Accordingly, because a lot of Todd and Audrey's automobile mileage is business related, it made financial sense to lease instead of buy their next car, and they would be able to appropriately deduct for tax purposes the lease payments as a business expense. Keep in mind that in this instance, leasing instead of buying the automobile was a good financial decision because the lease payments could qualify as a beneficial business tax deduction.

This new pretax dollar thinking about spending motivated Todd and Audrey to use a simplified cash management system and enabled them to stay on top of their spending patterns. After the first month, they were shocked about where their money was going along with the real cost of spending. They became even more motivated about intelligent cash management upon realizing how much their previous unmonitored and lackadaisical tax and cash management approach was ultimately costing them, their ability to retire in seven years.

Todd and Audrey were not planning to fail, they were just failing to plan, and the taxes were killing them. Remember that the tax laws are confusing, and the lesson to be learned from Todd and Audrey's story is that for the biggest tax reduction payoff, you might want to consider working with a *comprehensive financial planning advisor*, who is looking for tax *reductions*, as well as with a *tax preparer*, who is focused on looking for tax *deductions* when preparing your tax return.

You pay more federal taxes than corporate America does

Taxes at the federal level are collected from five sources, and their percentage breakdowns may surprise you.

1. Corporation Income Taxes   8.8%
2. Personal Income Taxes   55.3%
3. Social Security and Medicare Taxes   32.0%
4. Estate and Gift Taxes   1.4%
5. Excise (Consumption) Taxes   2.5%
                                                   _____
                                                   100.0%

The individual taxpayer, and in particular the high-income taxpayer, bears the brunt (approximately seventy-five percent) of all of the taxes collected by the above five areas of federal taxation. So, it merits paying attention to how you can reduce your tax liability and to how your tax money is being spent by the government.

Taxes permeate every aspect of your financial life. In the subsequent chapters covering investments, key employee compensation programs, risk management (insurance), business ownership, college planning, retirement, and estate planning, we will be discussing tax reduction strategies within the context of each of those planning areas. However, before moving on to the other specific planning areas, there are certain tax myths that need to be exposed.

Two Tax Myths That Can Hurt You

Tax myth number one

Deferring taxes is always good

There are two basic types of tax rates you have to deal with when you file your income tax return each year: taxes on your ordinary income (earned income and deferred income from retirement plans) and taxes on your capital gains (gains on investments held in a taxable account for at least twelve months or longer). The maximum capital gains rate is fifteen percent and much lower than the ordinary income rate, which is as high as thirty-five percent.

There was a time when the capital gains rate was twenty-eight percent and relatively close to the ordinary income tax rate, so it made financial sense to defer taxes. However, with low capital gains rates being so relatively low, it is not as compelling to defer the taxes on investments in retirement plans, regular IRAs, or annuities because the withdrawals from these investment plans are taxed at higher ordinary income tax rates.

Alternatively, an intelligently managed taxable investment account can be structured to benefit from the lower fifteen percent capital gains tax rate and can be made even lower by proactively offsetting taxable capital gains with capital losses throughout the tax year. In fact, intelligent investment management combined with intelligent tax management can at times effectively reduce the tax on capital gains to zero.

Therefore, with the lower capital gains tax rate in effect, deferring taxes is no longer a "given" best strategy even if you are able to contribute pretax dollars to a retirement plan. Of course, if your employer provides a matching contribution, you always want to contribute enough to receive the matched amount. Otherwise, with active investment management of a well-diversified portfolio combined with proactive tax-reduction management, it may be to your advantage to forego the immediate pretax contribution benefit of a retirement plan. In other words, you may be better off not taking the tax reduction opportunity on the smaller amount being invested, the *seed*, instead of looking toward the gain of a bigger tax break on the larger amount coming out, the *harvest*.

Another tax reduction planning opportunity that taxable investments offer involves making gifts. When gifting, it is always more beneficial to gift an appreciated asset than a depreciated asset or one that has had no increase in value. For example, you have a taxable mutual fund or stock that cost $5,000, and it is now worth $15,000, representing a $10,000 capital gain. You could liquidate the investment, pay the fifteen percent capital gains tax liability of $1,500, and gift the net proceeds of $13,500 to your place of worship or favorite charity. Better yet, you could donate the un-liquidated full $15,000 taxable investment, which would result in no capital gains tax being incurred for either you or the recipient. The result is that you lowered your tax liability and made a larger contribution, which makes the recipient even happier. A legal win-win all around, except for the IRS.

Another strategic tax reduction opportunity is to establish a uniform minor's account, which can be used as a gifting vehicle for highly appreciated assets owned by an adult who is subject to a higher tax liability than a minor child. Using the same example from above, if the appreciated asset is gifted to the minor child's account and then liquidated at the child's lower five percent capital gains rate, the tax liability on the gain would be reduced from $1,500 to $500, saving $1,000 in taxes.

Tax myth number two

Taxes paid go down during retirement

Start by answering this question. Are you intending to reduce your accustomed standard of living when you quit working? I do not think so! Also think about this. If you are going to live essentially the same way as you live now during your retirement in the future, you have to account for inflation. In order to keep up with cost of living increases, you are going to need to access larger amounts of dollars in the future.

Further, assume that all of your accumulated retirement money is in a tax-deferred 401(k), 403(b), IRA, or annuity. As you need to take out more and more never-taxed money just to maintain your purchasing power, your taxes will steadily *increase*. The more you withdraw to live on, the more you are taxed and at the higher ordinary income tax rates. This double-barreled blast of inflation and higher taxes can devastate your retirement program and is another reason to also be alert about tax myth number one, deferring taxes.

By now, you have gotten a glimpse of how taxes have an impact upon your entire financial life and your ability to accumulate and preserve wealth, both now and in the future. Accordingly, you need to be sensitive and intelligent about knowing and managing your taxes. You can start the process by using the Figure 6-3 Tax Awareness Worksheet to determine how much *actual* spendable income you have available to meet current living expenses as well as *actual* investable income for putting money aside toward college, retirement, and other investment objectives. You can also go to *www.quietmillionaire.com* for an online version to print.

Using your most recent income tax return, pay stubs, W-2 forms, and property tax assessments as information sources, fill in the numbers below.

FIGURE 6-3   Tax Awareness Worksheet

Gross Income: $ _____

Federal Income Tax: (_____)

State Income Tax: (_____)

Local Income Tax: (_____)

SS/Medicare Tax: (_____)

MINUS: Total Income Taxes and SS/Medicare: $ (_____)

MINUS: Property Taxes: $ (_____)

Net After-Tax Spendable/Investable Income: $ _____

Once you have completed the tax awareness worksheet and are aware of your actual net after-tax income that is available for you to spend, then you can establish a realistic spending and savings plan to use.

Resolve to follow the two cardinal rules for reducing taxes and managing your cash flow

As a high-income taxpayer, you have the most to lose by running your tax program on cruise control. Therefore, you should proactively plan how to reduce your taxes throughout the entire tax year and program your spending mentality to be in terms of after-tax dollars.

You may want to seek help from a *fee-only* professional advisor with no hidden agenda to sell you financial products offering supposed tax benefits. While certain financial products may be warranted, they should not be the motivating force and certainly should not be costly commission driven. Rather, an intelligent comprehensive tax reduction planning process as well as an after-tax cash management program should be put into effect. If you decide that professional help is necessary, the fee you pay to receive competent guidance should prove to be worthwhile.

Quiet Millionaire® Summary

- Understand the difference between taking tax *deductions* versus planning tax *reductions*.
- Understand the basic structure of the federal income tax system in order to reduce your taxable income.
- Abide by the quiet millionaire's® two cardinal rules for reducing your taxes and managing cash flow.

(continues)

Quiet Millionaire® *Summary* (continued)

■ Understand how the two tax myths can hurt you; plan and invest accordingly.

■ Complete the Tax Awareness Worksheet to know the actual amount of after-tax money that you have available to spend and save.

■ If necessary, seek expert *fee-only* professional assistance for tax reduction and after-tax cash flow management.

CHAPTER SEVEN

How to Be an Investment Winner

There are many proclaimed winning approaches to investing money, but few are consistently reliable. This chapter discusses in detail an investment approach that is founded upon Nobel Prize–winning research and that has practically proven to be the most successful approach that I have used during my forty plus years as a professional investment advisor. There are other investment advisors who advocate and successfully use the same approach but who use different financial tools to get the job done. I will discuss the strategies and tools that I recommend in order for you to be a successful investor during the good and not so good times.

Building a well-structured investment portfolio is in many ways similar to building a solidly built home that is just right for you, one that will not fall down when the first bad storm arrives. Doing so requires using the best set of tools available and having the professional knowledge and experience to do the job right. However, if you intend to build only one house, many of the required construction tools are too costly for you to purchase, and they require proficiency to operate properly. Just as with building a house, the same applies to the use of certain financial tools that are skillfully used by only a limited number of tried and true professional investment advisors.

You may see the need to hire a skilled professional to build the financial house you want constructed. If so, after you have interviewed and hired the qualified financial house builder who is right for you and you are comfortable and pleased with the finished result, then there is still the ongoing maintenance that must be done. Here again, specialized tools and knowledge are required, as well as a devotion of the time required to conscientiously keep your financial house in tip-top shape.

The quiet millionaire® knows that successful financial management and investing requires making ongoing decisions that are knowledgeable, businesslike, and not overridden by emotions. Managing your emotions can be your biggest challenge and obstacle to being an investment winner. Specifically, if you make investment decisions based upon greed during the good times or fear during the bad times, you are well on the way to losing at the investment game.

This chapter will discuss how a winning investment portfolio is well constructed and maintained. While the information is lengthy and detailed and most likely beyond what you can do on your own without professional assistance, having the knowledge is important. It is important because you must understand how this winning investment approach is accomplished in order to be certain that it is being practiced correctly. Furthermore, you will be prepared to identify and work with an advisor who not only advocates but also is experienced in using the approach.

Find the Right Professional for Investment Advice

■ Seek out a *registered* investment advisor who is regulated by either the Federal Securities and Exchange Commission or the individual state securities commission. Be sure to obtain a copy of the advisor's registration, which is required to be filed with the appropriate regulatory authorities.

■ Work with an advisor who is compensated on a *fee-only* basis, without receiving any commission income, in order to avoid possible conflicts of interest and hidden agendas to sell you costly financial products. Advisors who are paid commissions may recommend more frequent transactions for your portfolio than warranted or investments with unnecessary sales charges and high expenses, causing a negative impact upon your portfolio's investment return.

■ Understand and be comfortable with the advisor's investment philosophy and investment approach, and determine whether it relates closely to what is discussed in this chapter.

For further information about what to consider when looking for professional help, you can visit *www.quietmillionaire.com* or call 1-800-542-4198 for a free report titled "Ten Questions to Ask a Financial Advisor *before* You Hire Them"©.

Requirements for a Well-Structured and Properly Maintained Investment Portfolio

Plan and coordinate your investment program

Your investment program needs to meet your comprehensive financial planning goals and objectives. Always structure an investment program in the context of an intelligent comprehensive financial plan. *You will not get there if you do not know where you are going or how to get there.* You must have answers to questions such as:

- How much money will you need for achieving each financial objective and goal?
- Will you have enough saved?
- When will you need the money?
- How can you keep more by paying less in taxes?
- How will inflation and taxes impact the portfolio's purchasing power?
- What can you realistically expect for investment performance relative to making assumptions in your financial planning?

If you are uncertain, overwhelmed, or too busy to invest intelligently without emotion and in accordance with a coordinated comprehensive financial plan, then seek out a competent professional to help you with these answers.

Structure and manage your investment portfolio in a knowledgeable, disciplined, and emotionally controlled manner

The quiet millionaire® knows that there are neither shortcuts nor black-box formulas for successful investing and therefore tunes out all of the hoopla from the media, the investment gurus, and the stock pickers. Instead, he or she prefers an intelligently structured investment portfolio built upon a solid foundation that is proven to hold up his or her "financial" house through both the sunny and the stormy times. The following are some *requirements* for establishing a well-structured investment portfolio in order to manage it in a disciplined and emotionally controlled manner.

Realize that everyone is an investment genius in a raging bull market

During times when investment values keep going nowhere but up, cocktail parties and other similar gatherings often sport lively and boastful investment conversations. However, this is also the time for unrealistic investment expectations to occur and can be a reliable indicator for the foolish investor on the horizon. You will also notice that when investments start to perform poorly, no one seems to be openly discussing the results of his or her investment prowess.

The quiet millionaire® realizes that investment management is paradoxical because when investments keep going up in value, it seems straightforward and easy to make money. On the other hand, when investments start to turn sour, successfully managing money on your own becomes difficult and complicated. Successfully managing your money can be equated with successfully driving a golf ball long and straight up the fairway. It seems easy while you are in the middle of an open fairway, but it becomes difficult when you are faced with sand traps and water hazards. It takes knowledge, experience, and steady emotions to win at golf, and the same ingredients apply in order to be an investment winner. While investing may seem exciting when the investment environment is productive, it is when the going gets tough that uncertainty and fear set in, and it becomes more difficult to make smart decisions.

Know your tolerance for risk first before investing

Before starting to invest in anything, you need to understand and measure your tolerance for risk with respect to your investment program. This means going beyond nonmeasurable risk terminologies such as "conservative," "moderate," or "aggressive" that are often used to define an investor's risk tolerance profile.

Instead, you must get more specific by asking yourself questions such as:

- What is a reasonable average rate of return (reward) to expect?
- What volatility (risk) can be expected and is acceptable in order for you to achieve the expected rate of return?
- What is a proper time horizon for achieving the expected results?
- How should the portfolio be structured to assure that your planning requirements and performance expectations are accomplished in a way that provides you comfort?

And the most important question is:

- **What is the most amount of money you can stand or afford to lose in the single worst year of your entire investment time horizon?**

For some people, an investment loss of five percent in any single year is too much risk, while for others, a twenty-five percent decline in any given year would be acceptable. Having a negative result occur that is greater than expected for the performance parameters is what unnerves investors. However, if you know your risk tolerance level, you then can intelligently structure your investment portfolio based upon a personal risk tolerance assessment and thereby avoid disconcerting negative surprises.

QUIET MILLIONAIRE® WISDOM
If you lose fifty percent of your investment value, you must gain one hundred percent just to get back to even (and it may take many years to do it).

Meeting performance expectations that are realistic and established in accordance with your particular tolerance for risk is more important than whether the performance beats some arbitrary, unrelated news-reported index such as the Dow Jones Industrial Average (the Dow) or the Standard and Poor's 500 Composite (the S&P). If the portfolio is intelligently structured in a way that meets your reward and risk expectations, then you should be happy during the good times and not be anxious during the tough times.

Develop a written investment policy statement

The investment policy statement should provide specific investment guidelines for you and your investment advisor to follow. The policy should specify how the portfolio is to be structured, the targeted average rate of return, the time horizon for expected results, the risk tolerance level parameters, the amount and timing for anticipated contributions and withdrawals, and the emergency liquidity needs.

Having a written policy statement enables you to have a clear reminder about your personal expectations for the portfolio, and it will help to monitor the performance accordingly. By being organized and prepared, you are less likely to fall into the "emotional investor" category and more likely to be able to stay focused on monitoring the portfolio's performance relative to meeting your specific planning goals and objectives.

The Seven Biggest Investment Mistakes You Must Avoid

Mistake one

Focusing on the least important investment decision first

When most investors start investing, they try to decide which stock, bond, or mutual fund to buy, and while this is important, it is the least important investment decision that needs to be made. Sometimes the decision is based upon a hot tip from a friend or family member, or sometimes it is based upon the recommendation of a financial magazine, investment newsletter, or a money talk radio or TV program. Keep in mind that these media outlets are unregulated as to what they print or say and are unaccountable as to the advice they give.

Therefore, it is often best to regard media noise with suspicion. These financial mumblings may seem professional, informed, and convincing, but they can actually be misleading and harmful. Most often, the real agenda is not to educate but mainly to make money for the noisemaker by creating excitement or alarm in order to attract your attention. Even relying upon reputable investment rating systems and financial analyst recommendations can be harmful if not properly used, and here again you should recognize the fact that there is often a hidden agenda to sell you a product.

Mistake Two
Trading individual stocks

Many investors believe that they can successfully trade (buy low and sell high) a mishmash of high-expectation individual stocks. When stock prices are running up in value, making money seems easy and can be fun. While this may happen in the short run during an up market, it cannot be done consistently over the long run and ultimately is a losing investment approach.

The stock trading game can be almost as risky as gambling at the casino, and too often there is a time of having to reckon with more overall losses than gains. In fact, the odds are even more heavily stacked against you because when trading individual stocks, there are significant "hidden" transaction costs involved. While the brokers proudly advertise "low discount" fees for stock trades, they do not openly discuss the big impact of costs involving the unrecognized technical aspects of stock trading.

Discussion about these "hidden" costs goes beyond the scope of this book. However, it is important for you to become aware and fully understand the costliness of not receiving the "best execution" price and the narrowest "spread" between the "bid" and "ask" price when trading stocks. Furthermore, you have another "silent partner" to pay when trading stocks, the IRS. Remember that there are tax consequences on investment gains in a taxable portfolio, which can additionally challenge your chances for winning even more if you are unprepared and uninformed about how to deal with them.

Mistake Three
Attempting market timing

Sometimes investors foolishly try market timing by deciding when the best time is to buy and sell an investment. The problem is that negative and positive emotions and susceptibility to outside hype can rule many investment decisions. This means that many investors buy enthusiastically when things appear great (but usually it is too late), and they tend to sell fearfully when things appear gloomy (yet again it is too late).

There are endless examples that can be cited about how bad market timing has harmed investors, but incidents of mistimed investor behavior that occurred in 2001 and 2002 are notable:

■ In 2001, the two worst negative-performing months of the entire year for the U.S. stock market occurred in February and March, which prompted the largest single-month withdrawal of investor money from stock mutual funds for the entire year to occur in March. However, the very next month of April produced the very best positive-performing month of the entire year for the U.S. stock market, while investors had fearfully run for cover.

■ In 2002, the worst negative-performing month of the entire year for the U.S. stock market occurred in September, which prompted the largest single-month withdrawal of investor money from stock mutual funds for the entire year to occur in September. However, the very next month of October produced the best positive-performing month of the entire year for the U.S. stock market, while investors had fearfully run for cover.

Repeatedly, investors react to decreases in the value of their investment portfolio by liquidating to safer cash positions at the wrong time. The result is that they lock in their losses and miss opportunistic gains, which causes serious harm to their financial well-being. Ironically, typical reactionary investor behavior is often a predictable market timing indicator of exactly what not to do.

Caution: Do not be foolish enough to believe that professed market timing strategies are successful in the long term when compared to that of maintaining a fully invested, diversified portfolio approach. Investment research confirms that even the so-called "market timing gurus" cannot correctly time the movements in the investment markets on a prolonged basis. This is because when market shifts occur, they often do so very quickly and dramatically in brief spurts, and just one incorrect market timing decision can be disastrous for a long-term investment program.

Mistake Four
Emotional investment decision making

Investing your own money can be very emotional and can interfere with intelligent decision making. When an investment keeps going up and up in value, the experience can be exhilarating and make you greedy for more; when it keeps going down and down in value, the experience can be frightening and cause you to panic. Investment *greed* often turns to *grief*! These are powerful emotions that can distort your thinking.

The decision to sell a soured investment is too often made out of panic during disconcerting times rather than being based upon sound fundamental analysis of the investment and as part of a strategic plan for comprehensively managing the portfolio. Some investors hold on to a poor investment too long, hoping that its value will recover, but do so at the cost of missing out on better investment alternatives for increasing value.

The quiet millionaire® makes proactive business decisions, not reactive emotional decisions. This does not mean that he or she never makes an unprofitable investment decision, but when he or she does,

> QUIET MILLIONAIRE® WISDOM
> *If you would not buy the same investment you own today, then you probably should sell it.*

the decision to sell is treated as a lesson learned and considered an opportunity to make a more profitable investment decision next time. The key is that working with a professional investment advisor can help you take the emotions out of your investment decision-making process and therefore help you to obtain the performance goals for your portfolio.

Mistake Five

Not taking advantage of tax loss harvesting

Tax loss harvesting is not some special tax break for farmers. Rather, it is a very valuable tax reduction strategy. Many investors do not realize that by holding onto a soured investment in a *taxable* portfolio, they may be missing out on tax reduction opportunities enabled by selling the investment for a capital loss to offset future capital gains. This strategy is termed *tax loss harvesting*, which can save you thousands of dollars in taxes being paid on earned income and the sale of profitable investments.

Here is how tax loss harvesting works. Let's say that you invest $10,000 in an international mutual fund in January, and by January of the following year, it is worth only $5,000. That represents a $5,000 loss. But, now the international markets look very promising. You have two choices: either hold the fund and wait for it to go back up or sell the existing international fund, *harvest* a tax loss, buy a different, but similar, international fund for $5,000, and then wait for it to go up instead.

Now, let us say that at that same time you harvested the above $5,000 tax loss, you now have a health care mutual fund that has a $5,000 gain and that, after owning for a couple of years, you decide to sell. Upon the sale, there would be no tax on the $5,000 gain because you harvested the $5,000 tax loss from the sale of the international fund. And, because you still have an international investment presence with the replacement fund, you do not miss out on the opportunity to participate in the growth expected to occur in the international markets. This valuable tax planning strategy replaces an investment loss with a tax loss that lessens the tax bite when you go to file your income tax return, without sacrificing an investment gain.

What many investors can experience without tax loss harvesting is the really painful circumstance of having to pay a big tax bill on an investment that has decreased in value. This often occurs with taxable, actively managed mutual funds in a declining investment environment. When things get rough, mutual fund investors start to bail out. This forces the mutual fund manager to liquidate profitable long-term holdings for meeting cash redemption requirements and causes sizable taxable gains. The tax consequences are passed on directly to the fund's remaining investors, even if their investment in the fund has suffered a loss. It is not pleasant having to pay taxes on a losing mutual investment, but it can occur especially when the markets get shaky and investors are nervously withdrawing their downtrodden investment money.

Looking for opportunities to harvest tax losses should be monitored throughout the year by offsetting investment gains with losses. This makes taxable growth portfolios tax efficient and productive. A savvy investment advisor may be able to save you thousands of tax dollars using this strategy and provide you with a summary worksheet showing all of your capital gains and off-setting losses for the entire year. This makes for easier tax preparation, and hopefully your accountant will appreciate it so much that your preparation fee will be lowered.

Mistake Six

Not realizing that a negative investment environment can be positive

Ideally, while saving and investing money, you want to buy low and then sell high when you withdraw and use the money. However, this perfect market timing does not happen in the real investment world. Therefore, the surest way to capture the lows when they occur is by establishing an automatic savings deduction program whereby you "save first and live on the rest."

During the accumulation stage of any type of savings program, whether it is for college, retirement, or any other purpose, it is an advantage to be saving when the investment markets are down in value. By adding to your portfolio during that down time, you are able to accumulate more investment units because the unit purchase prices are relatively low and undervalued. You benefit from a lower average investment cost, and when the holdings increase in value, you benefit from owing more accumulated units. The result is that there is more money available for you to take out when you need it.

Mistake Seven

Losing too much investment value during down-market periods

If your investment portfolio loses fifty percent in value, it requires a one hundred percent gain just to get back to even, which can easily take years. Consider the following performance comparison of a $100,000 losing investment portfolio, consisting of some individual "hot" stock selections, with that of a $100,000 winning investment portfolio that is well structured with more diversification in order to lessen its volatility:

$100,000 Original Investment

| | Losing Investment Portfolio | | Winning Investment Portfolio | |
	Gain(Loss)	Balance	Gain(Loss)	Balance
Year 1	+50% +$50,000	$150,000	+33% +$33,000	$133,000
Year 2	+24% +36,000	186,000	+18% +24,000	157,000
Year 3	(-50%) (-93,000)	93,000	-13% (-20,000)	137,000
Year 4	+12% +11,000	104,000	+8% +11,000	148,000
Year 5	+15% +16,000	120,000	+12% +17,000	165,000
Average Annual Rate of Return	+10.2%		+11.6%	

The most significant thing to notice in the above illustration is that although the losing investment portfolio started out much stronger for the first two years (+$86,000 vs. +$57,000 gain) and outper-formed the winning investment portfolio in every year except for year three (-$93,000 vs. -$20,000 loss), the end result was much less rewarding ($120,000 vs. $165,000 ending value) because it lost too much investment value during the down-market period. The winning investment portfolio "won by not losing."

QUIET MILLIONAIRE® WISDOM
The investment psychology of a losing portfolio investor can be self-destructive.

The **losing portfolio investor** in the above illustration most likely considered selling "the hot stocks turned cold" and bailing out during year three. However, because so much dollar value had been lost, the investor in that situation typically holds on reluc-tantly and hopes for a recovery to occur before selling. However, the investment environment during a severe down-market period can be very unnerving when the mood is gloomy and clouded with pessimistic talk about corporate scandals, job layoffs, terrorism, recession, etc.

As the portfolio continues to sink still further underwater, the losing investor becomes fearful and anxiously hopes for it all to end. But, finally, not able to take it anymore, the losing investor often sells the downtrodden investments and heads to cash before everything is lost. Now, earning a safe one percent is more tolerable than losing any more money, and the new risk tolerance comfort level for the losing portfolio investor has shifted away from being aggressive to being overly conservative, just when things are beginning to brighten again. The losing portfolio investor's bad experience often causes him or her to remain immobilized on the sidelines in cash and miss the opportunistic growth spurts that occur sporadically and quickly.

The **winning portfolio investor** constructs and maintains a diversified investment portfolio that is comfortably protected against large losses of value during down-market periods. Therefore, he or she is willing and able to remain calm, patient, and fully invested during jittery, negative-performing investment times and to be ready to participate in future portfolio growth when it does occur.

How to Construct and Maintain a Winning Investment Portfolio

In 1990, economists Harry Marcowitz and William Sharp were awarded the Nobel Prize in Economics for their investment research, which produced the **Modern Portfolio Approach** for constructing a winning investment portfolio. This is the investment approach that has proven to produce winning results through my practical experience in using it for more than forty years.

Specifically, the Nobel Prize–winning Modern Portfolio research revealed that the individual investment selection (what stock, bond, or mutual fund to purchase) and market timing decision (when to buy or sell an investment) play only minor roles in an investment portfolio's growth. Instead, the research determined that more than ninety percent of a portfolio's total investment return is attributed to the asset allocation decision, how the portfolio is strategically allocated to various asset classes on a diversified worldwide basis. The following is a description of the major asset classes:

FIGURE 7-1   Description of Asset Classes

- **Money Market Funds:** *U.S. money market funds used to provide cash for ready liquidity and reinvestment.*
- **Domestic Bonds:** *U.S. corporate and government bonds having short-, intermediate-, and long-term maturities to serve as an anchoring stability element for the portfolio.*
- **International Bonds:** *Foreign government and corporate bonds that include either hedged or unhedged positions for managing currency fluctuations.*
- **Domestic Large-Cap Growth:** *Large U.S. companies possessing high-growth characteristics selected according to certain target criteria for sales growth, return on equity, i.e., fast growth and low or no dividends.*
- **Domestic Equities Large-Cap Value:** *Large U.S. companies possessing undervalued characteristics selected according to certain target criteria for per share market price relative to company earnings, i.e., low price earnings, low price to book, and possible relatively high dividends.*
- **Domestic Equities Mid-Cap Growth:** *Medium-size U.S. companies possessing high-growth characteristics selected according to certain target criteria for sales growth, return on equity, i.e., fast growth and low or no dividends.*
- **Domestic Equities Mid-Cap Value:** *Medium-size U.S. companies possessing undervalued characteristics selected to meet certain*

(continues)

FIGURE 7-1   Description of Asset Classes (*continued*)

target criteria for per share market price relative to company earnings, i.e., low price earnings, low price-to-book value, and possible relatively high dividends.

■ **Domestic Equities Small-Cap Growth:** *Small-size U.S. companies possessing high growth characteristics selected according to certain target criteria for sales growth, return on equity, i.e., fast growth and low or no dividends.*

■ **Domestic Equities Small-Cap Value:** *Small-size U.S. companies possessing undervalued characteristics selected to meet certain target criteria for per share market price relative to company earnings, i.e., low price earnings, low price-to-book value, and possible relatively high dividend payout.*

■ **Specialized Sectors Equities:** *Specialized investment sectors such as health sciences, financial services, energy, leisure, natural resources, technology, utilities, real estate, and certain geographically focused international equities such as the Far East and emerging markets.*

■ **International Equities:** *Companies located outside the United States.*

Each asset class has its own time in the sun to grow

The investment climate is not sunny all of the time for any given asset class. Therefore, you must create a portfolio asset mix where something is shining brightly at any given time, and you cannot expect all of the asset classes to be shining brightly at the same time. Another way of saying that the assets classes all have their individual time in the sun is to say that their performance correlates differently with each other. These different asset class correlations are historically measured and kept updated so that the results can be used as tools to structure an investment portfolio.

The timing as to when good and poor performance will actually occur for each asset class is not predictable. However, by statistically combining the historical performances and correlations of the asset classes, it is possible to reasonably predict how the overall structured portfolio will perform in the future. Accordingly, if investors know their own particular tolerance for risk, then their investment portfolio can be structured to perform within certain specified best- and worst-case ranges for risk and growth. This is comforting to investors because the portfolio performs in accordance with their expectations.

QUIET MILLIONAIRE® WISDOM
The asset allocation decision is the most important investment decision for achieving winning performance results.

Your tolerance for risk and expectations for growth determine how your portfolio should be strategically allocated to each of the individual asset classes. Accordingly, the most important part of the investment structuring process is the allocating of specific target percentages for each asset class comprising the portfolio.

Be aware that this investment process of measuring risk tolerance and determining the appropriate strategic asset allocation for an investment portfolio requires using financial tools available only through certain professional investment advisors. This is because, as discussed previously, purchasing the required analytical tools is cost prohibitive for the individual investor. Furthermore, it requires specialized professional knowledge and experience to skillfully interpret the information and implement the appropriate investment strategies. Therefore, you will need to find an investment advisor who can guide you through this Nobel Prize–winning Modern Portfolio Approach.

Use the Five-Step Nobel Prize–Winning Modern Portfolio Approach to be an Investment Winner

The following is the five-step process that is required to successfully use this winning approach:

1. Determine your tolerance for investment risk.

2. Structure a target investment portfolio with target asset class allocations that will enable the portfolio to perform in

accordance with your tolerance for risk and expectation for reward.

3. Fill the individual asset classes with low-cost mutual funds that are expected to perform better than their competitors categorized in the same asset class.

4. Measure and monitor your investment performance in a way that is meaningful and accurate.

5. Strategically rebalance (adjust) the portfolio's asset class exposure as required in order to assure that the results meet your tolerance for risk and expectations for reward.

Step One
Determine your tolerance for investment risk

Knowing your investment risk tolerance is important in order to know how to structure a portfolio that will perform in accordance with your expectations and comfort level. Figure 7-2 is a sample of one of the questionnaires that I use to determine an investor's tolerance for risk and can be printed off the *www.quiet-millionaire.com* Web site. There are no right or wrong answers to the questions, but rather the responses are intended to uncover inconsistencies and unrealistic expectations such as achieving a high rate of portfolio growth without having to assume the required amount of risk. While other advisors may use a different tool to determine an investor's risk tolerance, the outcome should be to establish realistic expectations for portfolio performance and to structure an investment portfolio that is not full of disturbing surprises.

Upon completing the answers on the questionnaire, you will probably wonder how you calculate your own risk tolerance level. The answer is that you should not expect to figure it out without help from a qualified registered investment advisor. Feel free to take the completed questionnaire to your advisor and ask for help in interpreting your risk tolerance in order to structure a winning portfolio that will perform comfortably for you.

FIGURE 7-2   Sample—Investment Risk Tolerance Questionnaire

This risk tolerance questionnaire is designed to assist in the structure of a target investment portfolio based upon your investment time horizon, risk tolerance, investment objectives, and liquidity needs. There are no right or wrong answers to the questions, but your responses as well as your reactions to certain investment scenarios are instrumental in determining a recommended target portfolio.

The following questions are used to evaluate your reactions to various investment scenarios. These include risk/return trade-off, upside potential and downside risk, volatility aversion, and impact of inflation.

Check (✓) the appropriate response.

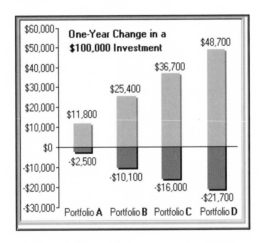

1. This graph shows the potential range of gains or losses of a $100,000 investment in each of four hypothetical portfolios at the end of a one-year period. The number above each bar shows the best potential gain for that portfolio, while the number below each bar shows the worst potential loss. Given that this is the only information that you have on these four hypothetical portfolios, which one would you choose to invest in?

   A. Portfolio A
   B. Portfolio B
   C. Portfolio C
   D. Portfolio D

   (continues)

FIGURE 7-2   Sample—Investment Risk Tolerance Questionnaire (continued)

2. Inflation (rising prices for goods and services) can have a significant effect on your investments by decreasing their potential purchasing power over time. Aggressive investments have historically outpaced inflation over the long run but have had more instances of short-term losses than more conservative investments. How do you feel about inflation and its impact on your investments?

    A. I am satisfied with my investments keeping pace with inflation. Limiting the potential for short-term loss is my main goal, and I am willing to sacrifice the potential for higher returns.

    B. I would like my investments to outpace inflation. I am willing to assume some potential for short-term loss in order to achieve that goal.

    C. I prefer that my investments significantly outperform inflation. I am willing to assume a greater potential for short-term loss in order to achieve that goal.

3. Suppose that a substantial portion of your investment portfolio is invested in stocks. If the stock market were to experience a prolonged down market, losing forty-five percent of its value over an eighteen-month period, what would you do (assuming your stocks behaved in a similar fashion)?

    A. Sell all of the stocks in your portfolio. You are afraid that the stock market is in a downturn, and you cannot afford the decrease in value.

    B. Sell half of the stocks in your portfolio. You think that the market may rebound, but you are not willing to leave all of your investment exposed to further loss.

    C. Hold the stocks in your portfolio. You understand that your investment may be subject to short-term price swings and are comfortable "weathering the storm."

    D. Buy more stocks for your portfolio to take advantage of their low price. You are comfortable with market fluctuations and assume that the stocks will regain their previous value or increase in value.

(continues)

FIGURE 7-2   Sample—Investment Risk Tolerance Questionnaire (*continued*)

4. Once again, assume you have a substantial portion of your investment portfolio in stocks. If the stock market were to gradually decline at an average of two percent per month, eventually losing twenty-two percent of its value over a year, which of the following would you do?

    A. Invest more now because stocks are selling for approximately twenty percent less than they were twelve months ago. You believe that the stocks will regain their value or possibly appreciate even higher over the long term.

    B. Sell the stocks in your portfolio and realize the twenty-two percent loss. You wish to avoid the risk of further loss.

    C. Sell half of the stocks in your portfolio. You are not willing to leave all of your investment at risk for further loss.

    D. Do nothing. You are comfortable waiting for the stocks to regain their previous value or to increase in value.

5. Aggressive investments have historically provided higher returns while exhibiting greater short-term price fluctuations and potential for loss. How do you feel about fluctuations in the value of your portfolio?

    A. I want to minimize the possibility of loss in the value of my portfolio. I understand that I am sacrificing higher long-term returns by holding investments that reduce the potential for short-term loss and price fluctuation.

    B. I can tolerate moderate losses in order to achieve potentially favorable returns.

    C. I can tolerate the risk of large losses in my portfolio in order to increase the potential of achieving high returns.

Step Two
Structure a target investment portfolio with target asset class allocations that will enable the portfolio to perform in accordance with your tolerance for risk and expectation for reward

In structuring an investment portfolio, it is important that target percentage weightings be established for the various asset classes.

By using the information gathered for identifying personal risk tolerance and expected rate of return, each investor has target asset class weightings designated specifically for his or her portfolio. Accordingly, the investor is able to see with a high degree of probability what to expect as a best- and worst-case performance scenario on a one-, three-, five-, ten-, and fifteen-year basis and can also see what average rate of return the portfolio should produce.

Figure 7-3 is a sample of a Target Investment Portfolio that I prepare after evaluating the investor's responses on the risk tolerance questionnaire. The Target Investment Portfolio specifies for the investor what best-/worst-case scenarios to reasonably expect for the portfolio's performance. The output is based upon constantly updated historical performances of the various asset classes comprising the target portfolio and should be considered only as a guideline and not as a guarantee of the expected results.

Once the asset class allocations for the target portfolio have been established and agreed upon, the most important decision has been made for structuring the investment program. As already mentioned, most investors think the first and most important decision is what stock, bond, or mutual fund to buy. However, with the Modern Portfolio Approach, that is the last and least important decision to be made; instead, it is the investor's weighted presence in each of the various asset classes that is paramount.

Figure 7-4 is a five-year Asset Class Performance Comparison between the Domestic Large Company Growth asset class and Domestic Small Company Value asset class, and it illustrates how the asset allocation decision is the most important one when structuring an investment portfolio and how only after that decision is made do you decide what stock, bond, or mutual fund to purchase.

FIGURE 7-3   Target Investment Portfolio Expected
              Risk Tolerance and Rate of Return

Target Asset Class Weightings

Asset Class	Target Holding Percentages
Domestic Bonds	13%
International Bonds	7%
Domestic Equities Large-Size Company Growth	16%
Domestic Equities Large-Size Company Value	16%
Domestic Equities Mid-Size Company Growth	4%
Domestic Equities Mid-Size Company Value	4%
Domestic Equities Small-Size Company Growth	6%
Domestic Equities Small-Size Company Value	6%
International Equities	14%
Specialty Sector Equities	14%
Portfolio Total Percentage	100%

Target Portfolio Summary

Original Portfolio Amount	$950,000
Expected Average Rate of Return	10%

Expected Range of Percentage Rates of Return

	1 Year	3 Years	5 Years	10 Years	15 years
Maximum	+34%	+24%	+21%	+18%	+17%
Minimum	-14%	-4%	-0.5%	+3%	+4%

Expected Range of Portfolio Values

	1 Year	3 Years	5 Years	10 Years	15 years
Maximum	$1,278,000	$1,823,000	$2,476,000	$4,951,000	$9,441,000
Minimum	$818,000	$848,000	$924,000	$1,231,000	$1,719,000

FIGURE 7-4   Asset Class Performance Comparison

$100,000 Initial Portfolio Investment

Year	Domestic Large Company Growth Asset Class		Domestic Small Company Value Asset Class	
1998	+42.2%	$142,200	-6.5%	$ 93,500
1999	+28.3%	182,443	-1.5%	92,098
2000	-22.1%	142,123	+22.8%	113,096
2001	-12.8%	123,931	+14.0%	128,930
2002	-23.6%	94,683	-11.4%	114,231
Average Annual Rate of Return	2.4%		3.5%	

Referring to the above chart, in the years 1998 and 1999, the Domestic Large Company Growth asset class, driven primarily by the high-flying technology stocks, was the best performing asset class for investors. It did not matter which stock or mutual fund you bought in that asset class; it mostly increased in value at the same high level. In fact, the *Wall Street Journal* reported that monkeys selected to randomly throw darts at a stock listing of the largest growth companies in the United States were achieving the same high rewards as professional investment advisors. In other words, you could do no wrong being in this asset class! Meanwhile, during the same time period, you could have been the most astute professional investment advisor buying Domestic Small Company Value stocks in that asset class, and most of your individual investment holdings within what was then the worst performing asset class were losing money. In other words, you could do no right being in this asset class!

Then, in the years 2000, 2001, and 2002, the gloomy clouds shifted to settle over the Domestic Large Company Growth asset class, which became the worst performing asset class; most of the investment holdings in that category were losing money for investors. Meanwhile, during the same time period, the sun shone brightly on the Domestic Small Company Value asset class, which became the best performing asset class; most of its holdings were making more money for investors.

Last, notice how the sunny and cloudy performance times for the two asset classes do not occur at the same time. In investment terms, this means that they have opposite correlations, which reduces the downside investment risk for the overall portfolio as well as the reward. By adding more asset classes to structure a diversified multi-asset class investment portfolio, you are able to further reduce the overall downside risk and thereby "win by not losing."

> **QUIET MILLIONAIRE® WISDOM**
> *Piecing together a well-structured investment portfolio is much like fitting together the pieces of a mosaic to produce a beautiful result.*

Many investment portfolios are an unstructured mishmash of security holdings that do not fit together properly. As a result, there is uncertainty about what downside risk and performance results to really expect. Often, the so-called *moderate-risk* portfolio is overloaded with negative surprises because of poor diversification. Furthermore, the so-called *conservative* portfolio, which is intended to be safe, can have a significant risk that most investors do not factor into performance, the risk of losing purchasing power as a result of inflation and taxes burying a low investment return. This unexpected outcome can be devastating for retirees who are depending upon their investments to keep up with increases in the cost of living.

The Modern Portfolio Approach to investing assures that more predictable performance results will occur during both the good and not so good investment environments. This is because a *well-structured* portfolio accesses multiple global economies for more investment diversification than can be accomplished with an *unstructured* portfolio consisting of too few asset classes and a limited number of individual holdings. The individual holdings within an undiversified portfolio typically have too high a degree of investment correlation, which means that all of the holdings go up or down in value at the same time.

It is more beneficial to *structure* a diversified investment portfolio by allocating a targeted array of low-correlation asset classes across the world's most attractive markets. This way, the various components of the portfolio that are performing well at any given time can offset some of the parts that are experiencing their time in the sun. The result is that you get a smoother ride on the path to successfully reaching your reward expectations because the component parts do not rise and fall at the same time, i.e., their values do not correlate with each other.

Using the Modern Portfolio Approach to assemble a diversity of target asset classes produces a well-structured portfolio that is most suitable and reliable for meeting your lifetime goals and objectives. Then, the remaining decision is determining what individual investment pieces should be used to fill the target asset classes.

Step Three
Fill the individual asset classes with low-cost mutual funds that are expected to perform better than their competitors categorized in the same asset class

Once the asset class structure for the portfolio has been determined, you need to decide what investment holdings will be used to carry out the investment performance objective for each asset class. For diversification purposes, this filling of the asset classes is most successfully accomplished by using high-quality, low-expense mutual funds that have a proven track record for performance that can be expected to continue.

Mutual funds provide a way for investors to *mutually* pool their money together in order to invest as a group by buying shares or units of the fund. The investment objective for each mutual fund placed within an asset class must match exactly the investment objective for the specified asset class. In other words, an international fund consisting entirely of foreign holdings outside of the United States should be used to fill the international equity asset class, and so forth for all of the individual asset classes.

There are more than six thousand mutual funds available to decide upon, so thorough, reliable research is required to screen the mutual fund universe for the most appropriate funds to use. Unfortunately, many providers of financial services and products, including mutual fund providers, often finesse their way around fully disclosing information about their true performance and internal costs. Furthermore, the disclosure materials (primarily a document termed a *prospectus*) that the regulatory agencies require to be given to investors for enlightenment are too overwhelming and not read by most investors.

Instead, investors more often rely upon investment newsletters and the financial media's magazine and TV hype, all of which are totally unregulated and unaccountable. It is important that you are not fooled with a false sense of honesty and trust provided by the financial "biggies" (mutual fund companies, banks, brokerage firms, insurance companies, etc.) with their huge advertising budgets and sales commission payouts— which are paid for by, guess who, you! Just realize that you have to be highly selective and savvy about which mutual funds are used to fill the asset classes in order to meet your portfolio objectives.

When deciding which mutual funds to select for constructing and maintaining an investment portfolio, investors should limit their selections to low-cost, no-load mutual funds that can be obtained directly from the mutual fund company without paying a sales charge. However, as part of deciding which no-load mutual funds are most appropriate for your portfolio, you also have to choose among funds that are either actively managed (**active mutual funds**) or passively managed (**passive mutual funds**), and both have their role to play in a diversified investment portfolio.

Active Mutual Funds

An *active fund* is actively managed to *outperform* or beat the performance of a particular market index benchmark for each asset class. As part of the mutual fund screening process, you certainly want to eliminate any funds that charge costly sales commissions, have high internal expenses, and produce relatively poor investment performance results, which is often the case with active mutual funds. There are three ways that a mutual fund company can impose costs upon its investor shareholders, which in turn decrease the amount of return earned on money invested in that fund.

■ Sales Charges

■ Marketing and Advertising Fees

■ Operating and Administrative Fees

Mutual Fund Sales Charges

Some mutual fund shares can be purchased directly from a mutual fund company without a sales charge (no-load), or some shares can be purchased *only* through a intermediary salesperson who is paid a commission and then the mutual fund company deducts a sales charge (load) directly from the amount of money that you invest.

The following is a description of the three categories of mutual fund shares that deduct a costly sales charge (load) directly from your investment, and you should avoid purchasing:

Categories of Mutual Fund Shares with a Sales Charge (Load)

- **A-Shares (charge one-time, front-end load):** When an investor purchases mutual fund A-Shares, a one-time, front-end sales charge (load) is assessed, which can be as high as seven percent of the amount invested. The sales charge is immediately deducted from the investment amount, and then the remaining net balance is invested.

- **B-Shares (charge one-time, rear-end load):** When an investor purchases mutual fund B-Shares, the full amount is invested but with the stipulation that a one-time, rear-end sales charge (load), which can be as high as seven percent of the amount invested, will be deducted if the investor withdraws the money within a certain number of years, typically during the first seven years.

- **C-Shares (charge ongoing, annual load):** When an investor purchases mutual fund C-Shares, the full amount is invested, but an ongoing annual sales charge (load), which can be as high as three percent, is deducted yearly from the amount invested and reduces the rate of return. Some C-Shares impose in addition a one-time, front-end sales charge (load), which can be as high as one percent of the amount invested. Because the annual load is imposed continually, this can cause a bigger negative impact upon the investment rate of return than the other two load categories.

Mutual Fund Marketing and Advertising Fees

In addition to imposing sales charges (loads), mutual funds (whether no-load or load) often charge ongoing annual marketing and advertising fees (12b1 fees), which can be as high as an additional one percent annually on the investment amount.

Operating and Administrative Fees

Besides imposing sales charges (loads) and 12b1 marketing fees, mutual funds (whether no-load or load) charge ongoing annual operating and administrative expenses, which can be as much as an additional two percent or more annually on the investment amount.

Passive Mutual Funds

The alternative to an active mutual fund is a passive mutual fund, which is passively managed and is also known as an index fund. An *index fund* is managed to passively *match* (as opposed to *beat*) the performance of a particular market index benchmark for each asset class. The most familiar index is the S&P 500, but you should be aware that there are numerous other indexes that are established for each asset class and for which the various index funds are managed to match. Investing in no-load passively managed index mutual funds is a way you can avoid sales charges (loads) and reduce to a minimum the amount of marketing, advertising, operating, and administrative fees that you pay.

Why should an investor consider a passive fund to match an index as opposed to an active fund to outperform an index? The reason is that eighty percent of the active funds actually "underperform"

QUIET MILLIONAIRE® WISDOM
When investing, accentuate the passive; be highly selective with the active.

their targeted index. This is because active funds have higher internal costs as discussed above and incur higher transaction costs because of more active buying and selling (turnover) of the investment holdings within the fund than do index funds.

Furthermore, you should also be aware that there is still another costly outcome occurring with most active mutual funds regardless of whether they are no-load or load. When your investments in an active mutual fund are situated in a taxable account (as opposed to being in a tax-deferred retirement account), the amount of taxes you pay can be much higher than when your investments are in a passive mutual fund, which is more tax efficient.

The higher tax liability occurs in an active fund because all mutual funds are required by law to annually pay out (distribute) to shareholders ninety percent of all the capital gains, interest, and dividends, which is taxable to them. Passive funds, because of fewer turnovers of their holdings, do not generate as many transactions that are taxable to shareholders. Adding insult to injury, these uncontrollable taxable distributions can occur and be especially painful when the mutual fund is at the same time losing value.

At this point of the discussion, you might be asking why any investor would select an active fund for his or her portfolio if the passive fund has more advantages. The answer is that through diligent and intelligent research, the best of the twenty percent of active managers that do outperform their target indexes can be discovered and be an important financial tool used to construct and maintain your investment portfolio.

The framework of a well-constructed, winning investment portfolio should consist of a core group of passively managed index funds that are then surrounded with a very select group of actively managed funds that are no-load and low-cost and that consistently outperform their comparable indexes as well as their fund peers. Here again is where a fee-only registered investment advisor can provide you with certain professional tools that are not available to the general public, the retail investor.

Locate a fee-only investment advisor who has access to low-cost, top-performing, actively managed *institutional* mutual funds that can be included as part of your passive/active portfolio structure

Because of all of the combined mutual fund charges that can significantly decrease investment performance results, it is important for you to understand that the higher the fund's costs, the less likely it is to perform well. However, be aware that if you work with a fee-only registered investment advisor to construct and maintain your investment portfolio, the advisor is able to access for you certain institutional mutual funds (as opposed to retail funds) that have no sales charges, no marketing and advertising fees, and the ongoing, annual operating and administrative expenses are extremely low.

Some of the top-performing institutional funds with the lowest costs and best investment performance are accessible only through a certain few registered investment advisors who must meet certain professional and financial criteria in order to use them. Institutional funds typically have minimal internal costs (as low as half a percent per year or less) and often require high minimum investment amounts (as high as $5,000,000 or more), which the individual investor can meet by investing through an approved investment advisor with large aggregate client investments. Accordingly, you can expect the investment performance to be high enough to more than offset the amount of the investment advisor's fee.

Selecting the most appropriate and best funds for each asset requires the investor to conduct ongoing research and possess investment expertise that is not influenced by advertising and media hype. Working with the right professional fee-only investment advisor can provide you with beneficial investment tools that are not available to you as an individual investor.

Step Four
Measure and monitor your investment performance in a way that is meaningful and accurate

Daily checking in on investment performance for a well-structured, diversified portfolio is really a useless waste of time.

People often ask me, "What's the market doing today?" My reply always is, "Which one? There are hundreds of them." Checking the Dow or S&P every day is meaningless and can drive you crazy. Instead, by being well diversified and participating broadly in the world's investment markets, you can focus your attention on what is happening during the three- to five-year full investment cycle and observe that every asset class does have its "day in the sun."

> QUIET MILLIONAIRE® WISDOM
> *The gains in percentage performance can be deceiving relative to the actual gains in* dollar value *performance.*

Investors evaluating their investment portfolio often simply want to know whether they had a gain or a loss during a certain period. They typically measure and judge the performance success of investments by percentage rates of return, which can be misleading and might not necessarily reflect the real return on the amount of money that they invested. Let's look closely at the performances for two portfolios, which demonstrate how the percentage rates of return can mislead you about the actual dollar gain for your investment portfolio.

$100,000 Initial Investment

Year	Portfolio #1		Portfolio # 2	
1	+35%	$135,000	+22%	$122,000
2	+30%	175,500	+14%	139,080
3	-14%	150,930	-1%	137,689
4	-16%	126,781	-4%	132,182
5	-22%	98,889	-5%	125,573
6	+29%	127,567	+16%	145,664
Average Annual Rate of Return	+ 7%		+7%	

Notice that both portfolios show the same seven percent average annual rate of return, which is calculated by totaling the percentages shown for each year and dividing by the number of years (six). However, also notice that the resulting portfolio dollar amounts are quite different at the end of year six, with Portfolio 2 being $18,097 further ahead. This is because the magnitude of ups and downs for Portfolio 2 was much less than for Portfolio 1. The smoother performance produced by Portfolio 2 demonstrates how important it is to "win by not losing" when you invest. However, the main point of this discussion is to show you that there are different ways to measure investment performance that result in different reported outcomes. You must be careful not to be fooled by percentage numbers when evaluating investment performance.

Many investors are completely unaware of how their portfolio has performed, individually or comparatively, and those investors who attempt to measure their rate of return are often confused about what the true results are. This discussion is necessarily lengthy and

> QUIET MILLIONAIRE® WISDOM
> *Different methods for measuring investment performance can produce different average annual rates of return results using the same input data.*

thorough in order for you to be knowledgeable about the methods for performance measurement—most investors are not. Understanding portfolio performance measurement is important in order for you to intelligently and accurately monitor your portfolio's performance and to make sure you are meeting your investment objectives. However, be aware that without having the professional skills or technological tools required, you will not be able to do the actual performance measurement calculations on your own.

There are three basic methods for measuring investment performance rates of return, and you need to understand how each differs as well as which one is most appropriate for you:

- Holding period return (HPR)
- Time weighted return (TWR)
- Internal rate of return (IRR)

Each of these methods measures investment performance differently and therefore produces different percentage rate of return results. The following illustrates how each of these methods, using the same data, calculates a different total and average annual rate of return at the end of a two-year period for a $100,000 investment portfolio.

Holding Period Return (HPR)

($100,000 Investment Portfolio)

Year one

Investment value beginning year:	$100,000
End of year value:	$105,000
Year one rate of return: +5%	+ $5,000

Year two

Beginning of year total value:	$105,000
Additional investment *beginning* of year:	+$95,000
Total value after investment:	$200,000
Year two rate of return: +10%	+$20,000
End of year value:	$220,000

The **Holding Period Return (HPR)** is the method used by most investors to intuitively measure their portfolio's average annual rate of return. It is the only one of the three performance measurement methods that can be calculated manually without using computer technology. For the illustrated portfolio, the investor would simplistically measure the performance in the following manner:

The total amount invested was:
$195,000 ($100,000 year one + $95,000 year two)

The portfolio value at the end of year two is:
$220,000

The gain is the total rate of return:
$25,000 ($195,000 + 13% is the *total* rate of return)

Therefore, the *average* annual rate of return for the two years is:
+6.5% (the 13% total return divided by the *two* years)

HPR Two-Year Average Rate of Return Performance Result: +6.5%

While HPR is a somewhat valid way to measure a portfolio's performance, it is too simplistic to be accurate because it does not account for how the performance is affected by the timing of multiple transactions (dividend and interest reinvestments, cash inflows and outflows) that can occur during the measured time period. Therefore, the more sophisticated performance measurement tools are required to be used for accuracy, and therefore you cannot do the calculations on your own without making daily computer inputs and calculations.

Time Weighted Return (TWR) is the preferred method by investment advisors to measure their performance for rate of return because it removes both the positive and the negative effects of cash inflows and outflows by the client on investment performance. Investment advisors cannot control the amounts and timing of cash deposits and withdrawals made by their clients, and these factors are what can make the performance result seem *better* or *worse*, depending upon the following cash flow circumstances:

■ Better performance result:
  Investments go up in value after cash *in*flow, more dollars going up.
  Investments go down in value after cash *out*flow, less dollars going down.
■ Worse performance result:
  Investments go up in value after cash *out*flow, less dollars going up.
  Investments go down in value after cash *in*flow, more dollars going down.

By stripping away the effects of all deposits and withdrawals made by the investor, TWR is the most pure method for performance measurement when the investor wants to accurately compare how his or her portfolio has done as a direct comparison with other money managers for the same period without the influence of any deposits or withdrawals to the portfolio. Accordingly, there is no difference in performance results regardless of whether the portfolio is worth $1, $100,000 or $1,000,000, and the following shows how the TWR performance is calculated for a $100,000 portfolio without any influence by cash flows.

Time Weighted Return (TWR)

($100,000 Investment Portfolio)

Year one

Investment value beginning year:	$100,000
End of year value:	$105,000
Year one rate of return: +5%	+$5,000

Year two

Beginning of year total value:	$105,000
End of year value:	$115,500
Year two annual rate of return: +10%	+$10,500

The investment advisor would measure the TWR performance in the following manner:

The total amount invested was:
$100,000

The portfolio value at the end of year two is:
$115,500

The gain is the total rate of return:
+$15,500 ($100,000 + 15.5% is the *total* rate of return)

Therefore, the *average* annual rate of return for the two years is:
+7.75% (the 15.5% total return divided by the *two* years)

TWR Two-Year Average Rate of Return Performance Result: +7.75%

The above TWR average annual rate of return calculation for the $100,000 portfolio does not factor in an additional $95,000 investment (cash inflow) being made at the beginning of year two, as was done in the previous HPR calculation. Therefore, be aware that when you see the published performance of a mutual fund or individual stock, it does not necessarily reflect the true performance of your particular investment in that mutual fund or stock. The difference in the reported performance can be worlds apart from your portfolio's actual performance because your performance depends upon when you buy and sell the fund or stock and how long you hold onto it. In order for your portfolio's performance to accurately match the reported result of a particular mutual fund or stock, you must have held the investment for the exact same holding period that is being reported, and you must not have made any deposits or withdrawals.

Be aware that in order to calculate the TWR, the performance data must be gathered and updated on a daily basis without fail. Therefore, the TWR calculation requires a computerized performance measurement program that can measure on a daily basis your particular portfolio without the effects of any and all cash flow transactions. Accordingly, also be aware that the TWR result may not be the actual performance result for your portfolio and that there is a third method to use in order to do that.

The **Internal Rate of Return (IRR)** enables investors to know how their own portfolio has done in terms of dollar growth and with respect to their desired or target rate of return for financial planning purposes. Therefore, the internal rate of return (IRR) measures the time weighted return (TWR) and takes into account a dollar weighted return (DWR) performance as well.

As discussed, the TWR measurement does not take into account inflows and outflows of cash; however, the DWR does. Therefore, the DWR calculates more heavily the periods when the portfolio is larger. This is because if a large amount of money is invested at the time the portfolio starts to perform well, the added money has more of a positive impact on the portfolio's measured performance.

The opposite negative effect can happen with a surge of new money when the portfolio's performance is struggling. Therefore, if you want to determine whether your particular investments are growing adequately for achieving your financial planning objectives, then combining both the TWR and DWR performance measurements to calculate the IRR is the most meaningful and accurate. Be aware that if there are no cash inflows or outflows for the time period being measured, then there is no difference in the average annual rate of return for the TWR and IRR because the DWR is not an influential factor.

The following shows two illustrations of how the two-year IRR is calculated for a $100,000 investment portfolio with only one variable being different: the timing of a $95,000 additional investment that is made at different times during the second year. Notice how dramatic an influence the timing of cash inflow has upon the calculated performance result.

Internal Rate of Return (IRR)

Different Performance Results Caused by Investment Timing

($100,000 Investment Portfolio)

	Portfolio One	Portfolio Two
Year one		
Investment value beginning year:	**$100,000**	**$100,000**
End of year value:	$105,000	$105,000
Year one rate of return: +5%	+$5,000	+$5,000
Year two		
Beginning of year total value:	$105,000	$105,000
Additional investment *beginning* of year:	**+$95,000**	0
Total value after investment:	$200,000	$105,000
First six-month rate of return: -10%	-$20,000	-$10,500
Total value end of first six months:	$180,000	$94,500
Additional investment *middle* of year:	0	**$95,000**
Total value after investment:	$180,000	$189,500
Second six-month rate of return: +22%	+$40,000	+$42,000
End of year value:	**$220,000**	**$231,500**

The IRR performance for each portfolio would be measured in the following manner:

IRR performance results caused by investment timing—Portfolio One

The total amount invested was:
$195,000

The portfolio value at the end of year two is:
$220,000

The gain is the total rate of return:
$25,000 ($195,000 + 13% is the *total* rate of return)

Therefore, the *average* annual rate of return for the two years is:
+6.5% (the 13% total return divided by the *two* years)

IRR Two-Year Average Rate of Return Performance Result: +6.5%

Notice that the IRR result for Portfolio One's two-year total rate of return (+13%) and the two-year average annual rate of return (+6.5%) are exactly the same as the results for the illustrated HPR-measured $100,000 portfolio. This same result occurred because both portfolios reflected a single $95,000 second investment being made at the *beginning* of year two vs. it being made at the *middle* of year two, as was done for IRR-measured Portfolio Two.

IRR performance results caused by investment timing—Portfolio Two

The total amount invested was:
$195,000

The portfolio value at the end of year two is:
$231,500

The gain is the total rate of return:
$56,500 ($195,000 + 18.75% is the *total* rate of return)

Therefore, the *average* annual rate of return for the two years is:
+9.4% (the 8.75% total return divided by the *two* years)

IRR Two-Year Average Rate of Return Performance Result: **+9.4%**

Portfolio Two's better IRR performance result demonstrates how the portfolio's rate of return benefited because the cash inflow (+$95,000) occurred after a negative performance period during the first six months of the second year (-10%) but participated with the additional dollars being invested during the positive performance period for the second six months of the year (+22%).

As with the TWR, be aware that you cannot manually calculate the above IRR performance result. It requires using a sophisticated computer performance measurement program that accounts for every transaction on a daily basis without fail for the period being measured.

Step Five
Strategically rebalance (adjust) the portfolio's asset class exposure as required in order to assure that the results meet your tolerance for risk and expectations for reward

Periodically rebalancing (adjusting) your portfolio's asset class exposure is a vital part of managing a diversified asset allocation program. By strategically rebalancing the out-of-balance differences in your portfolio's target versus actual asset allocations, you maintain the portfolio's basic structure in order for it to more reliably perform according to your expectations for risk and reward. The following is a portfolio target vs. actual asset allocation report that shows a portfolio that is out of balance and that may need rebalancing in order to adjust the differences.

Portfolio Target vs. Actual Asset Allocation

Asset Class Weightings

Asset Class	Target Holding Percentages	Actual Holding Percentages	Difference
Domestic Bonds	13%	15%	-2%
International Bonds	7%	6%	+1%
Domestic Equities Large-Size Company Growth	16%	12%	+4%
Domestic Equities Large-Size Company Value	16%	20%	-4%
Domestic Equities Mid-Size Company Growth	4%	2%	+2%
Domestic Equities Mid-Size Company Value	4%	6%	-2%
Domestic Equities Small-Size Company Growth	6%	4%	+2%
Domestic Equities Small-Size Company Value	6%	8%	-2%
International Equities	14%	12%	+2%
Specialty Sector Equities	14%	15%	-2%
Portfolio Total Percentage	100%	100%	

Looking at the above asset allocation report may not say much to you, but it does to a knowledgeable investment advisor who is making strategic decisions about managing your portfolio to perform in accordance with your expectations for risk and reward. The rebalancing process strategically takes profits from the asset classes that have become overweighted because of relatively strong performance (sell high) and reinvests in the asset classes that have become underweighted because of relatively weak performance (buy low). Portfolio rebalancing is not an attempt to *time* the investment markets but rather a process to *tune* the portfolio. In essence, the strategy is to sell high investments within asset classes that have increased in value and to buy low investments within asset classes that have not had their time in the sun.

Rebalancing should not be considered an automatic activity when the out-of-balance situation occurs because, strategically, it may be advantageous or prudent to delay or accelerate making shifts in certain asset classes. For example, if a particular over-weighted asset class is expected to continue its strong perfor-mance, it may be a good investment decision to let the asset class remain somewhat overweighted in order to have more dollars contributing added growth for the portfolio. Alternatively, if a particular overweighted asset appears to be overvalued and is expected to tumble, then the overweighted asset exposure might be prudently reduced to an underweighted status in order to assume a more defensive position for the portfolio.

With a well-diversified portfolio, you do not have to be right one hundred percent all of the time, but instead you have to make correct investment decisions only most of the time. However, at some determined point, rebalancing of the asset classes to be closer to the target allocation must be done in order to maintain the integrity of the portfolio's structure for achieving expected downside risks and upside rewards. Furthermore, when rebal-ancing, there may be tax conse-quences that have to be monitored and considered as part of the decision-making process.

> **QUIET MILLIONAIRE® WISDOM**
> *A diversified investment portfolio is a forgiving portfolio.*

You can be an investment winner!

By using the Modern Portfolio Approach as described in this chapter, you can be an investment winner. Be aware that there can be certain times when a hyped hot stock or mutual fund within a particular asset class may be outperforming your overall diversi-fied portfolio. But, be assured that the plodding, steady tortoise approach to investing always beats the rapid rabbit approach to the finish line of a long-distance run. It is only a matter of time before the rabbit wears out and investment *greed turns to grief*. You will be more successful if you *win by not losing*.

Quiet Millionaire® Summary

- Know the requirements for a well-structured investment portfolio and then wisely plan, coordinate, and know your investment program.

- Know your tolerance for risk.

- Know how to find the right professional for your investment advice.

- Use a fee-only advisor.

- Become knowledgeable on how to construct and maintain a winning investment portfolio.

- Be aware of the seven biggest investment mistakes you must avoid.

- Use the Five-Step Modern Portfolio Approach to construct and maintain a winning investment portfolio.

CHAPTER EIGHT

How to Get Maximum Results from Employer Stock Options and Other Key Employee Compensation Programs

Key employee compensation programs are offered by employers to their most important employees in upper-level positions. All of these programs are meant to attract and retain employees who are deemed as being vital for the company's future and financial success. However, intelligent and well-monitored financial management is required to maximize the results of these key employee compensation programs. They can be richly rewarding, but they also can turn out to be a worthless dud and worst of all can cause a disastrous financial heartache for recipients.

Key Employee Compensation Programs

The various forms of key employee compensation discussed in this chapter include:

- Stock options
- Restricted stock

- Restricted stock units
- Performance shares
- Stock appreciation rights
- Employee stock purchase plans
- Nonqualified deferred compensation

Stock Options

An employer can provide equity-based compensation to key employees in upper-level positions by granting them an option to *exercise* (financial terminology) their right to purchase a certain number of shares of the company's stock at a preset price within a certain amount of time termed the exercise period. Do not confuse key employee stock options programs with stock purchase programs whereby all employees (not just key employees) are eligible to purchase their employer's stock at a discount on a payroll deduction basis.

With stock options, if the employer's stock price rises above the option price, the options are deemed to be "in the money," and the employee can buy the shares at the locked-in discount option price. This can be a real wealth builder if the market price of the company's stock increases.

The employer's intent in offering stock options to certain key employees is for them to work hard to make the company as profitable as possible so that the company's stock increases in value as much as possible. If the share price goes up, the key employee has the option to purchase a specified number of shares at a preset lower price. Alternatively, if the stock falls in value and trades on the open stock market for a quoted price that is below the option price during the exercise period, the key employee's right (option) to purchase the stock has no value, and the stock options are termed as being "underwater."

Many key employees do not maximize the value of their stock options because they do not really understand the complex technicalities of stock options. Therefore, they fail to take full advantage of their optimal financial benefits. And as in most matters of money, making poor decisions about exercising your stock options can cause devastating income tax consequences and financial hardship, as the following story illustrates.

QUIET MILLIONAIRE® WISDOM
When to exercise or not to exercise employer stock options—that is the critical decision for building or destroying wealth.

In 1998, Doug and Betty lived in a comfortable and affordable home with enough living space and in an excellent school district to raise their two teenage sons. However, it was not their dream home, and they were restless about finding the house that was meant for them to live in, and they were always looking. For their children's benefit, they wanted them to stay in the same high school district before going to college, starting within the next two years.

Doug made good money working for a computer consulting company, and he had accrued a large number of stock options that were becoming more lucrative by the minute. In addition, he was buying on his own other tech stocks that were skyrocketing. Feeling excited with their net worth rapidly increasing, Doug had his sights set on retiring in seven years at age fifty-five.

One summer weekend in 1999 while out looking at houses, they found their dream house in the same school district, and even though their mortgage payment would double, "they could afford it." In order to buy the house and fix it up, they sold some of Doug's employer stock derived from his previously exercised stock options. When Doug and Betty moved into their dream home, they were enthusiastic about making improvements and decorating in a way they always envisioned their dream house to look.

Everything was going great until the beginning of 2000, when the tech stock bubble burst and things started to get worrisome for them. Doug's company started to lay off people, and he had to pick up the slack by constantly traveling out of town, being away from his family, and almost never being in his dream house. When they considered selling the house in order to relieve some of their financial concerns, they were shocked to learn that there were no buyers in their collapsing real estate market glutted with other anxious home sellers also hit by the high-tech collapse. If they sold, they would get less than what they owed on their mortgage.

In April, the IRS hit him with an unexpected huge tax bill resulting from the sale of his stock. To make matters worse, his remaining stock options had decreased more than seventy-five percent in value and were now "underwater." Therefore, the stock options could not be exercised in order to alleviate some of the building financial pressure. Even if the stock options were "in the money," the tax consequences caused by the immediate subsequent sale of the stock would only compound the financial problem.

Crushingly, the stock options no longer could be relied upon to fund college educations for their children, and Doug and Betty's plans for retirement were decimated. In addition, they had no way to pay the taxes they owed the IRS.

As Doug's employer continued to lose money, the value of the stock options was deemed permanently worthless. Then, worst of all, in 2001 Doug lost his job, and Doug and Betty had to file for bankruptcy. They lost their dream house and their dreams for retirement. Within the course of less than two years, they went from "riches to rags."

While this is an extremely disastrous stock option horror story, it is true, and there are many similar versions that have seriously derailed other lives. Therefore, if you have stock options, you need to know what type, the ground rules, the opportunities, and the hazards.

There are two types of stock options, nonqualified stock options (NSO) and incentive stock options (ISO), with different rules and tax treatments for each. Which type of stock option being offered to key employees is determined entirely by the employer, and the employee as the recipient has no choice as to which type. One of the main similar ground rules for both types is the *vesting period*, which is the time between the grant of the stock options by the company and the earliest the options can be exercised. Vesting periods of two or three years are most common.

Nonqualified Stock Options (NSO)

Of the two types of stock options, NSOs are less tax beneficial because although a NSO is not taxable when the option to purchase the employer stock is granted, it becomes immediately taxable when the employee purchases the stock (exercises). The tax is at the higher ordinary income tax rates (as opposed to the lower capital gains rate) on the gain between the option's lower exercise price and the current higher market price of the stock. So, for example, if the granted stock option allows you to purchase the stock at an exercise price of $100 per share and the stock is currently trading in the marketplace at $150 per share, you are immediately taxed on the $50 per share differential at ordinary income rates. Then, if you continue to hold the exercised stock for at least another twelve months, any subsequent appreciation is taxed at the lower capital gains rates when eventually sold.

While you do not have to come up with any money when the NSO is granted or while the option is outstanding, you do have to come up with enough money when the option is exercised in order to buy the stock at the option price and to pay the taxes owed. Some companies arrange for a cashless transaction whereby a brokerage firm buys the stock and immediately sells it, giving the employee the difference between the exercise price and the market price, minus the taxes.

Incentive Stock Options (ISO)

Although neither the ISO nor the NSO is subject to any taxation when the option is granted, the ISO is more tax beneficial than an NSO. This is because the ISO is not subject to taxation at the time the option to purchase the stock is exercised, while the NSO's gain is taxed when the option exercise occurs.

Furthermore, with the ISO program, if the purchased stock is *not* sold within two years of the grant of the ISO option and within twelve months after exercising the option, then *all* of the gains are taxed at the lower capital gains rates. However, a serious tax pitfall looms with ISOs if the stock is sold before the required holding periods are up. In that case, the ISO option defaults to an NSO tax treatment and is taxed at the higher ordinary income tax rates rather than the lower capital gains tax rate. Another iron-fisted tax liability, the alternative minimum tax (AMT), can become a major issue, especially when a substantial number of ISOs are exercised in a single calendar year.

The $500,000 College Tuition Cost

One of the biggest pitfalls with stock options can be exercising them too soon. Here is the story of how this caused John and Andrea to pay $500,000 for college tuition bills.

John and Andrea needed $40,000 to pay for their children's college tuitions. John had vested options to purchase 5,000 shares of his company's stock at $1 per share for a cost of

$5,000 while the shares on the open market were trading at $10 per share for a value of $50,000, a gain of $45,000.

John exercised the options, sold the shares for $50,000, and paid $10,000 in taxes on the gain. Therefore, he paid out $15,000 ($5,000 to exercise and $10,000 in taxes) and walked away with $40,000. If this seems like a nice outcome, here is the rest of the story.

Over the next four years, the 5,000 shares of exercised stock, which John had sold at $10 a share for $50,000 four years earlier, skyrocketed to $100 per share and would have been worth a total of $500,000 if he had not exercised and unloaded the shares. John and Andrea bemoan to this day that, in essence, it cost them $500,000 to send their kids to college!

Intelligent college planning would have revealed alternative ways to pay the tuitions without giving up the 5,000 shares and effectively using $500,000 to pay $40,000 in tuitions. Instead, if John had not exercised his stock options and sold the 5,000 shares of stock, the stock options would have appreciated with compounding gains in value on a pretax basis and would have increased John and Andrea's net worth by $500,000.

Five Things You Must Know to Get the Most Value from Your Stock Options

One: Building Stock Option Wealth Requires Intelligent Financial Leveraging

When you own a house (an asset) using a lender's money and the value of the house goes up, you are using a form of intelligent financial leveraging. Similarly, when you are granted stock options, you have an ownership right to an asset (stock) that can appreciate with "no money down" until you exercise.

Furthermore, at the time of exercise, you have to pay only what the stock was worth at the time of the grant in order to have full ownership of the stock at the current higher market value. Even better is that whether you continue to hold the stock or sell the stock to diversify, the low "original" cost continues to work for you.

Therefore, with a relatively little amount of money down to exercise and pay taxes, you are able to accumulate a lot of wealth. However, intelligent leveraging can be a powerful wealth accumulation tool only if you know how to use the tool, just as a carpenter must know how to use a hammer in order to build a very good house.

Two: Doing Nothing Is a Risk

With stock options, you do not actually own the stock until the grant is exercised, and there are ground rules for exercising the grant. If you do not abide by the rules, then the stock options can be permanently lost. Typically, there is a limited ten-year window of opportunity for the key employee to exercise granted stock options once the options *vest* (the time when you first become entitled to exercise). The options vest, or become exercisable, at various times during the ten-year exercise period and disappear entirely if not exercised. In other words, the stock options are lost forever if you do not exercise within the required ten-year period. However, once the stock options are exercised during the ten-year period and you actually own the stock, you can hold onto the stock indefinitely.

Be aware that there is now a trend toward shortening the ten-year exercise window period to a required six or seven years. This allows less opportunity to rack up gains or recover from a down market before the option exercise period expires. Some companies are now even establishing "cliff" vesting, whereby all of the options to purchase the stock become exercisable immediately upon vesting and there is no extended exercise window period.

More than ever, operating on cruise control is a hazardous way to travel the road of stock options. If you exercise too early and sell the stock, you may risk missing out on beneficial wealth accumulation. If your decision to exercise is delayed too long, you may risk losing flexibility for managing the exercise of your stock options as the deadlines approach, and you run the risk of paying unexpected and unnecessarily large tax consequences. The worst case of all would be for you to miss the exercise deadlines entirely, with wealth being lost and going out the window.

Three: *Lack of Diversification Is a Risk*

Exposure to high concentrations of a single stock can present an investment risk. If the employee's company stock is highly volatile, or if the company is not a worthwhile investment, exercising the options and selling the stock early may be best for intelligent diversification reasons. If the stock price drops permanently, your entire net worth could be seriously affected. Moreover, maintaining a highly concentrated stock position can also present serious problems if the stock price is down at the time you need to sell the stock in order to fund a financial commitment such as college educations, etc.

Last, be careful not to let foolish greed, excess employee loyalty, outdated company policy, and executive politics restrict you from making important investment diversification decisions. Whenever possible, sell off overconcentrated amounts of employer stock and strive for diversification to reduce your investment risk and to assure meeting your financial goals and objectives.

Four: *Taxes Can Gobble up Your Gains Even If You Do Everything Else Right*

Stock gains can be taxed in some ways more punishing than others can. Smart short- and long-term tax planning can preserve and maximize accumulated stock option wealth. The tax planning objective should be to avoid as much taxation as possible by being taxed at the lower capital gains rate instead of at the higher ordinary income tax rate. Furthermore, stock option executions can trigger the iron-fisted AMT, which can be avoided only by being well informed about what causes the AMT to occur.

Five: A Detailed, Managed, and Monitored Plan Is Required for the Most Intelligent and Profitable Stock Option Execution

Significant stock option wealth can be lost because of poor planning or no planning at all. Stock option planning cannot be done intelligently by using a cookie-cutter template, and there are no second chances if you make mistakes. Furthermore, during the execution process, there may be family pressures to use stock option money for discretionary purchases that may derail the overall financial accumulation success of the program. With knowledgeable planning, you can better weigh and access your priorities.

Therefore, the stock option planning process must be coordinated with all other comprehensive planning issues in your financial life such as future house purchases, college funding, and enjoying a secure and independent retirement. In addition, once the planning is in place with full understanding of the best strategies, then the program must be executed, managed, and regularly monitored for changes that require adjustments.

Up until 2005, stock option compensation was the most used form of stock-based pay for key employees because companies could bury the cost of doing so as a mere small-print footnote in their financial statements. Even though it is a cost of doing business, as are cash salaries and all other forms of compensation, the previous accounting rules did not require stock options to be shown as an expense. By this expense not showing in the financial statement numbers, stock options were offered plentifully while the true impact upon profitability of the company was not disclosed.

However, new accounting requirements effective in 2005 now require companies to show the cost of granted stock options as an expense on their financial statements. Because this can have a huge negative effect on the company's reported financial results, the heavy emphasis on using stock options to attract and retain key employees is now shifting somewhat toward other forms of key employee compensation.

Restricted Stock

As a growing alternative to stock options, restricted company stock is being issued by employers to their key employees. The stock is "restricted" in that it cannot be sold until a certain amount of time passes, as opposed to stocks bought and sold by investors on the stock exchanges, which can be traded with no restrictions.

With restricted stock, if the employee leaves the company before he or she has a vested right to the stock (typically a waiting period of three or four years), the shares may have to be forfeited. Because restricted stock consists of receiving actual shares of stock instead of an option to purchase the shares of stock, a lesser number of restricted shares are issued than stock options. Therefore, the upside potential for wealth accumulation is not nearly as lucrative.

However, there is less downside risk for employees with restricted stock compensation than for those employees receiving stock option compensation. This is because with restricted stock, even if the employer's share prices fall during the restricted period, once the shares become unrestricted and the employee has a vested interest, the shares are given to the employee to either hold or sell at any time. However, with stock options, the employee is not given the shares outright, as with restricted stock. Instead, the employee has the option to purchase the employer's stock from the employer during the exercise period, and that makes financial sense only if the purchase option share price is below the then-current market price for the company's shares being traded on the stock exchanges.

For instance, say you are given one thousand shares of restricted stock at $20 a share, for a total value of $20,000. If upon becoming unrestricted, the stock share price on the open market stock exchanges falls to $15 a share, you still receive the shares valued at $15,000 to sell. With stock options, if the option to purchase the shares is at $20 and the same share price drop occurred, the stock options would be "underwater" and worthless because you would end up paying $20 for a $15 stock.

Another advantage of restricted stock over stock options is that by having an actual ownership interest in the stock instead of an option to purchase the stock, the employee can receive any dividends paid on the restricted shares, even before the stock becomes vested by the employee and unrestricted. During the time while the stock is restricted, the dividends paid to the employee are taxed at ordinary income tax rates. However, once the stock becomes unrestricted, the dividends are taxed at the lower fifteen percent dividend tax rate.

There are other tricky aspects involving the taxation of restricted stock that need to be understood. Restricted stock is generally not taxed until the shares of stock are vested by the employee and the employer gives the employee the unrestricted shares of stock. However, once the restricted period is up, the value of the shares of stock is taxed as ordinary income regardless of whether the employee continues to hold or sell the shares. Therefore, if you have $15,000 of restricted stock that becomes vested and unrestricted in a given year, you are taxed as if receiving $15,000 in additional income during that year. If you continue to hold the shares, any gains in the share value thereafter are then taxed at the lower fifteen percent capital gains rate when the shares of the unrestricted stock are sold.

There is an alternative allowable option by the IRS for paying taxes on restricted stock. You can elect to pay the tax within thirty days from the time that the shares are issued instead of waiting until when they are vested. From then on, any increases in the stock's value are all taxed at the lower capital gains tax rate. The risks are that the stock value could drop and you paid up front a tax on the higher amount. In addition, you have irrevocably paid the nonrefundable tax even if you leave the company before the restricted stock is vested. Therefore, you had better be confident about the upside potential for the company's stock and certain about staying with your employer in order to choose this option.

Restricted Stock Units

Rather than issuing restricted shares of stock to key employees, some employers instead issue something less attractive, termed restricted stock units. The units are given in lieu of actual shares of stock but with a promise to the employee that he or she will receive the actual shares of stock at the end of the required vesting period. Furthermore, the vesting time for restricted units usually involves a longer waiting period than that for restricted stock shares, which means that the potential for a payoff takes even longer for the employee. In addition, the company usually does not pay dividends to the employee on the restricted units, as it does for restricted shares.

Performance Shares

One of the complaints about stock options by company shareholders is that the rewards to the key employees are tied more to the sometimes whimsical, sometimes maneuvered increase in value of share prices rather than on the actual financial performance of the company. In order to stop such criticisms, some companies now offer a form of restricted stock whereby the shares are issued only if the company meets certain performance targets and after a specified vesting schedule has passed.

Stock Appreciation Rights (SARs)

Stock appreciation rights (SARs) grant key employees the right to receive the increase in their company's stock value occurring between the time the grant is made and the time the grant is exercised. With SARs, the employee does not have an option to purchase or receive actual shares of company stock. Instead, the employee receives a "bonus" payout if the company's stock has increased in value at the time of vesting (when the employee has the right to exercise the benefit). The appreciated value amount is usually paid out in cash but can be paid out in the form of shares. Either way, when the employee exercises the right to receive the payout, the gain amount paid is taxed as ordinary income. If the payout is in the form of shares and the employee continues to hold the stock, then any gain in value from that point on is taxed as a capital gain. Often, SARs are granted in tandem with stock options to help finance the purchase of the options and/or to pay any tax due upon exercise of the options (sometimes termed tandem SARs).

Employee Stock Purchase Plans (ESPP)

The employee stock purchase plan (ESPP) is a program that allows employees to purchase company stock through payroll deduction at a discount to its fair market value. The company holds the stock in the employee's name until the employee decides to take actual possession of the stock or to sell it. At that point, the discount is considered additional compensation, and depending upon when the stock is sold, the discount and gain in value are taxed at some combination of ordinary income or capital gains rates.

Nonqualified Deferred Compensation

In addition to the various forms of stock equity–based compensation discussed in this chapter, some employers give highly compensated key employees an opportunity to defer a portion of their cash salary and bonus income. This enables top-paid executives to defer taxes and save more money for retirement beyond the restricted amounts they can contribute to a 401(k) plan, which is a *qualified* salary deferral plan by the Internal Revenue Code and the Employee Retirement Income Security Act (ERISA). By being qualified, this means that the company must include all employees in the 401(k) plan, the plan cannot be discriminatory, and there are limits on the amount that higher-paid key employees can contribute.

However, the company can offer, on a discriminatory basis, a *nonqualified* salary deferral plan for certain key employees only. Furthermore, unlike the 401(k) plan, the money contributed to a nonqualified deferred compensation plan remains a company asset and does not become an employee asset until after the money is distributed to the employee at retirement or termination of employment.

The deferred compensation is credited to an unsecured, interest-earning account, and all taxation is deferred until the money is actually received by the employee. However, there is an offset to the tax benefits derived by the employee in that the deferred compensation account is not protected from the employer's creditors if the company is sued or becomes insolvent. Therefore, the employee's deferred compensation is at risk.

The nonqualified deferred compensation account may be either actually funded or unfunded as a bookkeeping entry. If the account is funded, the money is generally transferred to a vehicle termed a "rabbi trust," so named because in the early 1980s, a synagogue received an IRS tax letter ruling that allowed tax deferrals for a rabbi who was the beneficiary of a trust established to pay him retirement benefits.

In order to encourage employee participation and savings, some employers offer a matching contribution. Some companies also provide more than an interest-earning account for the deferrals by permitting the employee to select from a list of mutual funds that typically mimic those available in the company's 401(k) plan. However, generally, the key employee should first contribute the maximum allowable amount to the 401(k) plan before contributing to the deferred compensation plan.

Key employee compensation can make you a quiet millionaire®

If managed intelligently, the benefits from key employee compensation can be highly rewarding, but there are also financial pitfalls that might be very costly. Figuring out the best ways to manage key employee compensation programs for maximum gain is often complex and "head hurting." The planning involved must be part of a coordinated, comprehensive financial planning process, and seeking competent professional guidance may warrant your consideration.

Quiet Millionaire® Summary

■ **Understand the rewards and pitfalls of employee stock options and the five ways to maximize and preserve their value.**

■ **Understand the rewards and pitfalls of all other forms of key employee compensation programs.**

■ **Plan and manage all key employee compensation programs as part of a comprehensive, coordinated financial planning process.**

CHAPTER NINE

Are You Prepared and Insured to Financially Survive Life's Risks?

Every day, we face the risk of something unexpected happening to us. When it is good, it is called a pleasant surprise, being lucky, or even a miracle. When it is bad, it is called an accident, a tragedy, or a catastrophic event. Life is full of different types of risks. Starting a new business or buying a hot stock is a risk taken for gain, but sometimes these risks end up being a loss. Some risks such as skydiving and horseback riding are taken willingly for pleasure and excitement. Other risks can be downright foolish such as smoking or drinking too much.

Certain risks are taken as a part of our everyday life, such as driving an automobile with the risk of an accident, getting married with the risk of divorce, having children with the risk of childbirth, or eating certain foods with the risk of becoming ill. Some people worry about risks that may never happen and live a very uneasy and sheltered life, while others may defy risks that are almost certain to happen and live life recklessly.

Risk management often involves purchasing insurance protection. This chapter discusses how to manage the different types of risk using the various forms of insurance available, as well as how to purchase the insurance you decide upon in way that is most cost effective.

Ways to Manage and Protect Against Risk

■ **Avoid:** You can try to avoid risk. If you never drive your car, you will never have an accident. Some risks cannot be avoided because they are certain to occur such as the risk of needing health care. You can try to avoid investment risk by keeping your money in bank certificates of deposit, but then you take on the certain risk of inflation and lessening the amount of time before you run out of money while living off of your investments. Avoidance of some risks is not always in your best financial interest.

■ **Control:** You can try to control or limit risk. Having a fire extinguisher in your home can put out the fire if it happens and can prevent the entire house from burning down. If you take medicine to control your high blood pressure to prevent having a heart attack, this is controlling a risk. If there is a fast-sinking investment that is causing you to have anxious sleepless nights, then you can sell the investment and limit further loss to control the amount of risk.

■ **Reduce:** You can reduce risk by replacing hazardous electrical wiring, getting rid of combustible materials in your home, driving defensively, or having routine health checkups. But, most important, you can reduce financial risks by reviewing and updating your financial plans.

- **Retain:** You can retain some of the risk of loss by having a high deductible on your health, homeowner, and auto insurance policies. This makes financial sense if you can afford the out-of pocket costs of the deductible amount in exchange for paying a lower insurance premium. Having no life insurance is a retained risk that may or may not be prudent depending upon whether survivors can withstand the outcome of a death without your income.

- **Transfer:** You can transfer the risk by buying insurance that protects you against having to self-fund the financial consequences of whatever risk the policy covers.

Most people do not understand insurance and pay too much for it. The quiet millionaire® researches the best ways to insure against risk and is insured properly. Intelligent insurance planning evaluates the actual need for transferring a risk and determines how to do so in the most cost-effective manner possible. However, people are usually uniformed and often misinformed about the most intelligent ways to transfer risk to an insurance company, and they end up paying too much for this form of risk management. This is because insurance products and their terminologies can be difficult to understand and because insurance agents are motivated to sell policies that pay them the highest commission.

Hopefully, this section will help you better understand how to intelligently plan with insurance products in order to manage a risk you cannot afford to assume or self-fund on your own. You will also learn what the common insurance verbiages mean and how to determine the right kinds and

> QUIET MILLIONAIRE® WISDOM
> *Intelligently use insurance to manage the financially catastrophic risks in life; do not overpay for the protection it provides, and be glad if you never receive a payoff.*

amounts of insurance you need in the most affordable manner.

Throughout this review of the different types of insurance products available for covering the various risks, keep these basic premises in mind:

◼ If the insurance premium or cost to insure is cheap, then either the chance of the risk occurring is low or the amount of the risk being transferred is limited.

◼ If the insurance premium is expensive, then the chance of the risk occurring is likely or the amount of the risk being transferred is high.

◼ If the insurance policy's deductible and co-pay provisions are high, this means that you have to pay more dollars out of pocket before the insurance company pays out dollars for its share of the risk incurred, and this lowers the premium amount charged.

Life Insurance

When considering life insurance, we tend to believe that death is a long way off. We live life as if we expect to live to be a hundred, and often we do not pay enough attention to the possibility that we might die tomorrow. Most likely, we will not die tomorrow or any time soon, but the risk is that we do not know for sure. Purchasing the proper type and amount of life insurance for the right price is an important part of the comprehensive financial management process. However, life insurance is usually acquired piecemeal, and the result is a costly mishmash. The purchase decision relies upon the insurance agent, whose incentive is to sell as much as the buyer can afford, which sometimes means purchasing policies that pay the most commission.

Here is a special warning for women about life insurance. They need to pay serious attention during the insurance decision-making process in order to make sure that intelligent insurance planning is accomplished. This is because according to the mortality statistics, women usually outlive men and are typically the survivors in a family situation. I once had a husband say to me in jest, *"I don't need life insurance because when I die, I want it to be a real tragedy."* Unfortunately, this is too often the actual outcome because of an uninformed and unplanned insurance program.

Let's look at some basic life insurance facts for understanding and intelligent planning. There are four parties involved with a life insurance policy: the insurance company, the policy's owner, the policy's insured (which is usually

QUIET MILLIONAIRE® WISDOM
Understanding life insurance can be as confusing and complex as a riddle wrapped in a mystery inside an enigma.

also the owner but not necessarily), and the beneficiary (which can be multiple). While most people think of life insurance mainly as a means to replace lost income in the event of a breadwinner's death, there are many other reasons for having life insurance. For example, life insurance proceeds, which are *not* taxable to beneficiaries, can be a means to provide cash liquidity for paying estate taxes or for providing financial resources to keep a business operating in the event of a key person's death. Sometimes life insurance can make sure that a surviving spouse will not run out of money during retirement. It also can be a way to fund a legacy such as providing a college education to grandchildren or contributing to a valued charitable organization or an alma mater.

Insurance companies use mortality statistics to figure out according to health, age, and gender when deaths usually occur, and they then price the insurance policy accordingly. The higher the risk of death, the higher the insurance premium or the likelihood of not being uninsurable is. Because women usually live longer than men, the insurance premiums are typically less for women. The premiums for smokers are always higher, which reinforces the warnings that smoking is a killer. Furthermore, because of the added mortality risks associated with obesity, being overweight requires a higher premium to be paid.

This section will describe the two main types of life insurance to choose from: term or permanent. The basic difference between term and permanent insurance is this:

■ Term insurance provides a *limited-time* death benefit only.

■ Permanent insurance provides a *lifetime* death benefit combined with a cash value investment component. There are three forms of permanent insurance policies that you can choose from and that will be described: whole life, universal life, and variable life.

Term Life Insurance

Term insurance is the most common type of life insurance offered on a group basis to employees by employers. It is also available for purchase on an individual basis outside of work. Term insurance is intended to cover a death risk for only a specified number of years, usually for terms of one year to thirty years, and it is anticipated that the need for the death benefit will be gone at the end of the specified term. The premiums for term insurance are cheap when you are young and increase as you age to where the insurance coverage becomes too expensive to keep. Therefore, most term policies are dropped and never pay a death benefit, except in the event of a premature death. Insurance agents are not thrilled about selling term insurance because the commissions paid to them stop when the term policies are dropped, and the commission amounts are meager while the policy is in force.

As mentioned, many people have group term insurance coverage offered to them through their employment. Because the insurance company underwrites the coverage as a group for all employees, people with health problems and smokers are included in the premium pricing. This causes the group term rates for each employee to be relatively higher than the rates for the employee who is individually insured as a healthy nonsmoker. Therefore, employees should always compare the differences in premium cost for their group coverage versus what it would be if they obtained their own individual policy outside of work.

Another disadvantage with group insurance is that you lose the coverage upon leaving the employment for any reason, and you may not be able to replace it individually if a health problem develops. This is another reason why any employee who is a healthy nonsmoker should consider opting for individual coverage that continues upon leaving the employment.

It is very important to remember that whenever you purchase individual term insurance, you should make sure that the policy is *convertible* to a permanent type of insurance without another underwriting being required, just in case a health problem should materialize in the future. Be aware that this convertibility feature is generally not available with group coverage. The Web site *www.insure.com* is a very informative place where you can obtain instant term insurance premium quotes from more than two hundred leading insurers, and you then have the freedom to buy your insurance directly from any of the companies that are most competitively priced for you.

Permanent Life Insurance

Permanent insurance is intended to remain in force for an entire lifetime and eventually pay out a death benefit amount upon the death of the insured. In addition to providing a lifetime death benefit, permanent insurance also has an investment component that builds up cash value inside the policy during the earlier years in order to keep the future premium amounts level and more affordable during the later years. However, in order to build up the cash value during the earlier years of the policy, the premium amounts for permanent insurance policies are much higher and less affordable than they are for term insurance policies with the same size death benefit.

Insurance agents prefer to sell more costly permanent insurance policies instead of term insurance because the premiums are higher and continue for the insured's entire lifetime. This provides the agent a more lucrative upfront commission as well as a longer sustaining commission payout on a residual basis. Furthermore, you should also know that if you drop a permanent policy early, there are costly surrender charges that can remain in effect for as long as fifteen years, whereby the insurance company keeps a significant amount of your cash value accumulated inside the policy in order to make sure it recovers the high commission payouts to the agent. Unfortunately, the sales practices and disclosures by agents can be misleading, and this makes understanding the true cost for the complicated components of permanent insurance difficult. To make matters worse, the regulation of the insurance industry is not sufficiently protective to the consumer.

There are three different forms of permanent life insurance: whole life, universal life, and variable life.

Whole Life (WL)

Whole life (WL) insurance is the original form of permanent life insurance, also known as ordinary or straight life insurance. With whole life insurance, you pay a level premium for your *whole life*. The size of the death benefit is a fixed amount agreed upon and approved by the insurance company when the policy is issued. A cash value amount accumulates in a tax-deferred fund that earns a relatively low fixed rate of interest. However, because the insurance company (as opposed to the policy's owner) assumes the full risk for the fund's performance being adequate to keep the policy from lapsing, the owner is never required to pay more than the originally quoted premium amount regardless of the fund's investment performance.

The accumulated cash inside the policy is considered to be an asset of the insurance company as opposed to it being a legally owned investment asset of the policy's owner. Significantly, this means that if the insurance company gets into financial trouble, the cash value can be confiscated by its creditors and lost to the policy owner. Therefore, it is important for you to know the financial strength and business practices of the insurance company that you do business with.

The policy's accumulated cash value can be borrowed against by the owner. However, if a policy loan is still outstanding upon death, the death benefit is lowered by the amount owed. Alternatively, the cash value may be withdrawn, but the policy might be terminated and subject to possible surrender charges and income taxes. WL insurance is the least flexible form of permanent insurance and limits your abilities to adapt the policy as a tool for meeting changed insurance planning needs in the future.

Universal Life (UL)

Universal life (UL) insurance evolved from the above WL policy and is also known as an adjustable or a flexible life insurance policy because both the death benefit and the premium amounts can be adjusted upward or downward. The death benefit can vary based upon the amount of premium paid and the interest rate earned on the policy's built-up internal cash value. A portion of each premium is deposited into a tax-deferred, fixed-income cash accumulation fund, with an annually adjusted interest rate, and the amount of the premium paid can vary depending upon the investment performance of the cash accumulation fund.

Harmful insurance sales abuses can occur when the UL policy is sold with an unrealistically high-interest-rate assumption for the cash accumulation fund in order to make the policy appear more attractive. The result is that the policy's owner shockingly has to increase the amount of the premium paid in order to prevent the policy from lapsing. This is because the policy's owner assumes the full risk for the fund's investment performance being adequate to prevent the policy from lapsing, which is unlike the WL policy, where the insurance company assumes the full risk. However, similar to the WL policy, the UL policy's cash value is considered to be an asset of the insurance company and therefore is subject to attachment by the creditors of the insurance company.

As is the case with the WL policy, loans can be made against the cash value of a UL policy, but the death benefit is reduced by any loan amount outstanding if the loan is not repaid during the insured's lifetime. Alternatively, instead of borrowing against the policy's cash value, a portion or all of the cash value may be withdrawn at any time, but then the policy might be subject to termination, surrender charges, and income tax consequences.

Variable Life (VL)

Variable life (VL) and a variation known as variable universal life (VUL) evolved from the above discussed universal life (UL) policy. The insurance industry developed the VL- and VUL-type policies in order to provide policyholders with more competitive and attractive investment options for their cash accumulation accounts. The main difference between VL and VUL is that VUL allows for flexible premium payments and the ability to modify the death benefit (same as UL), and VL does not. For purposes of this discussion, the term VL is used to describe both VL and VUL.

The descriptive word "variable" for these policies means that the investment results for the internal cash accumulation fund will *vary* for each policyholder. This is because each policyholder can specifically select where to invest premium contributions from a diversified array of stock and bond mutual fund options made available within the variable policy by the insurance company.

As is the case with the UL policy, the VL policyholder assumes the full risk that the cash accumulation account will earn an investment return that will be adequate to prevent the policy from lapsing, and, if not, then increased premium payments may be required to make up for any shortfalls. However, unlike the cash accumulation account with both the WL and UL forms of permanent life insurance, the cash accumulation within the VL form is kept completely separate from the insurance company's invested assets. Therefore, in the event the insurance company experiences financial problems, the policyholder's accumulated cash value is not in jeopardy.

VL is the insurance industry's version of "buy term and invest the difference." In order to sell VL, the agent must have a securities license as well as an insurance license—this is not the licensing situation for every life insurance agent. Very importantly, the money invested inside the VL policy must be proactively monitored just like any other investment program. However, too often the investments are not diligently managed after the initial policy sale is made, and they drift on cruise control. This can result in the policy's investment performance being riskier than is appropriate and possibly being underachieving. The outcome is that the policyholder may be required to pay additional premium amounts than originally intended in order to keep the policy from lapsing and losing the death benefit.

VL policies have relatively high internal operating costs because of the additional administrative and record-keeping requirements associated with maintaining the separate investment accounts. Therefore, in order to overcome these expenses combined with the life insurance mortality costs, VL policies require funding to the maximum allowable amount. The policyholder must commit to making sizable premium payments, an ongoing cash flow commitment that might be better directed elsewhere even though the accumulated cash value can be diversified to grow sheltered tax free inside the policy.

Nevertheless, if structured and managed properly, the VL policy can be considered a financial "Swiss army knife," meaning it can be useful for implementing comprehensive financial planning strategies. However, the appropriate implementation of VUL is complicated to structure and must include ongoing monitoring that requires maintaining up-to-date knowledge about the policy-holder's personal circumstances and staying on top of the changing insurance, investment, and tax environments. Too often, VL insurance policies are sold for inappropriate reasons and neglected after the initial sale is made.

The rationale used for VL is valid in that the policy does provide an income-tax-free death benefit and has internal investment options that can grow tax deferred, and the built-up investment accumulations are available for future use with favorable tax consequences. The problem is that these features and benefits are often misrepresented by VL salespeople and misunderstood by the policyholders, causing the planning concepts to be misused and poorly implemented without the required ongoing moni-toring being diligently carried out.

Frequently, VL is presented as a beneficial way to save for col-lege or retirement in a manner similar to that often proposed for using variable annuities (VA). However, keep in mind that both VL and VA are insurance products that have higher internal costs to overcome than do other financial tools available to save and invest your money. Therefore, you must be cautious about using insurance products for investment purposes and be certain that the rationale for using them as an investment substitute is legiti-mately compelling. In order to make sure that VL is the most appropriate tool for meeting your goals and objectives, you should work with a comprehensive *fee-only* registered investment advisor who is licensed for insurance and not selling the VL product in order to earn a commission.

How much life insurance is enough?

When doing an independent life insurance review for clients to evaluate their previously purchased policies, I find that the results have shown that most of the policies they have are the wrong type of insurance and for the wrong amounts of death benefit. By instituting an informed, cost-effective, coordinated insurance program that controls premium amounts, you can improve your cash flow for other beneficial uses while providing a sufficient death benefit for family survivors.

Using the rule-of-thumb approach and generalities to determine how much insurance you need is not appropriate. For example, people are often told that a multiple of anywhere between five to ten times their annual salary is a way of gauging how much insurance to buy. What if you are underpaid? Many stay-at-home parents are certainly more valuable than their annual salary and may need life insurance.

In order to know how much life insurance is an appropriate amount, what really must be determined is how much investment capital survivors will need. In order to do an accurate capital needs analysis, you will most likely require the guidance of an insurance planning professional. Keep in mind that a commission-paid insurance salesperson is often motivated to sell you as much insurance as possible regardless of your actual investment capital needs. For purposes of objectivity, it is usually best to seek the advice of a comprehensive *fee-only* financial planning advisor who is licensed for insurance and not motivated to sell you insurance for a commission.

The following is a checklist of what determinations should be included in a capital needs analysis in order for you to make an informed decision about life insurance protection.

Life Insurance Analysis Checklist

■ What is the estimated amount required for paying final expenses? Include all out-of-pocket medical costs, funeral expenses, taxes owed, and costs to settle your estate.

■ What is the total amount of outstanding debts? Be aware that it may be better for survivors not to pay off a low-interest-rate mortgage balance and instead to invest and use the life insurance proceeds to continue making mortgage payments.

■ What is the estimated total for survivor education funding costs? Adjust these expenses for inflation, which for college is averaging upward of about eight percent annually.

■ What is the amount of investment capital required to cover the survivor's (or survivors') annual living expenses *before* retirement? This calculation requires that adjustments be made for taxes and inflation. Offsetting this total capital need *before* retirement is the total amount of earned income and Social Security benefits expected for survivors *before* retirement.

■ What is the amount of investment capital required to cover the survivor's (or survivors') annual living expenses *during* retirement? This calculation requires that adjustments be made for taxes and inflation. Offsetting this total capital need *during* retirement is the total amount of pension income and Social Security benefits expected for survivors *during* retirement.

■ What is the total amount of investment capital that you currently have? Include all bank accounts, investment accounts, and retirement plans, but do not include any expected inheritances.

■ What is the total amount of current life insurance in force? Is any of this amount term insurance that will become too costly and need to be dropped or replaced? Do not include group life insurance, which is not portable upon leaving employment, or accidental death insurance policies, which do not include a death benefit for natural causes.

■ Based upon the above calculations, what *net* amount of investment capital is required from life insurance proceeds? Are you overinsured or underinsured?

A capital needs analysis should be performed at least annually in conjunction with a thorough review and update of all beneficiary designations and estate planning documentation.

Disability Insurance

As much as people are uncertain and uninformed about their life insurance needs, they are even more uninformed about how to survive financially with reduced or no earned income as a result of a disability. Understanding disability insurance is a complicated undertaking because the insurance companies load the policy provisions with subtle pitfalls that avoid or reduce their exposure to potential claims. Simplistically, keep in mind that if the disability insurance premium is low, the policy's fine print is likely loaded with wording to escape from paying the benefits you expect.

The loss of income as a result of a disability can destroy the lifestyle you are accustomed to living. Most people do not have any protection against lost income and live one paycheck away from suffering a financial disaster if they became disabled and unable to work. The financial cost of a disability can be far more devastating than the death of an income earner. This is because the disabled income earner is still alive as an added burdensome expense, but he or she is no longer able to contribute income unless that income stream was insured against disability. Even then, if insured, usually only sixty percent of the income is replaced by an insurance benefit. In addition, the disability income can be taxable as well, thereby further reducing the net available for meeting daily living expenses.

The risk of a disability occurring is greater than the risk of a premature death, an auto accident, or your house being

QUIET MILLIONAIRE® WISDOM
Incurring a disability is
more uncertain *than death*
but is more certain *than*
death during the income-
earning years.

destroyed. This is why the premium cost to adequately insure against disability is so expensive and why qualifying for disability insurance on an individual basis is very difficult.

Another reason is that the disability insurance industry has been shaken up by massive claim payouts because of its previous liberal underwriting and aggressive sales approach. Many of the biggest insurers have either involuntarily gone bust or voluntarily dropped out of the business. And, the disability insurance companies that are still around have dramatically tightened up their approval underwriting procedures.

Gone forever are the days of receiving a lifetime income payout due to stress, backaches, or chronic fatigue syndrome. Today, in order to be individually underwritten and approved for a disability policy, you MUST be in near-perfect physical and mental shape. In addition, if you do become disabled, then there are hoops you have to jump through in order to receive a benefit payout, which has limits for how much and how long.

Most people who have disability insurance protection usually obtain it through group coverage with their employer. However, here again the high cost restricts the number of employers that offer disability insurance as a benefit. Moreover, in most instances, the group coverage does not adequately replace lost income required for meeting current financial requirements and certainly is not sufficient to fund major financial commitments such as college and retirement.

Group disability insurance typically covers only fifty to sixty percent of your base monthly pretax earned income, not including bonuses. Furthermore, there are dollar limits imposed as to the maximum monthly income benefit paid that severely impact high-income families, and the benefit payout period rarely extends beyond age sixty-five. The disability insurance company wants to make sure that the benefit received is not lucrative enough to deter you from returning to work.

Another common restriction of benefits is that they may stop after a couple of years of receiving disability income because you cannot perform the duties of your own occupation, but you are deemed able enough to work at some other occupation. Depending upon how the policy is written, you might end up working at a chain discount store and not receive any more disability benefit payments.

There are also income tax ramifications to consider with respect to disability income received. To the extent that the employer pays the premium for the employee, the benefit is taxed as ordinary income, thereby making the actual lost income protection even less worthwhile.

Group coverage can be supplemented with a private policy that will increase overall disability protection up to seventy to eighty percent of lost earned income. However, obtaining disability insurance to replace that level of lost income is challenging because of today's tougher underwriting guidelines.

Social Security is mainly regarded as a source of retirement income from the federal government, but it also has a disability income benefit as well. However, more than eighty percent of the applicants fail to derive any income because it is extremely difficult to qualify for Social Security's disability benefit. Accordingly, there are lawyers who earn a nice living fighting through the disability appeals process on behalf of denied applicants. Even if you do qualify, the income received is below the government's poverty level guidelines.

Workers Compensation is a form of disability insurance that the individual states require most employers to provide to their employees. Insurance premiums are paid to the state by employers in order to fund the program, but a benefit is paid to the employee only if the disability is caused by a job-related incident. The workers compensation programs vary by state law, but the disability benefits paid are typically very low and last for only a few years.

Suffering a disability can be devastating financially and emotionally. Unless you diligently feather your nest with a combination of savings and disability insurance protection, drastic and painful lifestyle adjustments will be required in the event of lost earned income.

> QUIET MILLIONAIRE® WISDOM
> *Know and answer specifically: How and how long could you continue to pay your current and future bills without receiving a paycheck? (Can your family feel secure about the answers?)*

Understanding the intricacies of disability insurance and adequacy of coverage is complicated. Be alert to the fact that the protection is subject to tricky loopholes that can impact your expected coverage. Furthermore, the disability insurance review should be done as part of a comprehensive and coordinated financial management review. If you are confused and uncertain, seek guidance from a knowledgeable, independent, fee-only advisor who is not influenced by an insurance sales commission.

The following is a short checklist of the basic policy provisions to be considered when evaluating disability insurance protection.

■ What is the amount of the monthly income benefit? Are there provisions that allow for the income benefit to be increased as your earned income increases?

■ What is the maximum monthly income benefit amount payable? In particular, group insurance programs can have very low dollar maximums that are not sufficient to protect high-income earners. Even if the program's dollar maximum is high, you will be hard pressed to find a disability insurance company that pays a dollar amount greater than $15,000 per month. Furthermore, the maximum dollar amount is subject to the limitation that no more than seventy to eighty percent of the insured's earned income is being replaced.

■ In the event of a disability, is the benefit income amount fixed, or will cost of living increases be provided? Most disability policies have a fixed monthly benefit that does not increase once the benefit is being paid out.

■ What is the definition of a disability? Is it the inability to perform the duties of your specified own occupation (own occ), or is it the inability to perform the duties of any occupation (any occ) for which your education and training make you qualified?

■ What is the waiting period, or the amount of time you must be disabled, before benefits are paid? Waiting periods can range from one week to two years, and the longer you wait, the lower the premium cost.

■ What is the benefit period, or how long will you receive monthly income once the policy benefit starts? The benefit period can range from six months to age sixty-five and in rare instances for life. The longer the benefit period, the higher the premium to insure.

■ Does the policy have a rider that pays a benefit if you are able to return to work part time?

■ Does the policy have a Social Security offset rider that guarantees that if you qualify for disability payments under your insurance policy but do not qualify for Social Security disability, a common occurrence, the disability policy will also pay the Social Security disability amount?

■ Does the policy include an additional purchase option that guarantees you the right to purchase additional disability insurance in the future, regardless of your health at that time?

In summary, disability insurance is expensive, and the income benefit is usually inadequate to meet current expenses, causing financial hardship and painful adjustments in your accustomed standard of living. Therefore, any intelligent comprehensive financial management program must include a prioritized allocation of earned income to accumulate a financial reserve and insure against lost income.

Property and Casualty Insurance

Property and casualty (P&C) insurance protects you against the risk of property damage and loss and against liability in the event of a lawsuit. Having adequate P&C coverage for your residence, automobiles, and business ownership is required to protect and preserve your monetary assets and accumulated wealth. This review of P&C insurance will cover only the elements of *personal* P&C coverage, not information relating to commercial or business P&C coverage. However, you should be aware that because of terrorist attacks and the multiple catastrophic hurricane events that cause horrific losses of property and life, P&C insurers have adjusted their premium levels upward nationwide for personal and business coverage in order to take into account these higher insurance underwriting risks.

Your P&C cost and coverage should be evaluated and compared periodically to make certain that you are paying a competitive premium amount for the protection that you require. This why it is usually preferable to work with an *independent* P&C insurance agent who is reputable and experienced and who represents a number of different insurance companies for determining what specific coverage amounts are available and most appropriate for your particular situation.

However, be careful to look beyond the price comparison alone. It is extremely important that the insurer be financially sound, have a good claims paying record, and will not be quick to drop you after a claim is filed. In all cases, it is wise to limit your P&C insurance claims to the catastrophic, big-dollar event. Small claims or too many claims can drive up your premiums or cause you to be dropped as an insured.

There are many choices and decisions you must make, as well as many loopholes you must understand, with respect to P&C insurance. As you read the descriptions of the various P&C insurance policies and coverages, you will benefit by referring to the coverage declaration pages of your own existing auto, homeowner, and personal liability umbrella policies.

Automobile Insurance

Automobile insurance premiums have gone up with the increased sophistication and material costs associated with today's automobiles. In addition, most families own multiple cars, and in addition, the teenage driving risk is high. Typically, there are three component coverages within an automobile insurance policy: liability, medical, and collision and comprehensive.

Auto Liability: Liability insurance coverage is required by most states to protect you against the cost of property damage and bodily injury involved in an accident in which you are deemed to be responsible and liable. Liability is even required in so-called "no-fault" insurance states.

Auto insurance policy declaration pages reflect split liability coverage limits that are shown as split numbers. For example, the split numbers 50/100/25 mean your coverage limits for an accident are as follows:

- $50,000 for bodily injury caused to another person
- $100,000 for bodily injuries caused to everyone
- $25,000 for property damage

The cost for liability protection can amount to more than half of the total auto insurance premium. Each state has minimum liability coverage requirements; however, it is recommended that you insure to exceed these relatively low minimums for adequate protection.

A major premium cost consideration with respect to liability coverage is whether to purchase *un*insured motorist protection, which covers you when the other driver has no liability insurance, and *under*insured motorist coverage, which covers you for costs that exceed the other driver's coverage maximum. In most states, this coverage is optional. However, although uninsured and underinsured coverage is optional and does increase the liability premium, if you can afford the premium, you cannot afford to exclude this added protection. There are many uninsured drivers on the road, and if you are involved in an accident with one, you will not be reimbursed. At the very minimum, you should carry the same limits as your own liability coverage.

Auto Medical: Medical payment insurance coverage provides for the immediate treatment of injuries caused by a car accident. You, your family members, and other passengers in your vehicle are covered, regardless of who is at fault for the accident. Auto medical payment coverage is required only in certain states, typically the so-called "no-fault" insurance states. Be cost conscious about purchasing the medical component of an auto insurance policy if you already own a comprehensive medical insurance policy because you may already be adequately covered.

Auto Collision and Comprehensive: Collision coverage pays for damage to your auto in an accident regardless of fault. Comprehensive coverage pays for damage to your auto caused by something other than an accident (i.e., weather, theft, vandalism, etc.), including the loss of personal property within the car.

Collision and comprehensive coverage typically carries a deductible, the out-of-pocket amount for which you are responsible, usually between $250 and $1,000. The higher the deductible is, the less expensive the premium is. Keep in mind that making small claims may ultimately cost you more, with resulting increased premiums. Therefore, it is advisable to retain as high of a deductible amount as you can afford in the event of damage.

Having collision and comprehensive coverage is not mandatory. Therefore, with an older-model car, you need to weigh the premium cost against the salvage value because the cost to repair may be more than what the auto is worth.

Homeowner Insurance

Homeowner insurance covers the risks associated with damage to your home and its contents and provides liability and medical coverage as well. Homeowner insurance coverage is limited to owner-occupied dwellings of no more than two living units and does not include rental property that you may own. If you rent rather than own your residence, a tenant or renter's insurance version can be obtained to provide protective coverage for damage to the contents within the apartment.

There are different forms of homeowner insurance to select from depending upon which combination of risks, or perils, you are to be insured against. It is important that you carefully evaluate and understand what risks the policy covers and make sure that adequate coverage amounts are kept up to date. The following are the different homeowner (**HO**) forms of insurance available and the perils covered:

- **HO-1:** Fire, smoke, lightning, windstorms, hail, explosions, riots, civil commotion, vehicles, aircraft, vandalism, theft, and glass breakage.

- **HO-2:** Same as above, plus falling objects; the weight of ice, snow, and sleet; the collapse of buildings; accidental discharge or overflow of water or steam; the explosion of steam or hot water systems; frozen plumbing; heating units; air conditioning systems; domestic appliances; and power surges.

- **HO-3:** The most popular homeowner insurance package because it covers all perils, with the exception of earthquakes, floods, termites, landslides, war, tidal waves, and nuclear accidents.

- **HO-4:** Tenant insurance that is usually similar in coverage to HO-3.

- **HO-5:** Similar to HO-3, plus extended coverage to your personal belongings.

- **HO-6:** Condominium or cooperative insurance, similar to HO-4; make sure coverage fully supplements the condo's or co-op's insurance coverage.

Homeowner insurance replacement coverage can be either for the actual cash value or for the replacement cost of the asset. There is a significant difference in the premium amount and in the claim amount received. With the less expensive cash value replacement policy, the insurance company deducts a certain amount for depreciation from the cash value when it settles the claim in order to account for the fact that the asset was not new when damaged or destroyed. The actual amount determined may mean that you receive only $500 for property that costs $1,500 to replace, while with replacement coverage you would receive $1,500. While it is important to adequately insure personal belongings, it becomes especially important to monitor and maintain adequate **full replacement cost coverage** when insuring your house.

You should record and maintain an inventory listing of your possessions and their values. The most expeditious way to do this is to videotape or take pictures of everything inside and outside of your home. In addition, it is wise to keep receipts for the very expensive items. This kind of documentation can be invaluable for recollecting the multitude of accumulated possessions owned and for establishing monetary amounts in an insurance settlement.

Under the homeowner policy, you are able to purchase additional specific insurance coverage for precious valuables such as jewelry and artwork that can increase in value over time. The specified items are listed and valued on a separate schedule and should be kept updated with written appraisals that reflect current full replacement costs.

Personal Liability Umbrella Insurance

Personal liability insurance is an often overlooked form of P&C insurance even though it is relatively inexpensive. The premium is low because the likelihood of you actually using the insurance to protect against the personal liability risk is not great. However, if you have wealth to preserve, get it. Today's lawsuits are frivolous and high dollar, and if you are perceived to have deep pockets as an affluent high-income earner, you have a greater chance of being sued. Though not likely, it takes only one serious accident occurring in your home or automobile with you faulted for injuries or death to value this protection.

Most insurers require you to have both the auto and homeowner insurance with them in order to coordinate and put an *umbrella* over the underlying liability coverage. To obtain umbrella protection, the underlying amount of liability coverage for auto and homeowner insurance usually has to be at a level of at least $500,000 per accident. However, for a reasonable cost, you can obtain a personal umbrella policy to increase your overall liability protection for an amount totaling one million and up.

Quiet Millionaire® Summary

- Determine and then carefully balance the different ways to manage and protect yourself against the risks in life.
- Transfer as much catastrophic risk to insurance companies as you can afford to insure.
- Understand the intricacies of term and permanent life insurance, and purchase the right kind and amount of protection.
- Complete the life insurance analysis checklist.
- Know how much life insurance is enough.
- Do not overlook protecting against the risk of disability, which is more likely to occur than most other forms of risk.
- Acquire and maintain adequate automobile, homeowner, property, and casualty insurance protection.

CHAPTER TEN

Will Costly Health Care Wipe You Out?

Paying for health care is expensive and can be financially devastating. Receiving affordable and high-quality health care is a number one concern for most people. The future structure of the U.S. health care system is uncertain. What is certain is that the structure will change out of necessity. For your own certainty, the best advice is to proactively take charge of your particular situation, whether you are young and raising a family or elderly and living on a fixed income derived from your accumulated investment portfolio.

By becoming informed about your health care insurance options, you can plan how to manage and adequately fund your own specific needs for health care. This chapter will prepare you to understand and intelligently manage the many challenging decisions and changes on the horizon in how affordable health care is delivered, received, and paid for. Informed planning is the only sure way to make the most intelligent choices for you and implement affordable strategies that will prevent the costs of health care from financially wiping you out. This is why an entire chapter has been devoted to the subject.

Most people who have medical, dental, and vision insurance participate on a group basis through their employer, which helps make the protective coverage more available, especially if you have adverse health issues. This is because there is usually no individual health underwriting requirement in order to participate in a group plan. Also, group health insurance is usually more affordable because some employers contribute money to subsidize some of the out-of-pocket premium costs for their employees.

Another way that employers help employees pay premium costs is by offering a Section 125 "cafeteria plan." The name of the plan came about because the cafeteria plan offers a menu of expense options that the employee can pay for using pretax dollars. These expense options include insurance premiums for group medical, dental, and vision as well as group life and disability insurance. Some cafeteria plans also permit paying out-of-pocket expenses for medical and dependent day care with contributed pretax dollars. Contributions to the plan are tax deductible by employee participants, and the withdrawals are tax free. The only catch is that previously the pretax contributed money must have been entirely used before the end of the tax year or it was forfeited under the "use it or lose it" rule. This rule has been liberalized, with a now allowable extended two-and-a-half-month grace period beyond the end of the tax year for using the money before losing it.

Despite all of the benefits associated with group health insurance, there are some downsides to the plans, and there are no easy solutions to these problems. Take Bernie and Carolyn's story, for example:

> *Bernie and Carolyn are in their mid-fifties. They have raised two children, Heather, age twenty-six, and John, age*

twenty-four, both graduated from college and now out on their own. Because the kids are no longer a financial responsibility, Bernie, an engineer with a Fortune 500 company, would like to quit his stressful, unrewarding job. In fact, the only reason he became an engineer was because his parents insisted that he needed to become a responsible professional who earned a steady paycheck rather than a rock musician with an uncertain future. He has been a fish out of water for all of his adult working years.

Both Bernie and Carolyn love music and are talented musicians. Carolyn has taught piano lessons for years. Now they both long to open a music academy, Bernie to teach guitar and Carolyn to teach piano. There is only one problem, health insurance. In the past three years, Bernie has had two heart attacks, and Carolyn developed diabetes.

The result is that Bernie cannot afford to leave his employer and pursue his dream because he needs to keep his group health insurance coverage until Medicare kicks in at age sixty-five, nine years from now. Bernie is also worried that he will not even make it to then because his peers have been getting forced into early-retirement severance packages. He fears it is only a matter of time before he is next on the list.

Bernie's health insurance dilemma could have been avoided if he and Carolyn had done some planning in advance while they were both healthy. In their case, they knew, prior to their health issues developing, that once their financial responsibility for the children was over, they wanted to open the music academy. It would have been an intelligent strategy to have taken out a high-deductible and, therefore relatively inexpensive, individual policy earlier even though they had Bernie's group coverage. While he remained with his employer, they could have continued using the group health benefits and would not have submitted any claims against the individual policy. Then, when he quit his employer, the previously underwritten individual policy would have been there for them regardless of the health problems that materialized subsequently.

QUIET MILLIONAIRE® WISDOM
Affordable health insurance and good health are not guaranteed; you must be diligent about keeping both.

Retaining affordable health insurance coverage is a huge problem affecting a larger number of people who leave their employment because of career change, termination, or retirement. Many workers like Bernie are being forced to remain in jobs that they dislike because they would otherwise be without affordable health insurance. Losing affordable health insurance is a particular hardship for others who are being involuntarily "let go" from their employer and now must face a life without affordable health insurance until they are eligible for Medicare at age sixty-five. Those people without group health coverage always have the option to buy an individual policy; however, if you have a preexisting adverse health issue, an individual policy can be prohibitively expensive and can lack the full coverage if it excludes the preexisting condition.

The likelihood of needing health care is a matter of when, not if. This is why the premiums to insure against medical risks are high. In addition to the premium, there are often other out-of-pocket costs associated with medical insurance coverage. The *deductible* is a predetermined dollar amount that you have to satisfy every year before the health insurance company begins to contribute any money toward your medical costs. In addition to the deductible, there may be *co-payments*, where you are required to pay a certain dollar figure for each medical service provided, and/or *coinsurance*, where you are required to pay a certain percentage of your health care costs.

Medical insurance companies are protected by a "lifetime payout provision" that limits the total amount they will have to pay out over the lifetime of the insured. The amounts usually range between one to five million, and the higher maximum lifetime payout assures that the coverage will not be prematurely depleted

Types of Private Health Insurance

Deciding which type of medical plan is best to purchase, whether as a group participant or individually, is a confusing process. The following is a review of the features and benefits of the various types of plans available: indemnity, health maintenance organization (HMO), preferred provider organization (PPO), point of service (POS), and health savings account (HSA).

Indemnity Insurance Plan

Indemnity insurance plans are the *original* type of health plan, where the emphasis is on the treatment of unexpected illnesses as opposed to preventive medicine. The insured is allowed total control over the choice of physicians and hospitals to be used. After an annual deductible and co-pay or coinsurance is paid, the insurance company indemnifies in full for *any* medical service provided. While the indemnity type plan is the most flexible and provides payment benefits regardless of which physician and medical facility are used, it is the patient's responsibility for keeping medical receipts and bills and for completing the claim forms for payment.

The indemnity health plan does not usually cover preventive medicine services; fees for checkups, office visits, and shots are your responsibility. This can make indemnity insurance impractical for a large family that requires a lot of routine visits and preventative care. Because of skyrocketing health care costs and an emphasis on preventive medicine, managed health care has become the more prevalent medical service approach. While the managed health care form of insurance is a more affordable insurance alternative to the pure indemnity type plans, the offset is that there are restrictions in your choices for getting medical treatment.

Health Maintenance Organization (HMO)

HMOs paved the way for the development of managed-care medical insurance plans. Unlike the consumer-driven, higher-cost indemnity plans, HMOs are medical provider driven and, with controlled costs, are a lower-premium health insurance alternative. The basic concept is to manage care and control costs by limiting medical care access to an assembled preapproved network of physicians and hospitals.

From the network, you choose a primary care physician, who, acting as a *gatekeeper*, is responsible for your overall health care as well as for making referrals to specialists and approving further medical treatment. Usually, your choice of doctors and hospitals is limited to those that have contract agreements with the HMO to provide for your health care.

Because the HMO managed-care emphasis is on preventive medicine and treatment, most doctor visits, checkups, and shots are typically fully covered, with the possibility of a co-pay or coinsurance requirement for each service activity being the only out-of-pocket cost. Generally, there is a standard co-payment amount per doctor visit and a preapproved payment amount to cover prescriptions. No claim forms are required to be filed for services provided. Instead, as an HMO member, you merely present an ID card at the doctor's office or hospital, which then submits the service claim directly to the HMO for payment.

The drawback of any HMO policy is that no care can be received outside of the network without a highly restrictive prior approval being obtained. Therefore, except for emergency treatment, any medical service sought outside of the network is limited, and the expenses incurred are usually not fully covered, if at all. This restricted network referral process makes it difficult to access specialized care outside the HMO network, which can be a detriment to you receiving the best required medical treatment available without incurring a huge out-of-pocket financial cost.

Preferred Provider Organization (PPO)

The PPO is an evolved type of managed-care plan that is growing rapidly in popularity. It was developed to combine the lower cost of a managed-care plan with the greater degree of choice found in a traditional indemnity health insurance plan.

Although your health care is managed with restrictions, you are granted a more lenient degree of choice in providers. A PPO health insurance plan operates in a similar manner as an HMO in that you pay a fixed monthly premium, and in return you receive medical services from the health care provider network. However, a PPO does differ from the original HMO blueprint in that under a PPO insurance plan, a primary care physician or "gatekeeper" physician is not required. As a result, seeing a specialist does not require a referral.

If you need or want health care provided from *outside* the network, you are required to pay a higher co-payment than if the provider were from within the PPO network. In essence, each time you need medical attention, you can decide between a higher-costing indemnity plan format with freedom of choice for provider care or a lower-costing managed-care option that restricts your care to within the provider network.

PPO insurance is typically more expensive than an HMO managed-care plan. Even if the premium is comparable to an HMO, there are other out-of-pocket costs associated with a PPO. For receiving nonnetwork care, you must satisfy a deductible before the health insurance company begins payment benefits. After the deductible is met, you must pay coinsurance, which is higher than network provider coinsurance amounts. Furthermore, you might also be required to pay the difference between what the nonnetwork health care provider charges and what the plan deems to be "reasonable and customary" for the service. However, these extra costs associated with a PPO may be worthwhile to you because overall the PPO is less costly than an indemnity plan and more flexible about accessing provider services than an HMO.

Point of Service Plan (POS)

POSs are a lesser known type of managed health care plan operating similar to a PPO, but they are slightly less expensive and more restrictive about provider choices than a PPO. When you enroll in a POS plan, unlike the PPO, you are required to select a network physician who is primarily responsible for your health care and who is designated as your "point of service" physician. The primary POS physician is permitted to make referrals *outside* the network but with limited payments being made to the nonnetwork provider by the health insurance company. For medical visits within the health care network, there is no claims paperwork to complete. For services provided outside the network, it is your responsibility to keep track of health care receipts, complete the claims forms, and submit bills for payment.

Health Savings Account (HSA)

A health savings account (HSA) is not a health insurance plan unto itself. Instead, it is a tax-favored savings account that is used in combination with a PPO health insurance policy. The HSA is used for paying out-of-pocket medical expenses with pretax, nontaxable dollars. Here is how the combination HSA–health insurance policy works. The managed health care policy has a high deductible, which allows a relatively low premium. With the premium savings, the extra money available can be regularly deposited into the completely tax-free HSA. The maximum amount that can be contributed annually to the HSA is the lesser of the amount of the health plan's high deductible or the maximum specified by law, which is annually inflation adjusted. As of 2006, the maximum allowable contribution amounts to a HSA are $2,700 for individual coverage and $5,450 for family coverage.

The HSA includes a checkbook that may be used to pay for medical expenses using nontaxable, pretax dollars until the health insurance high deductible is met and the policy's benefits begin. Any HSA account funds not used during a given year remain in the account, invested to grow without taxation, and are available for future medical expenses or for retirement income purposes similar to a traditional IRA. Note: This is unlike the employer sponsored group Section 125 "cafeteria plan," which requires that all pretax contributed money must be entirely used within a given tax year or the money is forfeited under the "use it or lose it" rule.

> QUIET MILLIONAIRE® WISDOM
> *To control costly medical expense outlays, closely match and diligently monitor your health insurance plan benefits with your medical service needs.*

In evaluating whether to select a HMO, PPO, POS, or HSA health insurance plan, the following checklist of questions can be used as a guide:

Health Plan Evaluation Checklist

- How many doctors in the network are there to select from?
- What hospitals are available through the plan?
- Where are the offices and hospitals in the network located?
- Are my preferred doctors and hospital choices in the network?
- How are referrals to specialists handled?
- What is the coverage policy for emergency care?
- What health care treatment services are covered?

■ What preventive services are covered?

■ Are there limits on medical treatments or other services?

■ How much is the health insurance premium?

■ Are there deductible, co-payment, or coinsurance requirements?

■ What are the additional costs and restrictions for using non-network providers?

■ Is there an annual out-of-pocket maximum?

■ What is the lifetime maximum dollar benefit?

In addition, depending upon how much you want to pay or what your family health history is, you might want to include other less common coverage in your medical insurance policy. Some of these "extra" coverage areas might include:

■ Dental insurance

■ Vision care

■ Care by specialists

■ Care for mental health

■ Services for drug/alcohol abuse

■ Family planning services, OB-GYN

■ Chronic disease care

■ Physical therapy

■ Nursing home and hospice care

■ Chiropractic care

■ Maternity care

■ Well baby care (immunizations, etc.)

Specialized disease insurance policies are available for specified diseases such as cancer, heart attack, or stroke. These policies provide benefits only if you contract the specified disease. However, the policy will not cover the specified disease diagnosed in existence *before* you applied for coverage. Some policies will deny coverage if learned subsequently that you had the specified disease at the time of purchase, even if you did not know it existed. Importantly, be sure you understand what conditions must be met before the policy will start to pay your bills.

> QUIET MILLIONAIRE® WISDOM
> *Say "no" to specialized*
> *disease insurance.*

Purchasing specialized insurance is an emotional purchase decision, not an intelligent purchase decision. Although a comprehensive medical insurance policy has a higher premium than specialized insurance, it is a much better value because it covers all diseases and medical treatment needs. Buying specialized disease insurance is a waste of money. Agents who sell it play on the purchaser's emotions and often use misleading sales practices that are scrutinized by state insurance regulatory agencies.

Types of Government Health Insurance

Affordable health care is a growing social problem as a result of rapidly increasing medical costs and an aging population requiring more frequent and more expensive treatments. The managed-care approach has held down costs somewhat but at the expense of limiting consumer choices for health care providers and services. Each year, health care costs are consuming a larger amount of the consumer's spendable income. More and more people are living without health insurance coverage, and by necessity, the government's allocation of resources to subsidize this health care crisis appears to be increasing.

Currently, the main government programs for subsidizing health care are Medicare, which helps senior citizens pay for medical and prescription expenses, and Medicaid, which is a welfare program that provides custodial long-term care for patients who have no financial resources.

Medicare

Medicare is a federal health insurance plan that is the primary means for paying health care costs by most people age sixty-five or older and for some disabled individuals under the age of age sixty-five. Medicare consists of two parts: Part A (hospital insurance) and Part B (medical insurance).

Medicare Part A (Hospital Insurance)

Most people, if they qualify for Social Security benefits, are automatically enrolled for Medicare Part A when they turn age sixty-five, and no monthly premium is required. People who do not qualify for Social Security benefits may enroll for Part A but have to pay a monthly premium, which in 2006 is $393 per month. Part A does have in-patient, out-of-pocket deductibles but no coinsurance requirement. In 2006, the out-of-pocket deductibles are:

$952 *total* for a hospital stay of 1–60 days each benefit period

$238 *per day* for days 61–90 of a hospital stay each benefit period

$476 *per day* for days 91–150 of a hospital stay each benefit period

Beyond 150 days of a hospital stay each benefit period, you are responsible for all of the hospital costs.

In addition to paying for a portion of in-patient hospital care, Medicare Part A pays a portion of skilled nursing care, hospice care, and limited rehabilitative care provided in home or in a skilled nursing home facility. Be aware that Medicare does not pay for long-term custodial care requiring assistance with daily activities such as dressing, bathing, and cooking. Such long-term custodial care provided by a skilled nursing home facility or in-home care must be paid for out of pocket or by a long-term-care policy. The last resort for paying custodial care costs is Medicaid, which is government "medical welfare."

Medicare Part B (Medical Insurance)

Medicare Part B is medical insurance that helps pay for doctor services, outpatient hospital care, and other medical services that Part A does not cover, such as physical and occupational therapy and some short-duration home health care.

There is a premium cost for Medicare Part B, which in 2006 is $88.50 per month and can increase annually. In addition, there is an annual deductible requirement, which is $124 for 2006. Once the annual $124 deductible requirement is met, you pay twenty percent of the Medicare-approved amount for the medical services provided. Furthermore, there may be additional out-of-pocket costs if your doctor charges and requires you to pay more than the approved Medicare amount.

It is important to enroll in Part B when you are first eligible at age sixty-five. **The Social Security Administration recommends that you apply for Part B coverage three months before turning age sixty-five.** This is when the initial enrollment period begins, and it continues for seven months. If you delay enrollment, the Part B premium is permanently increased by ten percent for each year of delay. The only exception is if you are still working or have group health coverage after age sixty-five.

Medicare Part C (Medicare Advantage)

In many parts of the country, you have the option to select privately issued Medicare health insurance plans that are subsidized by Medicare, known as Medicare Advantage (formerly Medicare+Choice). The Medicare Advantage plans are available in various formats: indemnity fee for service, HMO, or PPO formats described before. Most of these plans generally provide extra benefits and lower co-payments than required by Medicare. However, you usually have to see doctors who belong to the plan and go to certain hospitals for medical care.

In order to sign up for Medicare Advantage, you first must enroll in Medicare Part A and B and pay the required Medicare Part B monthly premium. Besides paying the Medicare Part B monthly premium, there is an additional monthly premium charged, which varies among the private insurance companies providing Medicare Advantage coverage. However, despite the additional monthly premium, your out-of-pocket costs could be less than for Medicare because of lower deductibles and expanded coverage.

While Medicare Advantage plans provide Medicare Part A and B coverage, some might not include Medicare Part D prescription drug insurance coverage (discussed next), and therefore whether to purchase separate prescription drug coverage has to be decided upon. However, with Medicare Advantage coverage, there is no need to purchase a Medigap policy (discussed below). Be aware that if you ever become dissatisfied with the Medicare Advantage plan option, there is a safe harbor by being able to revert to Medicare.

Medicare Part D
(Medicare Prescription Drug Insurance)

Since January 1, 2006, Medicare recipients have the voluntary option to purchase Medicare Part D prescription coverage through a separate drug insurance policy for a monthly premium. For those Medicare recipients who already have prescription drug coverage that is better than Medicare Part D's, the coverage is termed *creditable*, and they can sign up for Medicare D later if at any point the coverage is no longer creditable. However, for those recipients who do not have creditable coverage and do not voluntarily enroll for Medicare D coverage when first eligible, there is a penalty assessed in the form of higher monthly premiums if they enroll subsequently.

In 2006, monthly premiums averaged $35 per month. The coverage typically required that a $250 annual deductible be paid, and then the insurance pays:

- Seventy-five percent of the next $2,000 spent for prescription drugs
- Nothing for the next $2,850
- Ninety-five percent for prescription drugs over $5,100

The deductible and cost-sharing limits are subject to upward adjustments in future years.

Medigap (Medicare Supplement) Insurance

Medigap policies (also termed Medicare Supplement Insurance) are health insurance policies sold by private insurance companies that generally cover the costs not covered (gaps) by Medicare such as deductibles, co-payments, and coinsurance that you must otherwise pay out of pocket. However, you must first enroll in Medicare Part A and B in order to purchase this insurance. **Anyone upon attaining age sixty-five should immediately apply for a Medigap policy before the initial, one-time-only, six-month open-enrollment period ends.** Waiting beyond the open-enrollment period may result in you being denied or charged more for this protective insurance coverage if there are health issues in existence.

The insurance companies must structure the coverage in their Medigap policies to comply with federal and state laws. Therefore, there are twelve standardized policies (plans A–L) that are available in most states, and what your Medigap policy covers depends upon which plan (A–L) you buy. Although the plans are standardized, the premiums charged vary according to each insurance company provider and by state of residence. Generally, the more benefits the policy provides, the higher the premium, which is in addition to the Medicare B monthly premium. When you receive medical care, Medicare pays its share of the benefits, and then your Medigap policy pays its share.

As of January 1, 2006, when the new Medicare Part D prescription drug benefit took effect, no Medigap policies sold after that date could any longer include prescription drug coverage, as was previously allowed. Therefore, all new Medigap policy purchasers must also sign up for Medicare D by enrolling in a separate Medicare D prescription drug plan that covers prescription drugs only.

For more information about Medicare and the other insurance plans that supplement and compliment Medicare, the following resources are available: *www.medicare.gov* (the official government Web site for Medicare information), *www.seniors.gov, www.aarp.org*, and *www.quietmillionaire.com*.

Long-Term-Care (LTC) Insurance

According to a 2004 MetLife Market Survey of Nursing Home and Home Care Costs, the average cost of a private room in a nursing home in the United States was $70,080 per year, or $192 per day. The study found that the cost of a home health care aide averaged $18 per hour nationally, which turns out to be $432 per day. Demographically, the need for long-term care is a growing social problem. More than fifty percent of people age sixty-five today will need long-term care, and if you are a woman, the likelihood is even higher. The following story about John and Christine shows the importance of LTC planning:

> *While John and Christine were still healthy and active and nearing retirement, they planned for their possible long-term-care needs. They had money, but they knew how expensive long-term care could be. The last thing they wanted to happen was to ever become a burden for their three grown children who had their own family responsibilities. They were also concerned that a long-term-care event could eliminate their retirement savings and cause them to run out of money and ruin their financial security and independence, so they bought LTC insurance. Because of their planning, there was no conflict or*

concern among their three children about how John and Christine spent their money during retirement.

After twelve years of paying combined annual LTC premiums of $5,000 per year ($2,500 each), John died as a result of a stroke after spending only one month in a nursing home. Until then, they had paid a total of $60,000 in LTC premiums, and their premium payments appeared wasted on John. But, looking at it from a positive perspective, thank goodness John did not suffer a prolonged illness in a nursing home.

However, Christine's need for LTC became an entirely different story. She eventually did need LTC after having paid premiums for fifteen years then totaling $75,000. She started out with home health care when she was diagnosed with Parkinson's disease and her health was failing. Christine now lived alone in her own home in Cincinnati. Although her one daughter Lisa lived close by, she was busy with her banking career and raising two teenagers. Christine's other two children, Michael and Jean, lived away in Dallas and Atlanta.

Eventually, Christine had to move from her home to an assisted-living facility, which took wonderful care of her. The assisted-living facility was ideal because it had a responsive, qualified staff and other seniors in similar situations for Christine to share living with. And, best of all, the living environment had a homey atmosphere, unlike a sterile nursing home, which was the type of facility that Medicaid would have paid for if Christine had run out of money. Her children visited as much as their busy lives and distance permitted. Just about every time they visited Christine, she said, "I'm so thankful that we have the long-term-care policy and that I'm here." Her children could not have agreed more.

Christine died after spending five years in the assisted-living facility. The LTC policy had paid out more than $375,000 in benefits. It took only one year of insurance-paid benefits at $205 per day before the entire $75,000 of out-of-pocket costs for paying the policy's premium were overcome. Christine would have never been able to pay that much on her own, and she would have outlived her money. In addition, Christine had LTC choices that she would not have had otherwise, and her children were relieved that she was being looked after with care and dignity. Planning had really paid off!

Because they planned ahead, John and Christine's LTC experience was better than those families who just drift into the event. In many cases, unpaid family members and friends provide much of the long-term care for the elderly. However, this is a challenging function, especially when undertaken by an elderly spouse. More often than not, the "free" caregiver gives out first.

Paying for professional long-term care is often the better or only option. Contrary to common misconception, Medicare *does not* cover the costs for long-term care beyond one hundred days, or less when the care provided is custodial and no longer deemed rehabilitative. Furthermore, the care must be provided in a nursing home and subsequent to a hospitalization. Of all paid long-term care, Medicare benefits account for only fourteen percent.

> QUIET MILLIONAIRE® WISDOM
> *Compare whether your retirement investment portfolio can survive paying for long-term-care expenses versus the alternative of paying insurance premiums to protect against financial devastation.*

You have the following three choices available to pay for long-term care: self-insure, privately insure, or apply for the government's Medicaid welfare program.

Self-Insure

If you decide to self-insure the costs of long-term care, you will need to accumulate a substantial amount of money because the costs for long-term care are overwhelming and the premiums to insure against the potential out-of-pocket costs are high. The cost for this care, whether given in the home, an assisted living facility, or a nursing home, can cost $60,000 or more per year, and that is after first paying taxes on the money! The magnitude of this can destroy your retirement plans and financial resources if paid out of pocket. Any competent retirement cash flow analysis must contingently account for this potential financial event. The analysis should compare how the cost of paying a premium versus the cost of self-funding will affect your retirement cash flow and deplete investment assets. Otherwise, you may find out the hard way that the costs of long-term care can devastate your planned retirement cash flow and accumulated resources.

Private Long-Term-Care (LTC) Insurance

Purchasing private insurance to pay for long-term care should be considered if you can afford the premiums and are relatively healthy at the time the policy is being underwritten for approval. However, do not assume that you cannot qualify for LTC insurance because you have been turned down for life, disability, or health insurance. The underwriting medical requirements for each of these types of insurance are different.

Since 1997, the federal government has provided tax deduction incentives on premiums for private long-term-care insurance. However, be aware that accessing the benefits for tax-qualified (TQ) policies are more restrictive than for non-tax-qualified (NTQ) polices. When deciding whether to purchase a TQ or NTQ long-term-care policy, make sure that you understand how the tax deductibility of the premiums affects the accessibility of the policy benefits.

Purchasing LTC insurance is confusing for most people. According to the Health Insurance Association of America (HIAA), nearly fifty percent of all people who look into LTC insurance do not buy it because they are confused about which policy is right for them. Furthermore, of the one hundred and thirty companies that sell LTC insurance, only a relative few of them are appropriate for consideration. A cheaper premium offered today by a company may cause heartache and hardship tomorrow when the premiums are subsequently increased dramatically or when small-print escape clauses enable a claim to be denied for your LTC need.

Another potentially harmful consequence with LTC is that while you might purchase a policy from one of the best LTC insurance companies, you could make a bad decision about the structure of the policy. Or, you could purchase a policy that is appropriately designed for your LTC need, but it is with an insurance company that will not be around in the future to pay the benefits as expected.

It is not within the context of this book to educate you sufficiently about LTC planning or which insurance company and policy structure is best suited for you. There are too many variables to consider in the decision-making process. Rather, the intent is to inform you about what factors to consider and where to seek trustworthy and competent guidance for making an informed decision that will best meet your particular LTC insurance need. Here is some advice:

■ If you can afford to pay a premium for LTC insurance protection, then you can afford to hire a fee-only financial advisor to evaluate your particular situation on a comprehensive planning basis without bias or motivation to sell you a policy. Then, once a well-structured LTC insurance needs analysis is completed, locate an *independent* insurance broker who specializes in selling LTC insurance and represents a number of different high-quality LTC companies in order for you to obtain a most suitable and affordable LTC policy. If necessary, ask the fee-only financial advisor to refer you to a qualified independent LTC insurance broker.

■ The best time to consider purchasing LTC insurance is when you are in your late fifties because the premiums begin to accelerate after that. The difference in premium amounts for a fifty- and sixty-year-old is not nearly as great as the difference in premium amounts for a sixty- and seventy-year-old.

■ Most LTC insurance consumers spend a lot of time deciding whether to buy a policy and which company to buy it from. However, once these decisions are made, they do not focus enough time on the most important decisions of how to properly design the policy to adequately cover their LTC risk in the most cost-effective manner.

■ The benefits of an LTC policy are triggered by the inability to perform certain activities of daily living (ADLs), which in turn requires custodial care. There are six standard ADLs: bathing, dressing, eating, continence, transferring, and toileting. Not all LTC policies list and require the same ADL loss. Bathing is usually the first ADL that most people cannot perform. Therefore, make sure that bathing is listed along with all of the other ADLs because a policy that does not include bathing will most likely delay triggering benefit payments.

> QUIET MILLIONAIRE® WISDOM
> *Your decisions about which long-term-care policy benefits to purchase are as critical as your decisions about which policy to purchase.*

The following are some guidelines for your consideration when designing a private long-term-care insurance policy:

■ **Daily benefit:** The daily benefit is the amount that an LTC policy pays for services per day. Typically, you can purchase a daily benefit that ranges from $50 to $350 per day in today's dollars. Determine the costs for daily LTC in your area, and deduct from this amount what you would be able to afford to pay out of pocket in the event of a need for LTC both before and during retirement. The difference is the minimum amount of daily benefit you should consider. However, remember to build into the calculation the effects of inflation. It is better to purchase a higher daily benefit than a longer benefit period because with most policies, whatever amount of daily benefit you do not use extends your benefit period. So, if your home health care costs $100 per day and you have a policy that pays $200 per day for two years, your benefit will actually last four years.

■ **Inflation protection:** Most LTC policies are sold without inflation protection because it significantly increases the premium. This is a very big mistake because without inflation protection, the compounding increases for the cost of LTC detrimentally erode the value of the policy. Inflation protection is available on a simple or compound benefit increase basis. The simple inflation benefit increases each year by five percent of the *original* daily benefit, while the compound inflation benefit increases five percent by each year's then-current benefit.

The compound inflation benefit is recommended over the simple inflation benefit, and the following example explains why. If in today's dollars, the LTC daily rate is $200 and assuming an annual inflation factor of five percent (the typical assumption for LTC policies), then in twenty years, the daily rate will be $505. The following demonstrates the difference between a zero percent inflation increase and a five percent simple and compound inflation increase for today's $200 per day daily benefit:

Policy Year	No Inflation	5% Simple	5% Compound
1	200	$200	$200
5	200	240	243
10	200	290	310
15	200	340	396
20	200	380	505

Notice how the compound benefit really starts to make a difference beyond ten years to keep up with the ever-increasing costs for LTC. If premium affordability is a factor, it is better to reduce the benefit period than to reject the valuable compound inflation protection.

■ **Elimination period:** The elimination period is the waiting period before the benefit payments start and is the equivalent of a deductible with a health insurance policy. Most policies have elimination periods between twenty and one hundred days. In order to reduce the premium amount, you should choose the longest elimination period you can afford before the insurance benefit kicks in. Keep in mind that Medicare does provide limited rehabilitative nursing home benefits for up to one hundred days of care upon discharge from a hospital stay.

■ **Benefit period:** This is the length of time that the insurance company pays for long-term-care services once your claim starts. The benefit periods available to select range from three years to a lifetime. If you have designed the policy according to the above steps, the proper benefit period is the one you can afford. Many people choose a three-year benefit because they are told that the average nursing home stay is two to three years. However, that average includes stays ranging from one month to ten or more years. Therefore, forget about the average statistics, and focus on purchasing what you can afford rather than the average.

The total amount of dollar benefit available within a policy is determined by multiplying your daily benefit by the number of days in your benefit period. For example, a policy that pays $200 per day with a three-year benefit has a value of $219,000 ($200 daily benefit x 365 days in a year x 3 years). In turn, a policy that pays $100 per day for a six-year period has essentially the same dollar benefit if you use it for the entire benefit period; if you do not, then the policy is less valuable. Again, this is why it is better to select a higher daily benefit for a shorter period if the premium cost to insure is a concern.

In the event you can neither afford to pay out of pocket for LTC nor purchase a LTC insurance policy, then applying for Medicaid welfare may be your only option.

Medicaid (Government Welfare)

Be careful not to confuse the government's Medicaid and Medicare programs. As discussed before, **Medicare** provides only very limited rehabilitative nursing home coverage for up to one hundred days after a hospitalization but usually is less once the care becomes custodial and is no longer deemed rehabilitative. **Medicaid** is a government medical welfare program that pays for more than forty-five percent of all long-term nursing home care in the United States. Be aware that Medicaid pays only for custodial care provided within a nursing home, not for in-the-home care. Furthermore, not every nursing home facility accepts Medicaid patients, and you or a family member could be forced to go for long-term custodial care at a facility many miles away from home and family.

The funding for Medicaid comes from the federal government and from each state. The benefits vary according to state and are available only to those who are considered destitute. This means that you must own next to nothing in assets and have negligible income. If you have assets, you must "spend down" almost all of your financial resources. With long-term care in 2006 costing $60,000 or more a year, this can happen fast and deplete all your retirement money accumulations.

Any allowable retained assets (*countable* assets) vary by state. However, the limits are usually (excluding home, personal belongings, and necessary automobile) less than $2,000 for a single person and $90,000 for a married couple (higher so that the non-Medicaid spouse is not impoverished). Strict eligibility rules are applied as to how the applicant's assets were used for up to a period of five years prior to applying for Medicaid. This is termed the "look-back" period, and the penalties are severe for trying to hide assets, with heavy fines and jail time imposed for Medicaid fraud. Any Medicaid planning is complicated and should never be done without the guidance of a qualified elder law attorney. For more information about Medicaid, go to *www.cms.gov/medicaid/*, *www.elderlawanswers.com*, or *www.quietmillionaire.com*.

Can affordable health care be achieved?

Our society is challenged to provide affordable health care for everyone. Health care has gotten so expensive because people live longer and expect to receive the highest quality health care available. The costs for research, development, and delivery of modern medical technology are astronomical. The amount of money spent on health care per person and as a percentage of our gross domestic product (GDP) is spiraling out of control.

There are conflicting interests that must be addressed and need to be overcome in order to stabilize our health care system. As medical service consumers, ideally we want affordable health care for any medical reason, large or small, on demand any time we want it and from the best physicians and medical facilities we choose to use. However, this ideal vision conflicts with that of the health care and insurance companies, which strive to control costs in order to be profitable. In addition, the government faces tough and politically unpopular budgetary decisions necessary to publicly subsidize this financially demanding social issue.

The challenge for affordable health care will have to be met, but as a society, we tend to address difficult issues in a crisis management manner as opposed to a proactive manner. We will be forced to respond to and implement a comprehensive system of more responsible administrative and financial management by all parties: the health care system, the government, and all of us individually. In the meantime, plan diligently to manage and fund your own health care needs in order to avoid depending upon others.

Quiet Millionaire® Summary

■ Know and understand the features and benefits of all health insurance programs offered, and understand the variety of plan formats offered: indemnity, HMO, PPO, POS, and HSA.

■ Do not purchase specialized disease health insurance.

■ Complete the health plan evaluation checklist.

■ Understand and do not confuse the different benefits provided by Medicare and Medicaid.

■ If affordable, consider purchasing long-term-care insurance to fund costs that cannot be self-funded out of pocket.

■ Diligently plan your own course for managing the costs of health care and the potential for financial hardship.

CHAPTER ELEVEN

Follow the Quiet Millionaire's® Path to Successful Business Ownership

Most quiet millionaires® are successful business owners. While not ALL are, statistically, most of them used this path to become one. Moreover, most quiet millionaires® seem to have some things in common: the willingness to risk it all; the possession of a strong, self-motivating inner drive; a burning desire to do "it," whatever "it" is, and to do "it" in their own way and on their own terms. This is not the easy road to take, but it is the one that can be the most fulfilling.

The risks for achieving successful business ownership are great. According to the Small Business Association (SBA), fifty percent of all new businesses fail in their first year, and ninety-five percent fail in their first five years. Running a business demands your commitment, your unwavering tenacity, and your passion in order to provide the energy and focus required to fulfill your dreams.

If you have previously attempted the business ownership realm without achieving your desired success, or even worse tried and "lost it all," or if you want to muster enough strength and courage to venture out on your own, then this chapter is for you. In order to truly enjoy your experience, you must be knowledgeable about how to intelligently create and manage a profitable business. Here you will find an overview of the stages that a business transitions through in order to achieve success, and hopefully this will help you to become and stay the quiet millionaire®.

First and foremost, if you own a business, it should be to make money and to enjoy what you are doing while making it. Otherwise, why do it? As the owner of a successful business, I love what I do, I help people, and I get paid for it. What better combination can you ask for than that? This does not mean that I did not fail along the way. I have, but hopefully you can benefit from my mistakes and the business knowledge gained from practical experience. By explaining the transitional path to success for nearly every business owner, hopefully your journey will be easier than mine.

My personal experience as a business owner has rewarded me in so many ways more than when I was employed as a banker with global money center banks. Although I was on a fast track during my banking career, my success depended more upon how quickly I outmaneuvered and outpoliticked my peers around a conference table than how much I helped actual clients, which was what I really enjoyed the most. I eventually saw how I had to compromise myself every day with other bank executives who were difficult for me to admire and respect, which in turn left me very unhappy at the end of the day. My spark for what I did and believed in was fading, and I knew I had to get out, but how?

Fortunately, I did learn a tremendous amount from that corporate experience. I not only developed my professional skills, but I also learned the importance of working in a healthy business culture based upon mutual respect and trust. Accordingly, my firm's environment is today structured as a place to work together harmoniously and supportively for the benefit of our clients, who are considered paramount. The key ingredient for business success, as well as personal career rewards, is meeting and ideally going beyond the expectations of the people you are serving.

But, usually this does not just happen in an easy way for the business owner. You need to create and work a realistic plan for owning and operating a successful business. And, the only way to do that properly is to have a *written* business plan that is monitored for results and updated regularly. Unfortunately, this is one of the most ignored aspects of business ownership because most business owners either do not know they should or do not know how to prepare one. And, even if you fortunately got to be a successful quiet millionaire® business owner without having a written business plan, you still need one for maximizing the outcome of the four stages of your business's transition.

The Four Transitional Stages of Business Success

There are four transitional stages of business success. Each stage presents exciting opportunities, crushing disappointments, and its own set of special challenges. Also, there is not necessarily a clear-cut delineation between the stages. Overlapping and regression often occur during the life stages of a business. Being aware of these stages will help you to know what to expect and how to intelligently manage your way through all four stages. I must warn you up front that most start-up businesses do not survive beyond the first two stages. They either fail or turn out to be nothing more than an expensive hobby. So, keep this in mind as you learn about the four transitional stages of business success.

Stage I: The Wonder Stage

The first business stage is the wonder stage. This is the time when you wonder such things as, "Should I start a new business from scratch, or should I buy an existing one? Do I want to own it alone or in partnership with others? What kind of business do I want? Should I be doing this? Am I doing the right thing? Am I going to make it?"

Know the success factors to be a quiet millionaire® business owner

As part of this early questioning process during the wonder stage, you must honestly determine whether you have what it takes to succeed as a business owner. A survey of millionaire business owners conducted by Dr. Thomas J. Stanley, who researched the characteristics and attributes of the affluent for his book *The Millionaire Mind,* revealed the following six categories as crucial factors to which the business owners attributed their success in becoming millionaires. Accordingly, the more of these categories that you can truly say apply to you, the more the likelihood that you will be and stay the quiet millionaire® as a successful business owner.

The first category is **social skills**. Being able to get along with people is paramount for business success. This enables you to develop loyalty and trust with the people you serve and work with and in turn enables you to leverage your time in order to grow the business. This requires motivational leadership qualities and the ability to effectively communicate ideas, products, and services. It is beneficial to have a reliable mentor and business advisory network in order to short circuit mistakes and speed up doing things the right way.

Second, you have to have **discernment toward critics**. This means that you cannot let the criticism of detractors affect your competitive spirit and enthusiasm during the tough times. Staying true to who you are and believing in your business mission sustain the self-respect, high energy, tenacity, and mental toughness required to overcome the cynics and doubters that can drag you down.

The third category is to keep your **integrity and moral values** intact. By always being honest and sincere with people, the truth prevails, and trust is developed. Having a supportive and interested spouse or life-sharing partner is important for being able to share success as well as to express disappointments and concerns. Also, having a strong religious belief can serve you in a way no one else can, keeps you humble, and is there for receiving guidance when times are tough and for giving thanks when times are good.

Creative intelligence is the fourth category. This means being able to see and seize specialized opportunities that are not apparent to others and being able to develop profitable business niches. This intuitive creativity more likely comes about when you love your career and business because of your constant heightened awareness of and receptivity to new ideas.

The fifth category represents the essential spirit within all entrepreneurial business owners, the need for **self-reliance**. Being able to invest in your own business with control over how to operate by being your own boss causes a willingness to take financial risks with the expectation of a profitable return. And, you must be willing to sacrifice if need be by living below your means in order to assure a successful outcome. However, keep in mind that being too self-reliant can be a hindrance. The quiet millionaire® business owner values good advice and appreciates the contributions from others.

And, last, **luck and discipline** have a lot to do with making a business successful. While you cannot entirely control how fortunate you are, good fortune is helped along by being well disciplined and organized. And, you must be willing to work harder than most people in order to help assure a "lucky" and rewarding outcome.

Have a business plan for success

If you determine during the wonder stage that you have what it takes be a quiet millionaire® business owner, then you need to plant the business seed and properly nourish it in order for there to be a harvest. A business evolves from an idea about a product or service for which there is an expected demand and a potential to make money. However, to make the idea happen, you need to know your destination and how you are going to get there and thereby lessen anxiety and reduce the chances of costly business failure during the wonder stage. The best way is to intelligently map out your course on paper before acting on the creation. This is called having a **business plan**, and to do one right takes a serious and knowledgeable effort. If you are destined to fail, it is better to fail on paper rather than through foolish and faulty action. In fact, not having a well-thought-out written plan is a primary reason why most businesses fail. It is a serious mistake to believe that you are the exception and ignore doing one.

The following is an extreme example of a less than credible business plan that was presented to me during my banking career by a hopeful business owner named Joe.

> Joe came into the bank to borrow money, and I asked him, "What's the purpose of the loan, Joe?" He answered, "I want to open a bar." "That can be a pretty risky venture, Joe. Have you had any experience?" I asked. Joe, with complete seriousness, said, "Oh, yes, I have lots of experience. I'm in bars all the time." Next, I asked, "Well, Joe, you might have the experience, but have you got a business plan?" Looking at me with a questioning look, Joe indignantly said, "Of course! My plan is for the business to make a lot of money."

Needless to say, by the end of the discussion, I was not convinced enough by Joe's business plan to lend him the bank's money, but that silly although actual example is often the planning extent with which many new business ventures are started. The business plan can realistically flush out the pitfalls and potential mistakes *on paper*, a better way to learn than from actual costly lessons that are a financial drain and possibly disastrous for the business.

Preparing a written business plan forces you to be knowledgeable about your capital requirements in order to survive the anxious times while more money might be going

> **QUIET MILLIONAIRE® WISDOM**
> *Uncertain cash flow can doom a highly profitable business to certain failure.*

out of the business than coming in. So, your business plan must include a good cash flow projection, which shows specifically how much cash will be required during the lean times and how any deficiencies will be funded to keep the business operating. One of the main things to remember when running a business is that *cash is king*. Your business can be operating profitably but can become bankrupt and be forced to be shut down because there are bills to be paid and no sources of cash to pay them. Therefore, know *in advance* the potential cash requirements and where the cash will be coming from.

Define your business's target audience and plan how to attract it

As part of the business plan, you need to develop and activate a marketing game plan for telling your target audience what your business has to offer. When I started my business, I thought, "Build it and they will come," just as Kevin Costner did when he built the baseball field in the movie *Field of Dreams*. Although I had a vision, a business plan, and a valuable service to offer, I learned first hand that if potential clients are not aware of your field of dreams, there is no game to be played. Fortunately, although with a lot of anxious moments, I finally attracted enough fans to support a winning team.

Locate resources for helping prepare your written business plan

Most business owners do not write a business plan either because they do not know they should or because they do not know how to prepare one. You can try to do it on your own, and there are inexpensive business planning software products available for purchase, as well as free information on the Internet to help you. However, you may instead decide to seek help with the business planning process. If so, keep in mind that it is your business plan, and the bulk of the work is still yours to shoulder. In the end, you are the one who is responsible for producing a plan that you can internalize, implement, and manage.

There are plenty of resources available to help you. Some are free for the asking and loaded with great business planning and management information such as SCORE® at *www.score.org* and the Small Business Association (SBA) at *www.sbaonline.sba.gov*. In fact, SCORE has volunteers consisting mainly of retired executives and business owners who will help you for free.

You can also seek help from CPAs and business consultants. However, in no way assume that all of them are competent. While they may have book knowledge and technical skills, they may not have the practical experience derived from taking actual hard knocks, which can be the most informative schooling of all. Also, just because an accountant can prepare your business tax returns and accounts for all of your income and expenses, it does not make him or her an authority on business planning. The business planning process requires devoted time to monitor and review the business plan for achieving expected results.

Banks may also be helpful to you, but when seeking help from the banker, keep in mind that the banker is a paycheck employee who probably never risked starting and managing a business. This is why the entrepreneur and bank lender typically seldom ever speak the same language. Furthermore, banks are not in the business of providing you with risky venture capital that may never be repaid. Instead, they make loans that are expected to be repaid. You have to satisfy them that the money they have rented to you will be returned with interest for its use. Nothing impresses a lender more than a written business plan that demonstrates that you know your business and that is convincing about how any borrowed money will be repaid. I know all of this from my experience as both a banker and a business owner entrepreneur.

Getting through the wonder stage requires intelligent courage and demands energetic persistence and a thorough understanding of the financial challenges to be faced. You will need these ingredients and many more in order to survive the hazards lurking in the next stage, which will either make or break your way to achieving business success.

Stage II: The Blunder Stage

The second stage is the blunder stage, which is when there are still a number of costly operating mistakes that must be learned from and corrected. It is the stage when the business's survival is at its greatest risk, the one when most businesses fail because the required adjustments could not be made in time. Having a written business plan continues to be an important tool because it can serve as a compass for proceeding in the right direction. By monitoring how the business is actually performing compared to what was set down in the business plan, adjustments can be made early to reduce mistakes and blunders and to operate more efficiently and profitably.

During the blunder stage, it is particularly important that ways be found to improve business development strategies in order to make sure revenues exceed expenses and to provide enough personal

> QUIET MILLIONAIRE® WISDOM
> *Business insanity is repeating the same blunders and hoping for different results.*

income. One of the crucial discoveries I made during this business stage was that certain marketing strategies being used were not producing a sufficient number of new clients to meet my business plan projections and requirements for survival.

Specifically, I was relying upon costly paid media advertising and direct mail programs to attract potential clients to my financial management seminars, with the result being disappointing attendance and a lot of "no shows." So, I decided instead to try *free* press releases to announce the seminars. Surprisingly, people started to *call us* to attend the seminars and actually showed up. The seminars were packed, and many attendees became new clients. The previous marketing efforts using expensive and unproductive promotional activities were costly blunders that were learned from and eliminated. Best of all, today my business enjoys the most productive form of advertising that no amount of money can buy: referrals from satisfied clients.

Intelligently leverage your time and business capacity

To reduce blunders, business owners need to smooth out their internal business operation in order to function more efficiently. It is beneficial to delegate more and use technology to improve operating capacity. Job functions that are burdensome and that can be done competently by others should be either delegated internally or farmed out in order to avoid wasting precious time. For example, the business owner should not be doing $10 per hour jobs at the expense of $200 per hour billing time or lost opportunities to increase new business. Too often, the excuse is "I can't afford the help" when actually it is quite the opposite in that help is required to improve efficiency and profitability.

Moreover, the business owner can maximize the benefits from today's technology to outcompete the monolithic corporations loaded with a bunch of nine-to-five employee attitudes. When I first started as a business owner, I did not even know how to turn on a computer. The computer and I just sat stalemated, staring at each other and trying to determine each other's worth. The technology did not start to work for me until out of desperation I hired a long-haired, dressed-in-black teenage computer geek to get things going. Today, that same long-haired geek owns a global computer consulting firm, sports a crew cut, and wears Brooks Brothers suits. We helped each other to succeed, and today my business is in the forefront because of the advantage gained by using technology to operate the business more efficiently.

Replicate the best to eliminate the worst and elevate business performance results

Achieving profitability is the financial measure of success for a business, and it is beneficial to know how well the business is operating relative to other companies similar in industry and size, including the most successful. Information about financial ratios and profit margins for specific industries can often be obtained from industry trade and professional associations as well as from the Risk Management Association (RMA), *www.rmahq.org.* Having this information reveals where the business's financial and operating performance might need to be adjusted for improvement. This information can be useful for developing a new or revising an existing business plan. If the business operation is profiled to match those that are most successful, then flattering imitation can help reduce blunders and produce similar success.

Because it is during the blunder stage when most companies fail, this is the time for an honest reality check. Is the business really viable, and do you, as the owner, have the resources and stick-to-it-ness to succeed? If the decision is to keep moving forward, then what specific adjustments might need to be made? Furthermore, as a business owner, your work should be fair to you. Your work should be for bliss and profit and should not be an agonizing, anxiety-causing cash cow that abuses you. Reaching the potential financial rewards available during the next business stages depends upon how intelligently you persist and how effectively you manage the business through the blunder stage.

Stage III: The Thunder Stage

The third business stage is the thunder stage. This is when the business is really starting to hum, more things are being done right than wrong, and the business is on its way to real financial success. However, be aware that too rapid business growth during this stage can present dangerous pitfalls. If the business fortunately reached the thunder stage without a well-structured business plan, now is still an important time to write one and act on it. The business may be doing well, but with a new or revised business plan, further continued success can become more assured.

Watch out for lightning bolts

Although the business activity may now be thundering, be aware that potential danger is lurking if the business is not sheltered from accompanying lightning bolts. For example, there could be the danger of having unmanageable growth, which destroys the business ingredients that made it successful in the first place. This is now the time to identify the ideal client/customer profile to serve and to manage growth and improve profitability. The following story about quiet millionaire® business owner Paul is an example of how this is done.

> Paul's printing company was thundering out of control and could not keep up with all of the customer orders coming in the door no matter how many new people were hired. Revenues were up, but profits were not increasing proportionately. Paul was working seven days a week and burning out. So, he decided to get in control of the business thunder by being more selective about which customers he wanted his company to serve.
>
> In evaluating the customer base, Paul found that eighty percent of the business volume was generated from the top fifty percent of the customer base. This meant the lower fifty percent accounted for only twenty percent of

revenues, and it became obvious that future growth should be directed toward the type of customer representing the top fifty–type customer.

Then, Paul compared the company's profit margins to those of other comparable printing companies and observed that the additional fee quotes for work taken on had to be more intelligently priced and that operating expenses had to be more closely monitored for better control. In other words, they should be working smarter, not harder. An informed business decision was then made to take on only new business that met certain minimum size and profit margin criteria and to let those that did not want to pay the bid job price go elsewhere.

Accordingly, Paul's company growth is now not being fueled by expanding the number of clients but rather by producing more revenues per customer. This also means that the number of employees does not have to be increased, and with increased profitability, more benefits can be provided for the existing loyal and highly regarded employees. In turn, this assures work quality and service continuity for customers to appreciate. All together, it is a win-win situation, and Paul is once again energized and enthusiastic.

The thunder stage is also the time when the business owner should refocus to spend more time working **on** the overall business and less time working **in** the business. At this point, the business

> QUIET MILLIONAIRE® WISDOM
> *A business operating without a vision is running blindly on a course to nowhere.*

owner needs to become a visionary about the destiny of the business and be less involved in the nitty-gritty daily operation. This should not be a problem if previous planning provided for hiring and training trustworthy people to operate the business.

As a visionary, the focus for the business owner should be on addressing important questions about the future growth of the company—questions such as: Should rapid growth be controlled, or should more people be hired to accommodate uncontrolled growth? Should maximum reinvestment in the business prevail for nurturing thunder stage growth, or should the emphasis be on transitioning into the fourth business stage, the plunder stage?

Stage IV: The Plunder Stage

The fourth stage is the plunder stage. This is when the business owner can really reap the rewards (plunder) for all of the personal sacrifice, risk taking, and hard work and is entitled to be the quiet millionaire®. Business owner plundering is meant to be taken in a healthy, positive sense, not in a greedy, negative sense. In fact, quiet millionaires® plunder responsibly and continue to live below their means. They choose to work even though they do not have to because they usually love what they do. The business is their baby that they birthed, nurtured, grew to maturity, and want to continue to care for so it stays healthy.

Reduce taxes, share rewards

With business success comes more taxes to be paid. But, what is the logic in making more money if too much of it is going to pay higher taxes? That money is better spent being reinvested in the business and paid out to reward employees for a job well done, and there are often tax incentives for doing so. Previously unaffordable, tax-deductible employee benefits can be provided for the "business family" in the form of health care, life insurance, disability, and retirement. An intelligent employee benefits program can derive tax advantages for the business while rewarding loyal employees and in turn better assuring their support for continued success going forward.

Use the business plan to save a successful company from an untimely death

During the plunder stage, the business plan becomes even more intertwined with the owner's personal estate planning. Succession planning and implementing an exit strategy for the owner(s) in the event of death, disability, or retirement becomes critical. Without a business plan covering these issues, the business may not survive beyond the founder because succession planning was left to chance. Furthermore, unless this stage is managed intelligently, families can be broken apart with bitterness.

The quiet millionaire® business owner recognizes the potentially disastrous problems that result from having an overinflated ego and self-worth or a denial about

> QUIET MILLIONAIRE® WISDOM
> *The business owner's epitaph too often is "I buried my business with me."*

his or her mortality and dispensability. Having this awareness is important because, statistically, only thirty percent of family businesses make it to the next generation, and a meager ten percent make it beyond that. Most often, the reason for an untimely death of a successful business during the plunder stage is because the owner is reluctant to release the reins of ownership and management and believes that the business cannot survive without him or her.

However, this potentially lethal circumstance can be avoided if a well-planned transitional succession plan and transfer of ownership are in place for the business to operate in the event of the owner's retirement, disability, or death. A properly prepared legal document termed a *buy-sell agreement* should be executed to address these issues. Moreover, it should be established in advance where the money will come from to fund the intentions and activation of the buy-sell agreement.

Another less frequently used planning technique to transfer the business ownership is an employee stock ownership plan (ESOP), which is a qualified, tax-deferred, defined benefit retirement plan that makes the company's employees partial or complete owners.

Contributions made to the ESOP by the employer and/or the employees *must* be used to purchase the company's stock, unlike contributions made to other types of retirement plans. This enables the purchase of part or all of the shares of existing owners and motivates the employees to increase their productivity and thereby share in the company's success.

The quiet millionaire® business owner also realizes that even if a succession and transfer of ownership plan has been established, there are often other unaddressed business planning issues that can cause problems. For example, the business successors may want to retain and reinvest money for the future growth of the business while the business owner may prefer to maintain the business status quo and instead use the money to maintain a personal lifestyle.

Business planning issues can also conflict with other family members who are not active in the business but who want their "fair share" of the money, which the business has to offer. Conflicting money issues can rip families apart with bitterness. A written business plan, proactive estate planning, and open communication among all interested parties help to diminish these pitfalls.

Another threat to the survival of a business occurs when there are too many greedy plunderers inside the business. This can happen when the successor generation is not willing to make the same energetic and financial commitments for the business to thrive as the original business owner did. Here again, business planning and implementation can direct the best course for the company and reveal the negative impact of subsiding too many personal materialistic wants by the business.

For business owners, their personal financial security often depends upon successful preservation and transition of their net worth from the *single stock* holding of their company to a more diversified investment portfolio that adequately supports their desired retirement lifestyle. However, the potential tax consequences from extracting business ownership equity for personal use can cause a sizable reduction in net worth. In particular, this can be the case if a business was started with an original investment consisting mainly of a dream and a lot of sweat equity and then evolved to make the owner a quiet millionaire®.

Furthermore, in the event of the business owner's death, without intelligent preplanning, there can also be an untimely death for the business because of a huge estate tax liability being owed, which can be paid only by liquidating the company. Even more hurtful is when this forced liquidation has to be done at a "fire sale" price and a still further loss of hard-earned wealth.

The following story describes how a quiet millionaire® business owner client of mine avoided a potential financial disaster and instead achieved rewarding success. The story does not include all of the potential business succession planning issues and strategies that can arise, but rather it is focused on the issues that related to John and Rita's situation. Hopefully, it will help you understand and appreciate the positive financial impact of proactive intelligent business planning instead of remaining passively on cruise control and ignoring important work.

John started his successful architectural firm forty years ago with an investment of $5,000, which he estimated had grown to be worth about three million dollars. He and his wife, Rita, still retained one hundred percent ownership. Their family included four married adult children with their own children. Jeff, their oldest son and the only child who was employed by the business, was deemed to be the successor owner. Although he had the title of president, he owned no company stock.

John and Rita initially contacted me to help them with concerns about their upcoming IRA distribution requirements and investments. The IRA was comprised of individual stocks recommended by their long-time stock-

broker. They found out the hard way that the investments did not match their tolerance for risk. The only other professional they used was a now semi-retired accountant who prepared both company and personal tax returns ever since John started the business.

As part of my comprehensive Financial Management Review process, I discovered some far more serious and costly issues that had never previously been addressed. In particular, planning for business succession and reducing a potentially huge estate tax liability could possibly force their company to be shut down and liquidated.

The preliminary estate tax calculation for their total estate, which was valued at approximately $5,000,000, including the estimated business value, determined that their federal and state estate taxes owed in the event of both of them dying during the current year would total $1,665,000, representing thirty-three percent of the total taxable estate. Owning only several small life insurance policies on John's life and because both John and Rita were no longer insurable at a reasonable premium cost, the only way the estate taxes could be paid was to either sell or liquidate the company. This would probably put their oldest son, Jeff, out of a job and negate the promise of him taking over ownership of the family business.

As is all too common, John and Rita's only estate planning documentation consisted of an outdated twenty-five-year-old will. They had never prepared durable powers of attorney for finances and health, living wills, or final letters of instruction. With respect to the business, they had no documentation for business succession in place. A probate judge would be the one to decide how their estate would be distributed to family members and to determine the fate for the business ownership if it was able to survive.

The first recommendation was to establish trusts in order to immediately eliminate $705,000 in estate taxes and to execute all of the other documents that should have been previously prepared. Then, a definitive buyout program was established to make sure Jeff would become the actual owner of the company as intended. Things were also arranged so that the other three children would not be shortchanged in any estate distribution of assets. The family members were now in control of their own destiny instead of being at the mercy of the lawyers and the probate court system.

Also, through doing a lifetime gifting program to children and grandchildren, additional potential estate taxes were eliminated. In addition, ways for reducing current and future income tax liabilities were implemented. During this plunder stage for the family, the potential plunder by the government's taxation was avoided, and the family was assured to retain its most valuable asset, the family business.

The potential financial problems and emotional hardship that loomed as in John and Rita's story are similar disasters often waiting to happen for many of those involved with a closely held business: the owners, family members, and employees. Conflicting personal and business objectives have to be addressed.

All of the rewards resulting from hard work throughout the business stages can be lost if continuous sound business planning, in combination with intelligent comprehensive financial planning and management, is neglected. Wunder! Blunder! Thunder! Plunder! By knowing what comprises the four transitional stages of business ownership, you will be prepared to avoid the pitfalls that spell doom for most businesses and to achieve the bliss and financial success derived from self-employment. Remember that there are times when owning a business can be hazardous, but it often is the path to becoming the quiet millionaire®.

Quiet Millionaire® Summary

■ Know the success factors of the quiet millionaire® business owner.

■ Understand the four stages of transition for a successful business.

■ Create and manage your business with a written business plan.

■ Compare and replicate your business with the best in your industry.

■ Discover the ways to make your business thrive.

■ Manage your success with a vision of destiny.

■ Preserve and share the rewards of your business.

■ Follow your bliss for work and make money to be the quiet millionaire®!

CHAPTER TWELVE

College Part I: How to Manage the College Experience *Successfully*

Managing the college experience is probably the least understood and most underestimated, time-consuming, and expensive financial commitment outside of managing the retirement experience. Some of you may be beyond or may have no personal interest in the college experience, and you might decide to skip these two college chapters. However, keep in mind that others in your family may be interested, and it could be beneficial if you share the knowledge with them. In particular, if you are a grandparent, you should be aware of the information in order to make college more affordable for your grandchildren.

The quiet millionaire® realizes that if you have a college funding problem, then you will also have a retirement funding problem because the two are closely intertwined. Trying to play the catch-up game to meet these financial challenges is playing high-risk financial roulette. The planning required for college and retirement is extensive and must be approached knowledgeably,

> **QUIET MILLIONAIRE® WISDOM**
> *If you have a college funding problem, then you also have a retirement funding problem.*

proactively, and with a long-term perspective using a multitude of comprehensive and coordinated financial management strategies.

The huge dollar-size commitment for funding college has a rippling effect upon all areas of your financial life from the day that your child is born to beyond the day that he or she graduates from college. College planning can be overwhelming, and unfortunately, most times it is done on a crisis planning basis. The college planning information that is presented here will give you a big-picture overview so that you can grasp what challenges you are facing, what needs to be done when, and what the logical approach to the entire college planning process is. By having this knowledge, you can decide whether to undertake the entire college planning process on your own or to seek competent professional help.

Unfortunately, sometimes even with professional advice, some of the best college management strategies often are not known or just not used. This is why it is important for you to do your

"YOUR FATHER ALWAYS TAKES IT HARD WHEN THAT COLLEGE TUITION BILL ARRIVES IN AUGUST."

© Reprinted with special permission of King Features Syndicate.

homework and to heed the college planning strategies presented here. These strategies have been tested and proven successful through applied experience and are geared especially toward high-income families who must overcome challenges for receiving college financial aid. College Part I discusses how to manage the college experience successfully; College Part II covers how to make college more affordable.

So what are your options for funding college? Save or pay as you go? Borrow or rely on scholarships? Attend the cheapest school possible? Not go to college at all? The best choices will result only through comprehensive college planning, which involves a serious commitment of participation by both the student and the parents. Let's first take a look at some facts about today's college costs and the trends challenging the affordability of college.

Trends Affecting the Affordability of College

Depending upon the information source, there are differing and confusing figures provided about what the costs are to attend college. This is because some sources refer only to tuition costs while others include *all* of the costs associated with college: tuition, fees, books, room and board, living expenses, travel expenses to and from college, and pizza money. When *all* costs are included, my professional experience has been that in 2006, the total *annual* cost to attend a public university averages about $18,000 per year. A private college costs anywhere between $23,000 and $33,000 per year, and some "prestige" schools can command as much as $45,000 per year. Keep in mind that these dollar costs are *after-tax* numbers, and therefore it is the larger pretax dollar amount that you must accumulate.

College costs are increasing at an annual inflation rate of eight to twelve percent depending upon the school. This rate is two to three times faster than the annual increases in earned income!

Unbelievably, some of today's grandparents attended college forty years ago for a mere $840 a year, and that included all costs. Even twenty-five years ago, the cost for college was around $2,600 a year. Yet, today, that same college is now costing $18,000 a year. Furthermore, state-supported schools are receiving reduced subsidies because of state government budgetary woes. As a result, the tuition costs for state schools have been increasing even more rapidly than for the private schools, while the financial aid assistance from the state schools has been decreasing as well.

Parents with college-bound students are overwhelmed by how much money it takes to fund a college education. Although the cost for everything increases because of inflation, the costs for college are inflating two to three times faster and consuming a larger percentage of the household budget. If this same inflation rate for college costs continues, twenty-five years from now, today's college that costs $18,000 a year to attend will cost $123,000 a year.

College costs per year for educating just one student can consume fifteen to thirty percent of a household's after-tax earned income; twenty-five years ago, it consumed only five to ten percent.

Let's put the percentages into a dollar perspective. Twenty-five years ago, if your gross annual income was $45,000 and your net take-home pay was $30,000, your annual out-of-pocket cost for a full year of college would have been $2,600, representing just nine percent of your net annual income. Using the inflation-adjusted dollar equivalents for today, you would need to be earning $150,000 gross annual income, with your net annual take-home pay being $100,000 and the annual out-of-pocket dollar equivalent for a full year of college being $18,000, representing eighteen percent of your net annual income. This means that in just twenty-five years, the percentage of net annual income required to pay for college has doubled from nine percent to eighteen percent, and the percentage amount required continues to increase.

High-income families must earn as much as $2 to pay for every $1 of college costs

Ironically, because of the higher tax bite, the cost of college today requires a proportionately higher amount of a high-income family's income and assets than that for a lower-income family. If you are in a high tax bracket, as much as fifty percent of your gross earned income is depleted by paying federal, state, local, Social Security, and Medicare taxes. This means that in order to pay for an $18,000 per year college bill, you need to earn $36,000 in *pretax* dollars.

Therefore, in 2006, funding the entire four years can easily cost a family $144,000 in *pretax* out-of-pocket dollars. Multiply this number by each additional college-bound child in the family, and the education commitment becomes financially challenging. Furthermore, the dollars required for college often skyrocket even higher because of the fact that only fifteen percent of all undergraduate students actually graduate within the allotted four-year time frame, and then there are those students who may go on to attend graduate school.

Most families are not financially prepared to pay for college, and the competition for college money is intensifying

Colleges, when determining the financial aid awards, have an *expected minimum education savings* amount that families need to meet for *each* child. Specifically, the colleges expect families to have saved at least one and a half percent of pretax income for *each* year before the child enters college. For example, if you earn $150,000 and have two children, you are expected to have saved $81,000 toward college over the eighteen-year precollege period ($150,000 x 1.5 percent x 18 years x 2 children). In actuality, only four percent of all college families have saved $5,000 or more for college, and a shocking fifty percent have saved nothing at all to educate their children.

**Today's higher college funding costs will force
many parents to delay their retirement, to reduce
their accustomed standard of living during
retirement, or to never retire at all**

Many parents delay having children to pursue careers and develop affluent spending habits. Even after having children, they continue to spend most of their current earned income and do not adequately save for college. Furthermore, any savings program for college must be intelligently invested because the lower the rate of return, the more money you are required to save.

Remember that every dollar used to pay for the high cost of college diminishes savings being allocated for funding retirement. Even worse, parents are often required to borrow or withdraw funds from their retirement plans or discontinue contributions toward retirement during the college years. When the college commitment ends, trying to catch up with retirement funding requirements is difficult because there is usually too little time left to accumulate sufficient amounts for living a desired retirement lifestyle.

Borrowing more than ever before is required to fund college

College costs have soared, and larger amounts of savings are required to fund attending college. However, parents typically do not save what is required, and the state governments have drastically cut back on subsidized funding to the state universities and colleges, making them less affordable. This inability for families to afford college has caused heavy borrowing to pay for college, an increasing problem intensified by how the federal government subsidizes higher education. Today, the federal government's subsidization of higher education has shifted from that of providing grants that do not have to be repaid to that of offering student loans, as well as providing education "tax breaks," for which most higher-income families do not qualify. The student loans required for attending college can be staggering, as illustrated by the following true story.

> *Audrey graduated from Ohio State University with $3,500 in student loans. Not bad considering that the average undergraduate student loan amount totals $18,900 upon graduation. However, Audrey then married Jim, who had obtained his law degree by borrowing $65,000 in student loans, which is again not bad considering that the average accumulated debt for law students totals $91,700. So, Audrey and Jim's combined student loans total $68,500. But, the good news is that the federal government allows them the option to repay all of the debt over thirty years at $400 per month. Jokingly, Audrey says, "Let's hope we stay married that long!"*

What Will College Cost You?

Here are some important questions about college costs that you should think about as early as possible.

- How much money specifically will it cost in future dollars to send your children to college?
- How do you plan to accumulate the required amount?
- How old will you be when your youngest child graduates from college?
- How much money specifically will be required in future dollars to fund your secure retirement?
- How do you plan to pay for college and still adequately fund your retirement objectives?

You will need intelligent answers and solutions for these types of questions in order to avoid having stressful money requirements during the college years and to prevent an anxious financial situation regarding your retirement years. Now is a good time to complete the college funding worksheet in Chapter Two for determining what college will cost you. With this completed data input, you can prepare a **College Funding Analysis,** and you should seek professional help if necessary.

Figure 12-1 illustrates a sample College Funding Analysis for a family with three children, ages five, three, and one. The parents have not yet saved any money for their children's college education, and they have a challenging financial commitment to undertake.

FIGURE 12-1   College Funding Analysis

Assumptions	Child 1	Child 2	Child 3	
2006 Annual College Cost	$18,000	$18,000	$18,000	
Annual College Inflation Rate	8%	8%	8%	
Current Age for Child	5	3	1	
Years until Start College	13	15	17	
Current College Savings	0	0	0	
Rate of Return on Investments	10%	10%	10%	
Future Scholarships, Loans, etc.	?	?	?	

				Combined
Results	**Child 1**	**Child 2**	**Child 3**	**Total**
Projected Four-Year College Funding Cost	$220,580	$257,295	$300,109	$777,984
Four Year Investment Funding Options				
Single Lump Sum	$63,897	$61,594	$59,375	$184,866
Annual Savings	8,178	7,362	6,729	22,269
Monthly Savings	688	616	559	1,863

Notice that in order to fund the total college financial commitment, the parents must prepare to pay a staggering **$777,992** for providing their three children with four-year undergraduate degrees. Even with a diligent college savings program, most families are not able to set aside the required amounts involved. Furthermore, each year that you postpone your college savings and investment program, the financial commitment becomes increasingly challenging. However, by starting early to plan and invest for college in conjunction with establishing a comprehensive and coordinated financial plan, you can make the financial commitment for college more manageable and less daunting. Furthermore, as part of your comprehensive planning process, you will know how your ability to retire will be affected and will be able to prepare an informed retirement funding analysis.

Affording College Requires Comprehensive Financial Planning by Parents and Proactive Academic Planning by Students

The college experience can be a very challenging and stressful milestone for both parents and students, especially when the family has not saved enough money. Procrastination and ignorance about the college planning process are why most families cannot afford the college of their preferred choice.

There are important college planning activities that require coordinated action by both parents and students. Parents need to plan financially and the students need to prepare academically for the college challenge. In college planning, timing is everything. Most families wait until the junior year or, even worse, the senior year of high school to start thinking about college. This is a serious mistake. Successful college planning depends upon important student academic decisions and family financial strategies being implemented throughout the entire four years of high school.

Furthermore, everyone involved in the college planning process should be aware of each other's responsibilities and should approach the process as a coordinated team effort. The number of college planning activities increases each year as the commitment becomes closer. Many of the activities, if started early, will set the groundwork for a successful outcome. Poor planning, or no planning, makes it impossible to manage everything that needs to be done before and after the critical middle of the student's junior year in high school.

Now the big question: How can you properly manage the college commitment and avoid very costly college planning mistakes? First, you should start by assuming responsibility for taking the actions recommended in this chapter. By doing what is recommended, you will save enormous amounts of time and money and will reduce the emotional and financial stress often associated with managing the college experience. Let's break it down into easy steps for the parent responsibilities and the student responsibilities.

Parent Responsibilities

Determine your financial commitment

If you do not know where you are going, you will not know how to get there. It is that simple. So, it is extremely important that you complete your **Funding for College** worksheet in order to do the analysis to determine what your financial commitment is.

Commit to a savings program that increases annually as your income increases

The compounding effect of investing over time is powerful, and delaying the savings program robs you of benefiting from it. Consider this: Let's assume that when the child is born, you decide to save $250 a month for a college fund, and then each year thereafter, you increase the monthly contribution amount by five percent (year two would be $262.50 per month and so forth). Furthermore, assume that you averaged annually a ten percent investment return on the contributions. By starting to save early, when the child is born, in eighteen years, the college fund would total $189,204.

Alternatively, using the same assumptions, if you start contributing later when the child begins high school, the college fund would total only $14,916 after four years. In order to accumulate the amount needed, $189,204 in four years, you now have to contribute a healthy monthly contribution of $3,167 per month. You can see how difficult it is to play catch-up and miss the power of compounding investment returns.

Understand the financial aid system

Financial aid determination starts with the calculation of your expected family contribution (EFC), which is the amount of money you are expected to pay toward college. Using a government-mandated federal methodology formula, the calculation is based upon data about family income and assets, family size, and the number of other college students in the family. The data is submitted to the Department of Education for processing on a form known as the **Free Application for Federal Student Aid (FAFSA)**. The first time this form is submitted occurs in January through March of the student's senior year in high school. The requested information includes financial data for both the student and the parents and uses the most current values for assets as well as income tax return information from the just-ended tax year (all of this is subsequently verified when the final tax return is completed). For each year thereafter that the student attends college, a FAFSA renewal form has to be submitted.

Many private colleges provide substantial amounts of financial aid using their own endowment money. Therefore, they may inquire even further about your

QUIET MILLIONAIRE® WISDOM
The best overview about the college financial aid system and higher education is provided by the Department of Education's Web site, www.ed.gov.

financial situation by using the institutional methodology in addition to the federal methodology to calculate the EFC. This entails submitting additional financial information by completing a **Financial Aid Profile (FAP)** application, also known as a **PROFILE** application.

By knowing the components and rationale of the EFC formula, high-income families can legitimately plan ways in advance to improve their eligibility for financial aid. For example, income earned by the student and investments in the student's name are much more heavily weighted and penalized under the EFC formula than are the parents' income and assets. Therefore, tax reduction strategies that advocate titling investments in the child's name may backfire in a costly way when financial aid eligibility is being determined. Later, financial aid strategies specifically for high-income families will be discussed.

Understand how a financial aid need analysis is conducted

A need analysis determines a student's eligibility for financial aid at a particular institution using the following formula.

COA (cost of attendance)
−EFC (expected family contribution)
=FN (financial need)

The cost of attendance varies according to each school and includes *all* costs encompassing tuition, fees, books, room and board, daily living expenses, and travel costs, all of which cause the financial need to be different for each school. Be aware that financial aid awards can be discretionary and discriminatory regardless of the calculated financial need. Suppose a school costs $20,000 to attend and your EFC is calculated to be $10,000. According to the need analysis, your eligibility for financial aid is calculated to be $10,000:

$20,000 (COA)
−$10,000 (EFC)
=$10,000 (FN)

However, just because your financial need is $10,000 does not automatically mean that you will be provided $10,000 in financial aid. While some schools might meet one hundred percent of your financial need, other schools might offer far less financial aid regardless of your calculated financial need. For instance, a school may offer a financial aid amount that meets only fifty percent ($5,000) of your financial need or an even a lower thirty percent ($3,000), or it might offer no financial aid at all. As will be discussed further, this is why part of your college planning process should be to select and apply to a number of schools having the financial resources and the willingness to offer you financial aid. Otherwise, you could end up paying your EFC *plus* a significant portion of your unmet financial need. In effect, any unmet amount can be considered a premium charged by the college for the student to attend.

Develop an intelligent comprehensive financial planning approach for college planning

It is important that high-income families plan for college as part of a comprehensive financial planning approach in order to be aware of the conflicting benefits and pitfalls that can arise when implementing various college planning strategies. For example, good tax reduction planning can often conflict with and harm opportunities for receiving financial aid, and the financial gains from taxes saved must be weighed against the potential effects upon receiving financial aid awards. Chapter Thirteen will discuss further how financial aid strategies interact with tax reduction strategies as well as how they are affected by investment programs involving 529 college savings plans, uniform gift to minors accounts, and retirement plans.

Shared Parent-Student Responsibilities

Most students lead hectic daily lives, with their time consumed by school, social activities, and family responsibilities. This often causes them to procrastinate and not take time out to plan for matters that are not immediately pressing. The same holds true for parents, and when the time comes to fund and manage major milestones in life such as a college education for their children, there can be emotional distress for the entire family.

Keep in mind that managing the college experience can be stressful for both the parents and the student. The student's transition of leaving family and lifelong friends to attend college away from home can be an emotionally unsettling experience. Insufficient planning for these transitional changes can cause the student to fail academically and be unhappy with the college experience and can possibly result in a costly waste of money for the parents. Allowing procrastination and uninformed decisions to dominate the college planning process unquestionably increases the risk for an unsuccessful outcome.

Prepare and support your student
for attending college

Part of the parents' college planning responsibility is to help the student prepare academically and socially for college. Remember, the student alone cannot be expected to do all that is necessary without guidance from his or her parents to supplement what the schools cannot provide in preparing for college. This is a process that should be considered and monitored throughout the student's high school career.

Unfortunately, parents are often consumed with managing their own life issues, are uninformed about the college needs of their children, and rely too heavily upon the schools to provide the required guidance. It is extremely important that parents communicate and support their student by working together closely on all college planning activities. This is a team effort, and there is a direct correlation between the student's success and the amount of parent interest and involvement in preparing the student for college.

Start academic planning for college early

Not every student is destined to attend Harvard. Accordingly, there should be a proactive and realistic assessment of the student's intellectual and academic capabilities. Ideally, this assessment should be accomplished by the student's first year in high school in order to determine what coursework should be selected throughout high school and to help avoid frustration and disappointment. Parents should be careful to guide, not direct, the student's decision-making process, and this is where the school's guidance counselor can be helpful. Be sure to fully utilize the resources of the high school's guidance department, and start early by meeting with the guidance counselor before the student starts the first year of high school. In order to best guide the student, it is important that the guidance counselor be familiar about the student's capabilities and education objectives, and often this requires that the parents and the student proactively interact with the counselor.

Review possible career interests and select appropriate college preparatory courses

Many students have no idea what they want to choose as a work career, while others seem to know from a very early age. It is important to stimulate thoughts about possible future ambitions. Open family discussion about the student's possible career interests should begin as early as possible. This enables parents to more intelligently participate with the guidance counselor about which courses should be taken throughout the four years of high school to best prepare the student for college entrance and career qualifications. For example, it would make no sense to load a student up with a bunch of math and science courses if he or she wants to be a journalist or to load up on art and English courses if he or she is headed toward the medical field. As the student begins to define career interests, have him or her research the qualifications and job activities for his or her career interests and interview people currently working in these areas to help further tighten career choices.

Develop productive study habits, time management, research and organizational skills

Parents, by providing for their student a study environment without tempting distractions such as television and non-study computer activities, will help assure academic competitiveness during high school. Students need to know how to research, study, and absorb large amounts of information and then regurgitate the knowledge for understanding and testing. This will pay even bigger dividends when the student is in the more challenging environment of college academics. Often, developing this discipline before college can mean the difference between academic success and failure when attending college.

Student Responsibilities

Participate and assume leadership roles in school and community activities

The message here is to make after-school hours count. By participating in group activities such as sports and clubs, students develop social and leadership skills and learn to both compete and cooperate. Keep in mind that there are many ways to be a "star" and develop talents that exist beyond athletic activities. Colleges take into consideration the impor-

QUIET MILLIONAIRE® WISDOM
A worthwhile education is one that teaches the student not only how to learn academically but also how to live responsibly and give unselfishly to others.

tance of the student's background, involvement in well-chosen activities, and leadership roles assumed.

The student should not neglect to participate in community activities that involve helping others either. Not only is this good as a college planning strategy, but also it helps develop the student's appreciation for a more beneficial living situation. This appreciation may also serve to reduce the stress associated with the student's materialistic peer pressure that is often thrust upon parents as well. With respect to controlling materialism and helping the less fortunate, here is a great opportunity for parents to lead by example.

Learn Managing Finances 101

Students need to understand that money accumulation is most often hard earned and needs to be managed intelligently. Unfortunately, many parents may not serve as good examples or role models for intelligent financial management. Furthermore, the schools do not teach it effectively if at all. As a result, many students go off to college and can't even balance a checkbook. Even worse, they typically get inundated with irresponsible credit card offers that can lead to trouble with reckless spending. Early learning of intelligent financial management will benefit the student as he or she evolves to living more independently while attending college and throughout life.

Develop a college entrance exam strategy to achieve the best possible test score results

The college admission process is competitive. Taking college entrance exams often causes the student anxiety and stress. Although the test scores alone do not determine an admission decision, a higher college entrance test score can make the difference in being accepted by a top-choice quality school, as well as being awarded financial aid. This is particularly the situation when the applications coming from students with similar grade point averages and comparable extracurricular activities are reviewed.

There are two not-for-profit college entrance exam sponsors, the College Board, which offers the SAT tests, and the American College Testing program, which offers the ACT test. Students often inquire about the differences between the SAT and the ACT and are usually concerned with how the scores on one test compare to the scores on the other. It is important to understand that some students do better on one test than the other. A student may be better suited to the English and Reading sections of the ACT if he or she has strong grammar and reading skills. A student with a stronger vocabulary may find the SAT Verbal section easier to handle. Math on the ACT tends to include some basic trigonometry, while SAT math does not go past basic geometry.

The best advice for students is to take both the SAT and ACT tests and determine the best outcome. Sample questions and exams are made available from the organizations that administer both tests. Because most colleges will accept either ACT or SAT scores, it is advantageous for the student to take both exams and submit the best comparative result. For example, if you score 1650 overall on the three-section SAT but a 29 composite on the ACT, you are better off submitting the ACT score. If the high school permits, taking these college entrance exams should ideally start during the sophomore year to gain familiarity with the testing environment and test content.

The Preliminary SAT/National Merit Scholarship Qualifying Test (PSAT/NMSQT®) should be taken in the sophomore year for familiarity and retaken in the junior year. Students attending high school for the full four years before entering college must take the PSAT/NMSQT in their junior year in order to enter the National Merit Scholarship Competition (NMSC). NMSC scholarships are awarded in the spring of the senior high school year. Registration for the test is done by the high school, not the student. Interested students should see their counselors no later than the beginning of their junior high school year to arrange taking the PSAT/NMSQT in October.

The National Merit Scholarship competition finalists have an opportunity to receive scholarship money from three sources. First, there are **National Merit $2500 Scholarships**, where finalists compete for these *one-time* payment scholarships that are awarded on a state representational basis. Second, there are **corporate-sponsored merit scholarships** for children of the company's employees, or residents of a community where a company has operations, or where the finalists have career plans that match what the corporate sponsor wishes to encourage. These scholarships may be either *renewable* for four years of undergraduate study or awarded on a *one-time* basis. Third, there are **college-sponsored merit scholarships** offered by sponsoring colleges to finalists who have been accepted for admission and have informed the NMSC within published deadlines that the sponsor college is their first choice to attend. These awards are *renewable* for up to four years of undergraduate study.

Regardless of whether the student takes the PSAT/NMSQT to qualify for the National Merit Scholarship Competition, the student should take both the SAT and ACT tests no later than the fall and spring of their junior year in high school. If necessary, a test preparation course should be taken to improve test score results. Be aware that test scores tend to be better the second time around as a result of increased comfort and familiarity. In any event, the best test results, regardless of when taken, are those used for purposes of college admission.

Diligently compose essays and a personal résumé for college admissions and scholarship awards

Many schools require that an essay be written as part of the application process, with the subject matter and length being specified. This important activity is often not given much effort by the student. It takes quiet blocks of time and a number of revisions to prepare these important written communications. Typically, the essay is a personal statement about a particular life event, a significant period, or a value that has influenced the student's very young life in a heartfelt and honest way. This is not the time to be artificial or contrived just to impress the reader. The structure and content should be well thought out for development and refinement in advance of submission. It sometimes helps the student to start a diary or journal to collect and recall significant life events for these essays.

Parents can also help the student brainstorm and compose essay topics, but they must be careful not to taint the creative process by doing too much or going beyond the student's comfort level with their participation. Usually, but not always because of time limitations, an English teacher's or a guidance counselor's involvement can be beneficial in helping with the student's essay.

Select and approach potential providers
for recommendations

The student should develop an interacting relationship with at least two teachers for deriving recommendations as part of the college admissions application process. It is also extremely important that the student's guidance counselor become familiar with the student's capabilities and college objectives. Parents would be wise to participate here too.

Hone the student's written and
verbal communication skills

Articulate communication is important throughout life. It is a fact that perception and judgment by others is influenced by how well we express ourselves via all means of communication. For students, good communication can improve the "marketing" of themselves in the written college admission requirements as well as in their scholarship opportunities. This will also benefit students during the interviewing process, which many college admissions require. Furthermore, beyond college, these developed written and verbal skills will go a long way toward establishing and advancing students in a successful career.

How to Select the Right College

Because of the lack of knowledge about the college selection process, surveys reveal that only fifteen percent of all college-bound students wind up completely happy with their choice, and for students to switch to a different school is costly. Choosing the "right" college that fits the student's personality and the parents' affordability is a very important decision. A good decision assures a smoother transition from high school and increases the probability that the student will graduate with an undergraduate degree and a job in four years.

Often, a poor college selection is made because it is based upon where friends or a high school sweetheart may be attending. With an inappropriate college selection, some students become so distressed or overwhelmed by the

> QUIET MILLIONAIRE® WISDOM
> *Selecting the right college is the most important decision in the college planning process.*

experience that they flunk or drop out altogether. These occurrences are costly in time and money. Even if the student decides to transfer to another school, most likely the earned coursework credits will be lost in the process, which then causes greater amounts of money to be paid for college than is necessary.

Sometimes it is not the student's fault that a bad selection is made. Parents often can adversely affect the decision because of their own preference, lack of knowledge, or disinterest. They may influence the decision because of some form of self-interest such as preferring the student to attend a college close to home, their own college alma mater, or the least costly school. While it is important to help guide the student, in the end, it should be the student's decision to make. Parents and students working together on the college selection process in a diligent, intelligent, and informed manner can greatly improve the chances for the college experience to be an academic and financial success.

Start the college selection process as early as possible during high school

It takes time to research and evaluate the many important criteria about colleges that are often overlooked in the selection process. If you wait to start your research until the latter part of the junior year or during the senior year of high school, there is a high degree of probability that you will not make the best college selection both financially and for the student's satisfaction. The following are some selection criteria to consider:

Cost: Although important, it does not have to be the driving force if intelligent comprehensive college planning is done.

Value: Weigh the benefits you expect to receive compared to the price you will pay. Choose an affordable college that feels comfortable and is academically challenging to provide a lifelong learning benefit.

Location: Should the student commute or live on campus? Is the distance from home satisfactory? Is the campus setting right: big city urban or quiet rural comfort in a college town? Warm or cold weather?

Size: Is the campus size right: large with thousands of students and a high student-faculty ratio or small with close personalized student interaction with professors?

Diversity: What is the student body background, geographic orientation, and cultural heritage? Is there a religious affiliation?

Academics: What percentage of faculty are PhDs? Does the college offer course majors that interest the student and prepare him or her for graduate school or a career choice? What is the attrition rate of students not graduating? Are there co-op programs? Is there job placement assistance?

Campus Life: What are student activities outside of class? Are living and eating arrangements acceptable? Safety? Alcohol and drug policies? Are there fraternities and sororities?

Athletic Programs: If the student wants to participate in a varsity sport, is it a realistic expectation? If not, is there intercollegiate participation, and are there opportunities for intramural and recreational sports?

Extracurricular Activities: Are there activities offered to meet the student's social interests, personal growth, and career aspirations?

Facilities: What is available? Do they include libraries, laboratories, student center, theater, arts, athletic center, and computer resources? How do they accommodate students with special needs or disabilities?

Financial Aid: What types and amounts of assistance are available? Does the school have money to offer if it wants to attract the student?

There is no single resource or easy way to gather information about the selection criteria. Preliminarily information is available by viewing college Web sites and accessing available published materials and software packages. But, in the end, the only way to complete the criteria evaluation process is by making on-campus visits. Remember that visits take place only after as much screening as possible has been done from home.

Select schools where the student profiles in the top twenty percent of all applicants with respect to grade point average and college entrance exam results

By choosing schools where your child profiles competitively on an academic basis with other students, he or she will be more suitably challenged by his or her education. The parents may be happier financially too because often schools will compete with money to attract more desired students. This is why some schools will not offer a competitive financial aid package if your student is not in the top twenty percent bracket.

Visit as many selected schools as possible before deciding whether to apply or attend

Keep an open mind with no preconceived notions about schools. Often, following a college visit, initial top choices drop from serious consideration to no consideration, and secondary or previously unknown choices rise to the top. Many high school students base their initial college desirability upon what their parents, guidance counselors, or friends recommend. College guides, magazines, media sports events, or college teams also maybe influence them. Regardless of how they initially decide upon their college choices, students must visit the campuses of these schools in order to get a true personal feeling about each school. Spring breaks and summer vacations offer valuable free time to tour campuses, ideally before actually applying.

Under no circumstance should a decision be made to attend a school without an on-site visit. Personal dialogue with the admissions and financial aid officers and relevant faculty members should take place. Ideally, getting direct feedback from students currently attending and even arranging an overnight stay on campus can be helpful as well.

Commit to using the four-year college planning checklist in order to pull the process together and to reduce errors and omissions

Figure 12-2 is a four-year college planning checklist prepared by the not-for-profit Higher Education Advisory Institute and can be printed at *www.quietmillionaire.com.* Both the student and parents should commit to using the checklist throughout high school. Notice how the number of college planning activities increases during each year of high school as the student gets closer to attending college.

Failure to develop and activate an intelligent college planning process can prove to be a very expensive mistake causing your out of pocket costs to attend college to be greater than necessary or even beyond affordability.

QUIET MILLIONAIRE® WISDOM
Affording college requires starting to prepare early using a proactive, comprehensive planning approach, knowing all entry requirements, and meeting all activity deadlines.

FIGURE 12-2   Four-Year College Planning Checklist

FRESHMAN YEAR

___**Student and Parents:** Explore possible career and college major interests.

___**Student and Parents:** Meet with guidance counselor for a recommended schedule of college prep courses to be taken throughout high school for careers and college majors of interest.

___**Student:** Establish good study habits and commit to a consistent study routine. Strive for a high GPA, especially in required college prep courses. Manage time effectively.

___**Student:** Learn to use the library effectively, including computer research. Enhance vocabulary skills and writing abilities.

___**Student:** Become involved in school and community service activities for use on résumé when applying to colleges and for scholarships. Strive for leadership positions.

(continues)

FIGURE 12-2   Four-Year College Planning Checklist (*continued*)

___**Parents:** Calculate your expected family contribution (EFC) to know whether eligible for need-based financial aid and whether legal repositioning of income and assets to increase eligibility is feasible and warranted.

___**Student:** Update guidance counselor about your career and college major interests and reaffirm that high school course selections remain appropriate. Formulate your sophomore year college prep course schedule.

___**Student:** Seek summer employment for income and savings for college.

SOPHOMORE YEAR

___**Student and Parents:** Begin college selection process. Review catalogs and Web sites of colleges that have preferred attributes and academic course majors of interest. Research their history for providing financial aid.

___**Parents:** Recalculate your EFC for determining and implementing appropriate financial aid enhancing strategies prior to the base year calculation.

___**Student:** Consult guidance counselor about registering for the Preliminary Scholastic Aptitude Test (PSAT). These scores are mandatory to be eligible for the National Merit Scholarship Program and certain other scholarships. Take the PSAT test in October for practice in taking college admission tests and to establish eligibility for scholarships.

___**Student:** Continue to participate in school and community service activities to be a more attractive college admissions candidate and improve opportunities for scholarship awards.

___**Student:** Update guidance counselor about your career and college major interests and reaffirm that high school course selections remain appropriate. Formulate your junior year college prep course schedule.

___**Student:** Seek summer employment for income and savings for college.

JUNIOR YEAR

September–December

___**Student:** Review your cumulative grade point average for possible improvement. Take advanced-placement (AP) courses.

(continues)

FIGURE 12-2   Four-Year College Planning Checklist (*continued*)

___**Student:** Register and take in October the PSAT test for the second time in order to qualify for National Merit Scholarship eligibility.

___**Student:** Obtain schedule for SAT and ACT test dates. Register and prepare to take SAT and ACT tests during fall, spring, and summer—the earlier the better to determine whether a test preparation class is needed to improve test score results.

___**Student and Parents:** Attend college night programs and college fairs. Obtain information about colleges of interest.

___**Student and Parents:** Narrow preferred school choices to between ten and twelve that include at least one resident in-state school, one safe school, one reach school, and six to eight "good" financial aid schools that meet your selection criteria.

___**Student and Parents:** Begin to schedule college campus visits. Research local resources for scholarships and grants through guidance counselor, church, employer, chamber of commerce, and local business organizations. Avoid scams that ask for money and offer guarantees.

___**Parents:** Recalculate your EFC. Last chance to reposition income and assets before the base year for determining financial aid calculations that start as of January 1.

January–May

___**Student:** Strive to achieve high GPA. Graduating in the top ten percent of the class can offset lower SAT and ACT scores and improve opportunities for being admitted and receiving financial aid from more schools.

___**Student:** Register to take the SAT and ACT tests in spring and summer if did not take in fall. Take test prep course if concerned about results. Have the scores sent to the schools being considered.

___**Student:** If enrolled in advanced-placement courses, take AP tests.

Summer

___**Student and Parents:** Research and review career interests. Interview people working in the careers of interest. Formulate course curriculum for senior year. Seek summer employment.

___**Student and Parents:** Continue to visit colleges being considered.

(continues)

FIGURE 12-2   Four-Year College Planning Checklist (*continued*)

SENIOR YEAR
September–October
___**Student:** Register and retake the ACT and SAT tests in October if necessary. Submit the highest test results to all schools of interest. Note: This submission involves a fee if not completed at the time of test registration.

___**Student:** Compose essays and a résumé for college admissions and scholarships. Seek out two teacher references, and make sure the guidance counselor is familiar with your capabilities and aspirations.

___**Student and Parents:** Firm up narrowed list of eight to twelve colleges for application. Make sure to include "good" financial aid schools that meet selection criteria and where the student profiles in the top twenty percent relative to all other applicants. Include at least one in-state fallback school.

___**Student and Parents:** Obtain admission applications and prepare to meet specified requirements for narrowed list of colleges. Determine and be prepared to meet admission and financial aid application deadlines. Start submitting through the guidance department the required admissions package for each school. Be prepared to encounter possible resistance from the guidance counselor for submitting the recommended eight to twelve school applications; guidance counselors typically prefer just two or three.

___**Student and Parents:** Continue to visit college campuses on the narrowed list. Thoroughly explore campus, classrooms, and dorms. Speak with students and faculty. Meet with admissions and financial aid officers. Include, if possible, the experience of a student on-campus overnight stay.

November–December
___**Student and Parents:** Complete and submit admission applications before all filing deadlines.

___**Student and Parents:** Obtain from guidance department the FAFSA and the CSS PROFILE financial aid forms. Prepare preliminary IRS tax return. Preliminarily, prepare the FAFSA and, if required, the PROFILE as well as other school specific financial aid forms for submission in order to meet all financial aid filing deadlines. Note: The FAFSA form cannot be submitted before January 1.

(*continues*)

FIGURE 12-2   Four-Year College Planning Checklist *(continued)*

January–May

___**Parents:** Finalize preliminary income tax return for answers on financial aid forms. Complete and submit the FAFSA and, if required, the PROFILE as well as other school-specific financial aid forms by no later than February 1. Keep copies. Meet all financial aid deadlines starting with the earliest.

___**Student:** Verify that midyear transcripts have been sent to each school receiving your application for admission.

___**Parents:** Monitor mail for the Student Aid Report (SAR) and, if submitted, the CSS PROFILE acknowledgment. Note your EFC amount. Review and make any corrections. Resubmit if necessary. If SAR is correct, retain and submit to your final-choice college for selections.

___**Parents:** Send verification and final IRS tax return to each college requesting verification.

___**Student and Parents:** Monitor mail for college acceptances and financial aid awards.

___**Student and Parents:** Review and compare financial aid offers for possible appeal. If housing deposit is required for more than one school, make sure to make any refund requests within deadline.

___**Student and Parents:** If appropriate, appeal financial aid awards in an intelligent, nonthreatening manner.

___**Student and Parents:** Review final financial aid awards and make final college selection by May 1. Send required deposit, signed financial aid award offer, SAR, and final grade transcript when available. Submit all pertinent loan applications. Notify other colleges of your final decision.

___**Student:** Seek summer employment, possibly at the chosen school's locale.

Quiet Millionaire® Summary

- **Realize that if you have a college funding problem, then you also have a retirement funding problem.**

- **Be aware of the trends challenging the affordability of college in order to plan successfully.**

(continues)

Quiet Millionaire® Summary (continued)

■ Take time to figure out early what college will cost you and commit to a savings program.

■ Start the college selection process as early as possible in the high school career.

■ Know and implement your responsibilities as a parent in the college planning process.

■ Know and implement your parent-student shared responsibilities in the college planning process.

■ Help the student know and implement his or her responsibilities in the college planning process.

■ Become knowledgeable about how to select the right college, the most important decision of the college planning process.

■ Make on-site college visits.

■ Commit to using the four-year college planning checklist.

CHAPTER THIRTEEN

College Part II: How to Make College Affordable

I f you intelligently prepare for managing the college experience as covered in College Part I, you are already on your way to reducing the financial stress of funding college. College Part II discusses how to make college more affordable. Parents and grandparents who are serious about saving for a child's or grandchild's college education have various options to decide upon, which include both intelligent and *not so* intelligent ways to accumulate money for college.

Intelligent Ways to Accumulate Money for College

529 Plan

Certainly, you should consider taking advantage of 529 plans, named after Section 529 of the IRS code, which codifies the plan and provides legislated tax advantages in order to encourage more savings for college. The plans are individually sponsored by the state governments and more recently by a consortium of private colleges. However, you must be cautious about which of the plans you choose to contribute to because there is a vast difference in the quality among the various state and private college sponsorships.

You are permitted to open multiple 529 plans and thereby choose to invest with the plans you deem are best for you. The student does not have to attend college in the state where the money is saved, and it is possible to transfer from one state's plan to another. Furthermore, at any time you are allowed to switch the student beneficiaries from one family member to another as college funding needs may change.

Money invested in a 529 plan is not subject to federal taxation and, depending upon the state, may not be subject to state taxation, provided the accumulated funds are used to pay for any *qualified* postsecondary undergraduate and graduate educational expenses. The expenses are considered *qualified* if the withdrawals are used to pay for tuition, fees, books, supplies, and equipment. Room and board expenses are also allowable if the student is deemed attending on a half-time basis or more.

Because there are no earned-income restrictions for contributing to a 529 plan, higher-income families are able to benefit from the tax breaks offered by these plans. This is significant because high-income earners are typically excluded from using most other tax breaks allowable for education funding.

Also, remember that the states compete with each other nation-wide for attracting investment funds to their state. Therefore, some states offer *only* their in-state residents a state income tax deduction on contributions, while other states provide matching contributions for investments made by their residents. Some states join with the federal government in not taxing the 529 plan investment gains when the withdrawals are used to pay for qual-ified expenses for colleges located within that state.

Be cautious about the lure of the individual state incentives because they may not be as beneficial as perceived. The 529 plan investment options are limited and vary in quality. Some plans are substandard and have made deals with big-name investment companies to offer the plans through commissioned salespeople, resulting in excessive operating costs that should be avoided. If the investment options perform poorly and the plan's internal administrative costs are high, the incentives and tax benefits may be offset and meaningless.

529 plans come in two basic forms, and depending upon the state, you can use either one or both types of plans. One type is termed a **guaranteed prepaid tuition plan**, whereby the contribu-tions are placed in an account that the state "guarantees" a rate of return that will keep up with tomorrow's inflated tuition costs.

The other type of 529 plan is termed a **college savings plan**, which has investment options for you to select from, but the options do not guarantee a performance rate of return. The con-tributions can be invested in a restricted selection of mutual funds for potential additional growth that is not guaranteed but that is intended to outperform the guaranteed option. In both types, the contributions grow tax free.

Another advantage offered by the 529 plan is that parents or grandparents can be the owner of the account rather than the child, and therefore they retain control of the investment money. Furthermore, when determining the financial aid awards, the colleges thereby consider the 529 plan to be a parent or grand-parent asset rather than a student asset, which is less penalizing. However, many colleges are now starting to assess the saved money as a student asset when structuring their financial aid awards regardless of the titling.

The 529 plan is also an especially useful estate planning device for removing large amounts of taxable money rapidly from estates. Ordinarily, individuals can exclude from gift taxation only up to $12,000 annually for each student, or $24,000 for gifts made by married taxpayers. However, if the money is contributed to a 529 plan, five years' worth of annual exclusion gifts can be accelerated into one year. This means that married taxpayers can contribute up to $120,000 ($24,000 x 5 years) to each student within one year without being concerned about a potential gift or estate tax liability. But, **the contributor must be sure not to make any other monetary gifts to the student during the five-year period.** Also, if the contributor dies before the end of the five-year period, the estate would include the prorated remaining balance of the contribution for federal estate tax purposes, but the earnings and appreciation would be ignored.

The allowable 529 plan maximum amounts that can be contributed for each student are set by each state. Most 529 plan limits range from $250,000 to $300,000 per student beneficiary. The account value can exceed the limit resulting from accumulated investment earnings and appreciation, but no future contributions can be made for the student once the account value reaches the plan limit.

Coverdell Education Savings Account

The Coverdell Education Savings Account (formerly known as an Education IRA) is named after the late Senator Paul Coverdell, who sponsored the legislation that created the account. Withdrawals from the Coverdell can be used to pay for qualified college expenses as well as qualified elementary and secondary school expenses, both public and private schools. The 529 plan withdrawals can be used to pay for only qualified college expenses. Qualified Coverdell expenses include room and board, tutoring, computer equipment, uniforms, and extended day care program costs.

Contributions to the Coverdell are not tax deductible, are limited to $2,000 annually per each student under the age of eighteen, and can be made as late as the April 15 tax filing deadline. Although the contributions are not tax deductible, the withdrawals are tax free as long as the money pays for qualified education expenses. Coverdell funds must be used by the time the student turns thirty, or else the account owner is assessed a ten percent penalty and taxed on the investment gains.

Allowable contributions to the Coverdell are phased out for married taxpayers with an adjusted gross income between $190,000 and $220,000 and for individual taxpayers with an adjusted gross income between $95,000 and $110,000. Therefore, high-income earners may not be eligible to contribute to the Coverdell but can contribute to a 529 plan, which has no income restrictions. However, if eligible for both, contributing to a Coverdell does not limit your ability to simultaneously contribute to a 529 plan. This ability to contribute to both enables a more diversified investment approach for college savings because the Coverdell does not restrict where the money can be invested as the 529 plan does.

However, be aware of the possible costly gift tax consequences that can occur if gifted money exceeds the gift tax exclusion limits of $12,000 annually per student from individual taxpayers or $24,000 from married taxpayers. For example, if $2,000 is contributed in any given year to a Coverdell, you must make sure that the combined total monetary gift amounts made to a 529 plan as well as any other monetary gifts do not exceed the gift tax annual exclusion limits. Otherwise, the excess amount gifted to the student is considered a taxable gift, and a federal gift tax return is required to be filed by the gifting taxpayers.

With respect to financial aid eligibility determinations, the Coverdell account is automatically assessed as a more heavily weighted student asset, whereas the money in a 529 plan can be considered as a less penalizing parent or grandparent asset. Furthermore, control of the money in a Coverdell is automatically transferred to the child at age eighteen, whereas control of the money in a 529 plan is never relinquished by the adult owner.

With respect to financial aid planning, if the student is not expected to receive need-based financial aid, and if you are eligible to contribute, then the Coverdell account should be considered for use as a college savings vehicle because the contribution amount is limited to only $2,000 per year for each student. Therefore, the relatively small amount of money accumulated in a Coverdell account will have little influence upon any financial aid determination that is not based upon need.

Taxable Investment Account (not tax deferred)

The investment gains and income earned in a taxable account are subject to taxation each year and are not tax deferred. However, with intelligent investment and tax management, the annual tax consequences for a taxable account due to capital gains, dividends, and interest can be kept low and sometimes can be a better way to save for college than saving in either a 529 plan or a Coverdell account. This is because money in a taxable account that is in the name of a parent, grandparent, or business, instead of in the student's name or designated as a college savings vehicle, can have a lesser negative affect upon financial aid award determinations. Furthermore, an appeal can be made to the financial aid office that the use of the money in a taxable account is necessary for retirement or for purposes other than college funding, which cannot be a valid appeal for money in a 529 plan or Coverdell. Certainly, your investment program for college funding should include taxable accounts for this reason, and it gives you flexibility to use the money for any purpose, including college if required.

Roth IRA

The Roth IRA is primarily intended for use as a retirement savings account, and every effort should be made to keep Roth money for use during retirement and not use it for college funding. However, the Roth IRA can be an effective savings tool for college funding, and money inside a Roth does not affect financial aid awards. Certainly, anyone who meets the income eligibility requirements to contribute annually to a Roth IRA (adjusted gross income less than $160,000 married filing joint, $100,000 married filing separate, or $110,000 single filing) should do as Joel and Betty are doing.

> *Joel and Betty recently had their first child, Adam, and they wisely wanted to start their college savings program early. The financial advisor for Betty's parents suggested that Joel and Betty each open a Roth IRA for their college savings because the money would remain forever tax free, could be flexibly used for either college or retirement funding, and would not be counted in the college financial aid calculations. Furthermore, if Betty's parents wanted to, they could help Joel and Betty to fund the $4,000 maximum annual contribution for each of their Roth IRAs.*

> *Best of all was that by contributing $8,000 every year to their Roth IRAs for eighteen years, and if they earned an average investment return of ten percent, Joel and*

Betty would have $364,793 that grew tax free to use for college expenses.

With respect to making withdrawals from a Roth IRA to pay for college expenses, because the contributions are made on an after-tax basis, the *principal* (the amount contributed) portion of the withdrawal is tax free and penalty free at anytime. Similarly, with respect to the *investment gains* portion of the withdrawals from a Roth IRA, there are also no taxes or penalties for paying college expenses if the Roth has existed for at least five years from January 1 of the year you made your first contribution and you are at least 59½ years old. Otherwise, the investment gains portion (only) of the withdrawals for paying college expenses is taxed as income, but the ten percent penalty for early pre-59½ withdrawals is waived.

You should be aware that parents can contribute an amount up to $4,000 a year to a Roth IRA for their college-bound student, provided that the student earns a comparable amount up to $4,000. This is worthwhile because if the Roth money is not used by the student to pay for college expenses, up to $10,000 can be withdrawn both penalty free and tax free for a first-time house purchase, or, alternatively, the money can be allowed to grow forever tax free and be used by the student for future retirement.

Traditional or Regular IRA

A traditional IRA can be used the same way as a Roth IRA to fund college and with the same restrictions. However, there is a significant disadvantage in using the traditional IRA because the contributions made to a traditional IRA are usually done on a pretax basis instead of on an after-tax basis as done for the Roth IRA. This means that the *entire* pretax amount of any with-drawals from a traditional IRA is subject to income taxes, while only the *investment gains* portion of taxable withdrawals from a Roth are taxed.

Not So Intelligent Ways to Accumulate Money for College

There are some not so intelligent ways to save for college that should be avoided because they can harm your chances for receiving financial aid or because they are not the best type of savings vehicle for college or any other long-term accumulation purpose.

Uniform Transfers to Minors Act (UTMA) or Uniform Gifts to Minors Act (UGMA) Account

A minor's account is a way to maintain control of money for minor children until they reach the legal age of *maturity* at eighteen or twenty-one, depending upon state law. Often, the motivation for opening a minor's account is to accumulate money in the child's lower tax bracket with less income tax consequences. However, you have to be aware of the "kiddie" tax that comes into play until the child reaches age eighteen. As of 2006, the "kiddie" tax rules allow a child under age eighteen to receive $850 in investment income (interest, dividends, or capital gains) free of any income tax. The next $850 is taxed at the child's low tax rate, and any investment income above that for the child is taxed at the parents' higher income tax rate.

Using a minor's account to reduce taxes can backfire on financial aid planning strategies and in the end can be more costly than the tax savings gained. This is because college financial aid awards are more negatively affected by accumulated money being titled in the student's name rather than in the parents'. In essence, the attitude of the school is "Spend the child's money first, and then we'll talk to you about financial aid."

Another major disadvantage of a minor's account that often causes regret for parents is that the money in the account legally becomes the child's at the lawful age of maturity, age eighteen or twenty-one, depending upon the state. The child is free to take the money without parental consent and spend it any way he or she desires. In fact, there are instances where children have sued parents who have refused to give them their gifted money.

Often parents are not aware of these disadvantages associated with a minor's account. When considering putting money in the minor's name, all of the pros and cons must be knowingly measured and weighed. Money that is already in a minor's account can be transferred to a 529 plan, although it could be considered a taxable gift and should not be done without professional guidance.

Annuities

Annuities are sold by insurance companies mainly to accumulate savings on a tax-deferred basis for retirement income. However, the financial use of annuities is sometimes misused and abused by annuity salespeople by being sold as a way to save for college without reducing financial aid awards. Their rationale is that annuities are deemed a retirement asset by the colleges and therefore are not considered in the financial aid determinations. While the argument used to frequently work, the college financial aid offices have become wise to this practice, and they now often reduce their financial award amounts by the dollar amounts tucked away in annuities.

Some salespeople even suggest that you save for college using an annuity, yet they know that you will have to make penalizing withdrawals to pay for college by incurring income taxes and a ten percent early-withdrawal penalty on the growth of the money. The misguided rationale used is that the benefits of tax-deferred investment growth and the limited impact of the accumulated money upon financial aid awards offset the income tax and penalty consequences. However, be very careful about using this approach as a college funding strategy because, as mentioned, the colleges are wise to this maneuver for financial aid purposes.

The result is that the cash invested in an annuity for college will probably be considered as being available to pay for college;

therefore, you accomplished nothing beneficial. As discussed, there are more intelligent ways to save for college than using an annuity. In fact, annuities do not usually merit being used as a savings vehicle for college, retirement, or any other purpose, and they should be avoided because of their high costs and the better investment alternatives that exist.

Life Insurance Policies

Life insurance policies that accumulate *cash value* inside of them (whole life, universal life, and variable life insurance) are commonly known as "permanent" insurance policies as opposed to "term" insurance policies that are in force for only a specified number of years. Here again, as with annuities, insurance salespeople are motivated by the higher commissions earned by selling permanent policies as compared to the much smaller commission amounts derived from less costly term insurance policies, which have lower premiums for the same size death benefit.

For college planning purposes, the claim for cash value life insurance is that the cash built up inside the policy accumulates in a tax-sheltered environment, is available for use without penalties whenever you want it, and will not be factored into the financial aid formulas. As with annuities, cash value life insurance policies have questionable merit for use as a college savings vehicle.

Instead of using permanent life insurance to save for college, it is better to institute a less costly term insurance program whereby you can increase the amount of cash flow available to go toward college savings because of the lower premiums while also providing an even larger death benefit for family survivors. When combining a need for life insurance with a need to save for college, buy term insurance and invest the money from the lower insurance premiums (the difference) in a combination of the previously discussed intelligent ways to save for college.

U.S. Government Series EE Savings Bond

U.S. Government Series EE savings bonds earn interest that is tax free if the bond is used to pay for qualified education expenses and if your modified adjusted gross income (MAGI) is less than $124,700 for married filing joint income tax payers or less than $78,100 for all other tax payers (inflation adjusted annually). However, the interest earned on EE Bonds does not keep up with the increasing college costs. Let's put some actual numbers to this statement. The inflation rate for college costs averages about eight percent per year. This means that a college today costing $18,000 a year to attend will double in nine years to cost $36,000. Meanwhile, $18,000 invested for nine years in Series EE savings bonds earning an average interest rate of four percent per year would grow to only $25,620, leaving a shortfall of $10,380 for paying the $36,000 college cost. Obviously, this is not the best way to save for college.

Bank Certificates of Deposit and Savings Accounts

Bank CDs and savings accounts earn similar low rates of returns as the above described U.S. Government Series EE savings bonds, plus they have the added disadvantage of the interest earned being taxable, regardless of your income level. Low-interest-paying bank accounts should be utilized only for funding short-term cash needs of less than one year and not for a longer-term college savings program that requires more growth.

Alternative Ways to Make College Affordable If You Have Not Saved Enough

Attending college is expensive. Saving enough to cover the entire cost is a challenge, even for high-income families. However, there are alternative ways to help make college more affordable that enable you to avoid borrowing excessively or affecting your retirement objectives.

Attend a community college or a state university

A student can attend a community college or a state university for the first two years and then transfer to a preferred choice or more expensive college to complete the four-year undergraduate degree. This alternative can reduce college costs and still enable the student to receive a degree from a preferred school. However, there are downside risks. If the student does not attain high grades in transferable course credits while attending the community college or state school, the course credits may be lost with the transfer. This would cause additional expense to obtain the undergraduate degree and offset intended cost savings. Furthermore, schools often do not offer their best financial aid packages to transfer students. Keep these risks in mind when using this strategy.

Attend a college that offers a cooperative education program

Approximately nine hundred colleges and universities offer cooperative programs whereby the student while attending college alternates periods of full-time classroom study with periods of full-time employment. The cooperative employers are college approved and offer intermittent periods of full-time employment in job fields that the student is interested in pursuing upon graduation. The student usually makes enough money to pay for a good portion of the college costs and often has a preferred opportunity for employment with the cooperative employer upon graduation.

The downside to the cooperative education approach is that the full-time employment periods typically extend the graduation time to five or more years. Cooperative education programs should not be confused with the government-sponsored work-study financial aid programs that provide students with part-time jobs on campus or in the local community.

Have the military pay for college

There are two military options you can consider. The first option is the Reserve Officer Training Corps (ROTC), which has branches at many colleges. To qualify for a ROTC scholarship, the student must apply in the senior year of high school and should also have a satisfactory grade point average as well as above-average test scores on the SAT and ACT exams. ROTC scholarships usually cover full or partial college tuition and provide a monthly spending allowance in exchange for required military service after graduation.

The second option for having the military pay for a college education is by attending one of the service academies. However, gaining acceptance is extremely competitive. To apply, the student must have excellent grades and high test scores on the SAT and ACT exams. The student must pass the physical requirements and have a recommendation from a congressman or senator. If all of this is accomplished, the student can receive a free college education in exchange for required military service upon graduation.

Attend Advanced-Placement (AP) or College Level Examination Program (CLEP)

Students can obtain a four-year undergraduate degree in less time by participating in the Advanced-Placement (AP) and the College Level Examination Program (CLEP). The AP program enables the student to earn college credits by taking advanced courses in high school that are acceptable toward degrees at most colleges and universities. AP courses also allow the student to explore more in depth a universe of knowledge covering nineteen subject areas that might otherwise remain untaught in the high school curriculum. This helps the student to gain an edge in college preparation, stand out in the college admissions process, and broaden intellectual horizons.

The CLEP provides students of any age or grade level an opportunity to show college-level achievement by taking exams in undergraduate college courses. The student can satisfy a proficiency requirement by demonstrating a mastering of the content of required degree courses such as basic math or a foreign language. Passing CLEP exams can jump-start obtaining required college credits and is also beneficial for dual-degree candidates or students just a few credits shy of college graduation requirements. There are 2,900 colleges that grant credit for advanced standing by passing CLEP exams.

Information about both the AP and CLEP programs can be obtained from the high school guidance department and the Web sites *www.collegeboard.com* or *www.quietmillionaire.com*. In conjunction with these programs, another way to further reduce college time and cost is for the student to take extra course loads during each semester and, if necessary, attend summer sessions offered by the college.

Purchase a rental property located where the student attends college for income and tax benefits

The student has to live somewhere, so purchasing rental property near the college provides the student a residence and rental income from other students and derives tax benefits for owning rental property. If the rental property appreciates in value, it can be subsequently sold at a profit, which can then be used to help pay for the cost of college.

Hire the student if you own a business

As an employer, you can pay your student up to $4,700 income per year without incurring income taxes and can deduct it as a business expense. In addition, you can contribute up to $4,000 a year to a Roth IRA in the student's name.

Take advantage of education tax credits and deductions

Education Tax Credits

There are two forms of tax-reducing education tax credits available to help offset the costs of higher education, the Hope Credit and the Lifetime Learning Credit. Be aware that both credits cannot be taken simultaneously for the same student in the same tax year, so there may be times when you have to determine which credit is more advantageous to use in any given tax year. Furthermore, both of these tax credits are entirely phased out if your modified adjusted gross income (MAGI) exceeds $105,000 for married taxpayers or $52,000 for individual taxpayers. In addition, if any free scholarship money is received, then this will also stop any eligibility for taking either of the credits. Keep in mind that the various education tax breaks are loaded with interactive restrictions and knowing how to use them optimally is confusing.

The **Hope Credit** allows eligible taxpayers to claim a maximum annual credit of $1,500 per eligible student for qualified college expenses paid during the student's first two years of college. The credit equals one hundred percent of the first $1,100 of expenses, plus fifty percent of the second $1,100.

The **Lifetime Learning Credit** allows taxpayers to claim an annual tax credit equal to twenty percent of the first $10,000 in total qualified college expenses for all eligible students in the family. Unlike the Hope Credit, you can use this tax break beyond the first two years of college, but you are limited to only one $2,000 Lifetime Learning Credit per tax year regardless of the number of students attending college.

Education Tax Deductions

Interest paid on education loans, up to a maximum of $2,500 per year, is tax deductible, provided your modified adjusted gross income (MAGI) is less than $135,000 for married filing joint tax-payers or less than $65,000 for all other taxpayers.

Consider college distance learning

College distance learning is becoming more prevalent. With college populations rising, it is becoming impossible to place all college-inspired students physically on campus. Distance learning, where the student and teacher are connected by Internet technology rather than the classroom, is becoming a very viable alternative. According to research from the International Data Corporation (IDC), the number of students enrolled in distance learning courses totals 2.2 million, representing fifteen percent of all higher education students. Internet distance learning is less costly for both the student and the educational institution, and now eighty-five percent of all two-year colleges and eighty-four percent of all four-year colleges are offering distance-leaning courses. This enables more students, especially many part-time working students, to obtain a college education and not to be burdened with a lot of debt to repay after getting their college degree.

How to Get Financial Aid

Now that you have learned about the ways to save for college and make it more affordable, it is now time to proceed to the next step, getting financial aid from the colleges. Knowing about realistic financial aid planning strategies can help you narrow the funding *gap* between what you have accumulated for college and what needs to be paid out of pocket in order to make college more affordable. For high-income families in particular, this is challenging but doable if the financial aid planning process is started early and approached intelligently.

The increasing number of students attending college is causing many colleges and universities to expand their faculty and facilities, which is straining the operating budgets and financial resources of the schools. To make matters worse, the federal and state governments have also reduced their subsidies for higher education. In addition, the type of financial aid being provided today is more in the form of loans that have to be repaid rather than grants and scholarships that do not have to be repaid. This combination of circumstances means that there is less money available today for an increased number of students seeking financial assistance, while simultaneously the costs to attend college are rapidly soaring.

Focus on comprehensive college planning strategies and do not waste time and energy searching for private scholarships

Private scholarships account for only one percent of all financial aid money, and they come mainly from local companies, organizations, associations, and employers of family members. Inquire with the high school guidance counselor about which local scholarships might be available and apply to those first. Be aware that private scholarships are often taxable and can jeopardize the financial aid awards provided directly from the school.

The other ninety-nine percent of financial aid comes from the federal government, your resident state, and the schools to which the student applies. Most scholarships provided for high-income families are derived from the colleges directly. Therefore, if you are serious about receiving financial assistance, it makes more sense to spend your time and energy going after the ninety-nine percent rather than the long-shot one percent.

It is also important that you determine each school's policy regarding the receipt of outside scholarships. Some schools will consider the receipt of any outside scholarship money as a replacement for the scholarship money that they were going to award. Alternatively, other schools may instead allow outside scholarships to replace the financial aid loan money instead of their scholarship money.

Select colleges that use financial aid to attract students who do not need it

The determination for need-based financial aid awards is primarily based upon family income levels, and this means that most high-income families are deemed to make too much money. However, because of the increased need and demand for larger amounts of financial aid, some colleges prefer to allocate their financial aid resources to attract students from high-income families who require less financial aid. The result is that students from high-income families who can afford to pay more for college sometimes have an edge in receiving financial aid over equally qualified students who have more of a financial need. While this may not seem fair, keep in mind that operating a college is, in essence, like operating a business, which is meant to be profitable—if it is not profitable, it will go out of business.

In fact, there is a new profession that has erupted on the college campuses called the enrollment manager, whose job it is to enroll the most desirable students for the least amount of cost to the college. The more richly endowed *private* colleges use the term "professional judgment" to offer money to students they want to attract, which means that it is possible for many high-income families to receive financial aid awards that enable the student to attend a higher-priced college for an out-of-pocket amount comparable to that of attending the less financially endowed public universities. Moreover, the colleges will compete for a student they want to attract by offering non-need-based financial aid. However, for this to happen, an informed college planning and selection process must be implemented.

Know where the student profiles academically relative to other school applicants

In order to improve financial aid opportunities, you should pick schools where your student profiles as being in the top twenty percent of all the incoming freshmen with respect to grade point average (GPA) and SAT/ACT scores. You can usually obtain this information from the school's admissions information and Web site. Although schools offer financial aid based upon need, they definitely give preferential treatment (i.e., more free money, fewer loans) to students who profile in the top twenty percent of the incoming class. This is done to attract the academically better students to their school. Be sure to use this to your advantage and include those schools in your search where your student profiles high academically relative to other like applicants.

Apply to a sufficient number of schools to include those considered good potential providers of financial assistance and those motivated to use it to attract your student

All colleges are not financially equal and generous. Higher-priced private colleges typically have more money to attract students than do the lower-priced state-supported schools. You should research the historical financial aid track record of the colleges to which your student is applying. The College Board (*www.collegeboard.com*) publishes a College Cost and Financial Aid Handbook, which itemizes the costs to attend each college as well as its financial aid history, typical financial aid packages awarded, average percentage of need met, average student debt, etc., for more than 3,000 two- and four-year colleges. However, be aware that this data is generalized. If the student profiles high academically and the school wants the student to attend, more money can become available even from schools that supposedly have poor financial aid track records. Therefore, you must select and apply to a diversified array and adequate number of schools in order to shake the award money loose.

Every school to which the student applies is shown on the financial aid FAFSA application submitted to the processing center. As a result, all of the schools know whether they have to compete financially to attract the student. The student should apply to six to twelve schools that meet criteria for academic major, geographic location, size, etc., and should include as many as possible of those schools having a good financial aid history. This should be done even if the student has a predetermination to attend a particular school in order to generate competing financial aid awards. Furthermore, very often the student's top choice will change during the selection process.

Be prepared to have resistance from the high school guidance departments about processing applications to more than just several colleges. This is because they have a limited amount of time to devote to this activity, and they do not always understand the beneficial outcomes for the student. You may have to be assertive to obtain their cooperation. In the end, it is not the guidance department but the student who has to be happy with the school selected, and it is the parents who have to manage the financial commitment for college.

Apply for financial aid even if you think that you will not qualify

The variables that influence financial awards are numerous, and high-income families should always plan on applying for financial aid. Let's look at an example of a how a college might award financial aid to a high-income family that is determined by a school to have no financial need.

$20,000 (cost of attendance)
−$50,000 (expected family contribution)
$ 0 (financial need)

Does this mean that the high-income family will not receive any financial aid and might as well not even apply for it? Definitely not! You should apply because each college can award discretionary "professional judgment" money that goes beyond the formula's financial need results. The professional judgment decision may be based upon a multitude of criteria such as the student's ethnic and cultural profile, athletic ability, grades, or geographic background. Some combination of the criteria is what motivates the school to attract the student to attend by offering financial aid regardless of need. However, **financial aid forms must be submitted in order for the colleges to make offers of non-need-based money designed to attract the student.** Many high-income parents do not fill out the financial forms because they assume that it will be a waste of time. This can be a costly mistake.

Understand early how your financial information is evaluated by the colleges

High-income families can also benefit by understanding early how their financial information is evaluated. The way that assets are titled and which family members earn how much income can make a significant difference in the EFC calculation and can influence the amount of financial aid offered on a professional judgment basis. Specifically, investments titled in the student's name and income earned by the student are weighted much more heavily than if in the parents' name.

Assets

After allowing for an exclusion of a certain amount of assets, the parent assets are assessed at a low graduated rate between 2.6 and 5.6 percent, while the student's assets are assessed at a much higher fixed rate of thirty-five percent, with no asset exclusion allowance. Assets owned and titled in the name of a business count less heavily in financial calculations than do those titled as personal assets. Furthermore, certain assets are not included at all in the financial aid formulas. For example, the FAFSA does not ask questions involving the value of the personal residence, retirement plans, annuities, and cash values inside life insurance policies.

Be aware that tax reduction planning may often conflict with financial aid planning. Many tax advisors do not understand the conflicting interaction of the tax laws with the financial aid rules. For example, you may be advised to title investments in your child's name using a uniform minor's account to reduce parent tax liability. While this advice may help reduce taxes, it can seriously reduce potential financial aid awards in an amount greater than the dollar amounts saved on taxes. Furthermore, the tax laws prohibit the child's money in a minor's account from being taken back by parents or anyone else who gifted the money. You should seek the advice of a tax advisor before any money is withdrawn from a minor's account in order to improve financial aid eligibility.

Earned Income

Parents are allowed to exclude a greater portion of their earned income from the financial aid calculations than the student can. Furthermore, the parents' income is assessed at a lower graduated rate ranging from twenty-two to forty-seven percent vs. the student's income being assessed at a higher fixed rate of fifty percent. Always be aware of how the various financial and tax planning transactions affect levels of income, and know that good income tax planning may harm financial aid opportunities.

For example, with the increasing graduated assessments being applied to parent income, converting from a traditional IRA to a Roth IRA during the student's base year for the EFC calculation should be avoided. This is because the amount of the converted traditional IRA is shown on the tax return as additional taxable income occurring during the year. While this might be a smart tax and retirement planning maneuver, it will often require explanation to the college financial aid office and could reduce financial aid awards.

Investment Income

As is with earned income, investment income is assessed at the different rates as shown above for parents and students. Furthermore, income occurring from gains on the sale of profitable investments during the initial base year for financial aid calculations can adversely impact awards. It is better to wait until either before or after the base year to liquidate profitable taxable investments having gains. This is because the financial aid formulas penalize income more heavily than investment assets being held.

Financial Position

Even if you do not qualify for need-based financial aid, you should position your finances in a manner that allows professional judgment to be used. For example, the college financial aid office may be better able to justify using professional judgment if investment assets are titled and deemed for meeting parent needs rather than for use by the student. However, make certain that all positioning of assets and income for financial aid purposes is carefully implemented in a manner that is both legal and ethical.

Fill out financial aid applications correctly and do not miss college submission deadlines

The starting point for processing financial aid requests to the colleges is your completion of the **FAFSA** form, which is used to submit your family and financial information through a central processing center operated by the federal government's Department of Education. The FAFSA application has a section for you to list all of the schools where you want the central processing center to forward your processed information. In addition to completing the FAFSA, some private schools will require you to also fill out a **Financial Aid Profile (FAP)**, also known as a **PRO-FILE** form, as well as their own financial aid forms requesting specific financial information they may want to see.

The FAFSA is not available for completion until January 1 of each year. However, it must be processed promptly in January in order for the processing center to get your information to each of the schools in time to meet their financial aid application deadlines. Each school has a specified deadline for submitting financial aid requests. You must be prepared in advance to complete and submit all the required forms within very short allowable time frames in order to be considered for financial aid.

Generally, the colleges that have the most financial aid money typically also have the earliest submission deadlines. When completing the FAFSA, the school that has the earliest financial aid deadline dictates the timing for completing the FAFSA processing. Even though current income tax information is requested on the forms, waiting until the tax return is completed may cause you to miss a substantial number of early deadlines. Accordingly, the required tax information must be assembled and submitted on the financial aid forms before the return is prepared. Then, when the final tax return is completed, it is sent to the colleges that request to see it for verification of the data you previously submitted on the financial aid forms.

Mistakes made in completing these forms can cause processing delays and missed deadlines. One of the major reasons critical financial aid deadlines are missed is because more than ninety percent of the FAFSA forms are sent back by the processing center because of seemingly harmless errors and inconsistencies in the answers. Minor mistakes such as correcting application errors with Wite-Out and omitting Social Security numbers can cause costly delays in the processing of your information.

Other costly mistakes occur in deciding what assets to include and what values to use on the financial aid applications. For example, when valuing your real estate property, are you properly valuing your residence and any other real estate such as rental property? While the FAFSA form does not request information about the primary residence, most of the other financial aid forms do inquire about how much equity value is in your home.

Often, home values are overstated on the financial aid forms because families are not familiar with an alternative form of market valuation using an approved "housing index multiplier" formula. The housing inflation index calculates your home's market value based upon the original purchase price and the date of purchase. You might be better off using the "multiplier" value on the financial aid forms instead of providing an estimated value based upon real estate comparables. Of course, if special particulars to your house warrant stating a lower market value, that valuation should be used as long as it can be substantiated.

Follow up after submitting the completed college financial aid forms

If the FAFSA form is submitted properly during the first go-round, you should receive within approximately four weeks a multipage document from the federal processing center titled the **Student Aid Report (SAR)**, which is a computerized printout of all of the personal and financial information answered on the FAFSA form. The SAR shows your calculated **expected family contribution (EFC)** number, which is the amount that you are expected to pay toward the student's college education. However, the EFC amount shown on the SAR is *not* the number that many private colleges use in their calculations for making financial aid awards. Private schools instead often use the "institutional methodology" rather than the "federal methodology" to calculate your EFC, which typically results in a higher EFC number.

The SAR printout information should be reviewed, and you should make corrections to any wrong information that you submitted on the FAFSA. In addition, if you used *estimated* income and tax information when originally submitting the FAFSA, the actual final tax return numbers can be submitted on the SAR. You should return the corrected SAR to the processing center and should also contact the financial aid office at each of the schools that received your original FAFSA information to find out how they want you to submit the corrected SAR information to them.

Within two to four weeks after you submit the corrected SAR to the processing center, you should receive an updated SAR reflecting all of your changes. Review the SAR again to make sure the information is correct, and also contact the schools to confirm that they have all of the information required for them to send you a financial aid award letter. Some schools will require you to send them a completed copy of your tax return before they will offer you a financial aid package. Therefore, it is recommended that you prepare your income tax returns as early as possible.

Furthermore, some financial aid forms are randomly selected for "verification," which is the equivalent of being selected for an audit by the IRS. If you are selected for verification, you will be asked to supply a copy of your tax returns and additional documentation confirming the income and assets you listed on the financial aid forms. Do not be concerned if you are selected for verification; it is a commonplace activity for determining financial aid awards.

By adhering to the above, everything should proceed satisfactorily, and you can expect to receive financial aid award letters during March and April of the student's senior year in high school. May 1 is the usual final date that the student must decide whether to accept the financial aid award and attend the college.

Determine the school's financial aid policy about providing assistance during the entire four years

While no school will ever provide a four-year financial aid guarantee, the initial award at most schools usually establishes what can be expected unless the family's financial circumstances change significantly. However, some schools award students a higher amount of financial aid for the first year in order to attract them to attend. Then, in years two, three, and four, they offer a much lower package. The school figures the student will be reluctant to transfer after having attended the school for the first year.

It could also become a serious problem if family financial circumstances change after the first year and the school will not adjust a student's financial aid package. You should ask the school about its policy for making adjustments if financial adversity should occur for the family or when other younger family members subsequently attend college simultaneously. Knowing what to expect up front can avoid difficulty later.

Sometimes it makes sense *not* to apply for financial aid during the first year if proper planning for improving financial aid eligibility has not been done. However, this could backfire because many schools have a policy of giving priority financial aid consideration to incoming freshman and to students who are already receiving financial aid. If this is the case, you may be excluded or may receive an insignificant amount relative to what might have been awarded with intelligent advance planning.

Do not reject federal work-study awards

The federal work-study program is a form of financial aid that provides part-time jobs for students to help pay for their educational expenses. A set amount of federal funds is made available by the government to the school for disbursement at its discretion to pay for student work. Some schools do not like to see rejection of their work-study offer, and this can influence their decision about offering other forms of financial aid.

The jobs can be on campus working for the school or off campus working for the community with a private nonprofit organization or public agency. However, some schools may have federal work-study arrangements with private for-profit employers, but the jobs must be judged as relevant to the student's course of study. The earned income is not taxable and is not included in the financial aid calculations as earned income by the student.

For parents concerned about the work-study program affecting their student's academic achievement, studies reveal that students actually do better academically because they develop more efficient time management and study habits. Furthermore, when assigning work hours, the financial aid administrator and employer consider class schedule and academic progress, and there is a limit as to how much time can be committed because the amount earned cannot exceed the total federal work-study dollar amount awarded.

Do not apply for an "early decision" acceptance and thereby lose your leverage for appealing financial aid awards

By applying for an early-decision acceptance from a college, the student must sign a binding agreement to attend if accepted. Not only does it commit the student to enroll at the college if accepted, but the student must also agree not to apply anywhere else and to withdraw all other applications if accepted. Because the school knows that there are no other colleges in competition for the student, it can allocate its financial aid money to attract other students that remain uncommitted. Therefore, it can be a very costly decision to apply for an early-decision acceptance from a college and lose leverage to appeal for the most possible financial assistance.

Be prepared to appeal financial aid awards

If a school that your student is interested in attending has not offered a competitive financial aid package, be prepared to appeal misawards and underawards from the colleges. Most parents assume that the initial amount of financial aid awarded by a school is final. However, if a school has financial aid resources and really desires the student to attend, it will offer tuition discounts and other forms of financial assistance to attract the student. However, the school will probably not be motivated to compete beyond its initial award unless you can show more generous award letters from other academically competitive schools. This is why it is important to research and apply to a number of schools that are likely to offer your student financial aid.

An informed selection process can also help you determine whether a particular school has offered a misaward or underaward and whether an appeal for increasing the school's initial financial aid award is warranted. The appeal process must be approached intelligently and in a nonthreatening manner. If you have selected colleges with financial resources and a desire to compete for the student, there is often an opportunity to increase the amount of money provided.

Use special family circumstances to increase financial aid awards

There are special circumstances when a family situation does not fit into the "norm." This includes divorced or separated parents; parents owning a business or farm; parents being unemployed, disabled, or deceased; minority students; gifted students and athletes; students qualifying as "independent" students without parent financial support; or families burdened with excessive medical expenses. Many families, in one way or another, do not fit into the statistical norm, and they should be aware of how this affects their opportunities for financial aid. The following are explanations of the special family circumstances that can affect the amount of financial assistance received.

Divorced or separated parents

If the student's parents are divorced or separated (or will be soon), there are a few key things they should know before completing financial aid applications. Only the financial information for the custodial parent with whom the student lives for the majority of the year should be provided on the financial aid forms. This can be done even if the custodial parent does not claim the student as a dependent on his or her income tax return. Custody, rather than financial support, determines financial aid eligibility.

For planning purposes, it might be beneficial having the student reside the majority of the time with the parent who has a less favorable financial situation according to financial aid calculations. Private colleges may request information about the income and assets of the "other" divorced parent. While this can impact the amount of the school's own funds awarded, it will not reduce the amount of federal financial aid awarded. If the parent with whom the child resides remarries, information about the income and the assets of the new spouse must be included as if he or she were the biological parent. This may not seem fair, but it is the way the financial aid system works.

Putting a financial commitment to fund college for children in a divorce decree can prove harmful to financial aid awards. While this financial assurance cannot always be avoided because of mistrust between ex-spouses, any legal commitment to pay for college is part of the questioning on the financial aid forms. Obviously, this can negate the perceived need for financial aid by a custodial parent to whom the college funding commitment is made.

Parents owning a business or farm

When determining financial aid awards, business assets and farm assets are given less weighting than personal assets. Therefore, it may be beneficial to retitle certain personal assets such as taxable retirement accumulation investment accounts and investment rental properties into a business entity such as a corporation or limited liability company (LLC). Furthermore, as a business owner or farmer, you have an ability to control the amount of your income shown during the years that your student is in college. This income flexibility can increase your financial need amount.

Family loss of income because of unemployment, disability, or death

If the family's breadwinner becomes unemployed, receives notice about potential unemployment, or if as a business owner experiences adversity, you should inform the college financial aid office about the change in financial circumstance. The same applies when a parent becomes disabled or dies. If the school has financial resources and is motivated for the student to attend, extra help may be provided during the period of financial hardship. Expected income, rather than the levels of earnings, will be used to calculate the EFC and the amount of the financial need.

Academically gifted students

High-achieving students academically are always a preference for colleges, and many private schools try to attract top students by offering academic scholarships and grants. Qualifying for a National Merit Scholarship can serve as an announcement to the colleges for the academically gifted student and can provide financial scholarship support that does not decrease the amount of other financial aid awards.

Athletes

Athletic scholarships are tough to come by and should not be relied upon. In most instances, athletic scholarships do not pay for the entire cost of college and should be sought after only as a supplement to other forms of financial aid. That being said, the student does not have to be at top Division I sports caliber to be awarded a scholarship. Division II or III schools will also offer preferential financial packages. Make certain to contact the athletic department and meet with the appropriate coach at each college you visit. Also, have the student's high school coach write letters of recommendation to each college. Keep in mind, however, that there is life after sports for the student, and the academic quality of the school should not be ignored.

Minorities

If your child is African American, Hispanic, Native American, or any other deemed minority, contact the colleges and find out about the availability of scholarship programs for minorities. Although there is controversy over awarding discriminatory types of scholarships, there are some colleges that offer them, and these types of scholarships should be taken advantage of if the student qualifies.

Independent students

An independent student is awarded financial aid based upon his or her financial situation as opposed to that of the parents. Before thinking you will make your child appear to be independent, here are the six criteria you must be able to overcome:

1. Is the student going to be twenty-four years of age or older before December 31 of the first year of college?
2. Is the student a veteran of the armed forces?
3. Is the student an orphan or ward of the court?

4. Does the student have legal dependents?

5. Is the student a graduate or professional student?

6. Is the student married?

If the student's situation does not fit into any of the above circumstances, then he or she cannot be considered independent. The schools will look to the parents' financial data even if the student is entirely out on his or her own financially.

Excessive medical and disability expenses

Some families are burdened with high medical bills that take a disproportionate amount of earned income. The financial aid office may take medical hardship into consideration in determining how much money to award, and the circumstances should be brought to the office's attention.

> QUIET MILLIONAIRE® WISDOM
> *Financial aid decreases the amount of college out-of-pocket costs and thereby increases the amount of money available for funding other financial goals.*

Do not underestimate the financial impact of college upon your ability to adequately meet other financial needs and objectives in life. You must be diligent about your college planning in order to reduce your financial commitment and make college more affordable. Most high-income families do not receive financial assistance without including financial aid planning as part of their comprehensive college planning process. Every family situation presents different financial aid generating opportunities, and you need to plan accordingly. The discussion thus far has been about the best ways to save for college and alternatives to make college more affordable if you have not saved enough, as well as how to get financial aid. However, it is likely that you still have a *gap* to fund, which is the amount of money you owe the college beyond what you have saved and received in financial aid.

How to Fund the "Gap"

When all of your college planning activities, accumulated savings, and financial aid awards in the form of "free money" grants and scholarships are still not enough to pay for college, you have what is termed a funding "gap." Paying out of current cash flow to fund the gap may be an option for some high-income families but often does not make financial sense when low-interest-rate student loans can be used as an alternative.

Most families end up having to borrow money to finance college today. Borrowing the wrong way can add thousands of dollars of interest costs to the financial burden of paying for college. Intelligent choices must be made about the best ways to borrow and who does the borrowing, the student or the parents.

Loans in the student's name usually have more favorable interest rates and repayment terms. The student can borrow from both the government and "alternative" private loan sources to finance the funding gap of a college education. Federal- and state-sponsored student loans are the least costly way to borrow for college, but

© Reprinted with special permission of King Features Syndicate.

they often are not sufficient to cover the entire funding gap and need to be supplemented with borrowings from private lenders. The following is an overview of all of the government and private loan options available to students and parents.

Student Loans for College Funding

Federal Loans to Students

The federal government lends students two types of college loans (Perkins and Stafford) that have low interest rates and do not require credit history or collateral.

Perkins Loan

The money for Perkins loans is funded by the federal government but disbursed at the discretion of the colleges to undergraduate and graduate students having *exceptional* financial need, and therefore most families are not eligible. The interest rate is fixed at five percent, and the government subsidizes (pays) the interest costs until nine months after the student graduates, when the loan repayment period begins for as long as ten years.

> **QUIET MILLIONAIRE® WISDOM**
> *The most intelligent borrowing strategy for college funding is to borrow in the student's name and for the parents, if able and warranted, to help repay the student loans.*

The Perkins loan amount that the student can borrow is determined by the school's financial aid office. For undergraduate students, the amount can be up to $4,000 per year with a cumulative maximum of $20,000; for graduate students, the amount can be up to $6,000 per year with a cumulative limit of $40,000 for the combined undergraduate and graduate Perkins loans.

Stafford Loan

There are two forms of Stafford loans: subsidized or unsubsidized (by the federal government). The **subsidized** Stafford loan is approved for students determined (by federal formula) to have a financial need, and therefore the federal government subsidizes (pays) the accruing interest costs for the student while attending school. The **unsubsidized** Stafford loan is approved for students determined *not* to have a financial need, and therefore the federal government does *not* subsidize (pay) the accruing interest costs while the student is attending school. However, the student can defer paying the accruing interest costs until the loan repayment period begins after graduation by letting the accruing interest be added into the unsubsidized loan amount.

The Stafford loan interest rate is fixed at 6.8 percent while the student is attending school as well as during the repayment period after graduation. After graduation, all of the individual Stafford loans (subsidized and unsubsidized) can be consolidated into one loan with repayment options from ten years up to as long as thirty years. Stafford loans are worth considering even if you do not need to borrow for college because during the time that the Stafford loans are outstanding you may be able to leverage a higher investment rate of return than the lower tax deductible 6.8 percent interest rate charged.

Unfortunately, the allowable borrowing amounts for Stafford loans are small. Undergraduate students can borrow a combination of subsidized and unsubsidized federal Stafford loans as follows: freshman year $2,625, sophomore year $3,500, junior year $5,500, senior year $5,500, with a cumulative limit of $23,000. There are very limited circumstances when the undergraduate student can borrow additional amounts each year, with the cumulative limit being increased to $46,000.

Graduate students can borrow $18,500 per year, with a cumulative limit of $65,500, which is a combined limit for both the undergraduate and graduate Stafford loans. There are very limited circumstances when the graduate student can borrow additional amounts each year, with the combined cumulative limit being increased to $138,500.

Eligibility for Stafford loans is made automatically by completing the FAFSA form, which is used to apply for all forms of financial aid. Depending upon determined need subsidization, the full allowable Stafford loan amount can be divided between subsidized and unsubsidized portions. Even though the unsubsidized Stafford loan is available to all students regardless of financial need, you must still submit the FASFA form in order to be eligible for any Stafford loan money. Furthermore, if additional private student loans are needed, it is required that the Stafford loan be obtained first in order to receive supplemental private student loans.

Stafford loans can be obtained either directly from the federal government or through an approved lender. The financial aid office of the college that the student is attending will direct you as to where and how to process the paperwork for the Stafford loan.

Upon graduation, the student has the option to use the Federal Consolidation Loan program to consolidate all accumulated Stafford loans into one low-interest-rate loan with a variety of extended repayment schedules available, which makes repayment more manageable. Keep in mind that the Federal Consolidation Loan program consolidates only Stafford loans and does not include any supplemental private-lender student loans.

State Loans to Students

In addition to providing free money grants and scholarships on a limited basis, many states offer low-interest-rate student loan programs, primarily to finance and retain in-state resident students who plan to pursue certain careers such as social work, medicine, law enforcement, and teaching. Part of the borrowing and financial aid seeking process should include contacting your state's higher education agency to determine what special financial assistance programs may be offered to in-state resident students. However, keep in mind that most of the financial assistance offered by the states is done mainly by supporting state universities and colleges directly in order to provide lower tuition costs for the in-state resident students.

Private Loans to Students

Private-lender student loans, also termed alternative student loans, are uncollateralized loans that typically have higher interest costs than student loans offered by the federal and state government. However, the interest rates and repayment schedules are usually more attractive when compared to the loan options that parents have available for borrowing. Applying for these loans is easy. The Internet offers numerous Web site sources of private student loans, which can be applied for online. However, it is very important to compare private student loan lenders for the lowest interest rates and loan fees available.

Remember that private student loans are not available without first having submitted the FAFSA form to obtain the federal Stafford student loan. The private loans combined with the Stafford loans can be used to finance one hundred percent of an undergraduate and graduate college education. Private student loans accrue interest, which can be added into the loan (capitalized) while the student is attending college. Repayment of the private loans is deferred until after the student graduates, at which time the accumulated private loans can be consolidated into a single loan for one monthly payment amount. The private loan consolidation process is entirely separate from the Federal Consolidation Loan program.

Parent Loans for College Funding

Federal Loans to Parents

Parent Loan for Undergraduate Students (PLUS)

Parents can borrow up to one hundred percent of the cost to attend college from the federal government with the Parent Loan for Undergraduate Students (PLUS) program. PLUS loan interest starts to accrue immediately and cannot be added back (capital-ized) into the loan amount. The interest rate is fixed at 8.5 percent and up to $2,500 of the interest costs is tax deductible annually even if you do not itemize.

Repayment of borrowings usually begins sixty days after each dis-bursement of funds is made to the school. However, some PLUS lenders may permit loan repayment to be deferred until after the student graduates. The repayment term can be up to ten years, but this is not recommended because parents should be striving to have the PLUS loans repaid in full before their retirement.

PLUS loans are the financial responsibility of the parents, not the student. Unlike loans to the student, the parents must be credit-worthy. If parents are denied a PLUS loan for credit reasons, the student becomes eligible for higher Stafford loan limits.

PLUS loans show up on the parents' credit report and could cause interference with their other borrowing needs such as mort-gage and auto financing. Therefore, federal loans in the student's name with lower interest rates and more extended repayment terms are recommended instead of the parents borrowing to fund college. Parents still have the option to repay the college loans in the student's name if they are able and it makes financial sense.

Private Loans to Parents

College Funding Loan

Private loans approved specifically for parents to fund college (also known as alternative loans) are really not any different from other types of credit rating–based loans. These loans should not be used to finance college because they show on your credit report and interfere with your ability to borrow for other purposes such as financing a house or automobile purchase. As already dis-cussed, it is more desirable that all borrowing for college funding be done in the student's name. Furthermore, if the parents do borrow for college funding, the PLUS loans discussed above or the home equity line of credit, which is discussed next, are preferable alternatives, but neither is recommended to be done.

Home Equity Line of Credit

As discussed in Chapter Five about debt management, home equity lines of credit can be used to finance any funding need, including college. The interest costs for home equity loans up to $100,000 are tax deductible if you itemize deductions on Schedule A of Form 1040 and provided that the borrowing under the line is not used to pay for the same college expenses paid by another tax-deductible interest borrowing such as a student loan. In other words, there is no double tax deduction benefit for the same college expenses.

Furthermore, parents who do not have enough itemized tax-deductible expenses on their Schedule A to exceed their standard deduction amount cannot deduct the home equity line of credit interest costs. However, they can take a student loan interest deduction up to $2,500 a year for interest paid on college loans in their name *provided* that their modified adjusted gross income is less than $130,000 for married taxpayers who file jointly or less than $65,000 for individual taxpayers. This limitation usually makes high-income parents ineligible to take the student loan interest deduction and is another reason to borrow in the student's name instead of the parents'. Upon graduation, the student's earned-income level will most likely allow the maximum tax deduction of up to $2,500 annually for the student loan interest paid.

Retirement Plan Loan

If your group retirement plan at work permits (not IRAs), you can borrow for college up to fifty percent of your vested interest in the plan, up to a maximum of $50,000 by law. However, this could present a costly problem if you leave the company under any circumstance with loans outstanding. All borrowings from a retirement plan must be immediately repaid with funds outside the plan or else the loan is considered a distribution subject to all taxation and penalties that would normally apply for withdrawals. Retirement plans are intended to fund retirement, and every effort should be made to avoid using that money to pay for college expenses.

Where to Find Competent Advice and Guidance for Your College Planning

Determining how to intelligently plan for college, how to select the right colleges, and how to minimize your out-of-pocket costs for college is a complicated process. There is a lot to learn and understand about the "business" aspect of college, how colleges approach filling their student enrollment quotas, and how financial aid is given out.

Both the student and parents must be savvy about college planning. Parents also have to be knowledgeable about comprehensive financial planning and tax strategies to make college more affordable. If managing the college experience is done improperly, it usually causes the student to select the wrong school to attend and the parents to pay unnecessarily large amounts of money out of pocket to fund college at the expense of achieving other financial objectives.

Guidance Counselors

Guidance counselors can play an important role in helping the student structure an academic program to prepare for college. They can assist in identifying colleges of academic interest and coordinate the college application process to include high school transcripts and letters of recommendation.

Guidance counselors can also serve as an advocate for the student when the colleges want additional background information about the student and the high school's curriculum. Accordingly, it is very important that both the student and the parents establish an ongoing interaction with the guidance counselor in order for the counselor to be an informed and willing advocate.

Do not expect or rely upon high school guidance counselors to provide the comprehensive college planning that is required to make college more affordable. Although most guidance counselors are willing to assist in any way possible, the guidance departments are too busy with many other roles beyond college counseling. This limits the amount of proactive and personal assistance they can provide. Furthermore, they are not knowledgeable about all of the complex financial planning, tax planning, and financial aid planning strategies that require a coordinated comprehensive approach for achieving the best results.

The high school's financial aid nights provide too little information too late with respect to financial aid planning. The most that can be expected is merely a last-minute overview of completing the financial aid forms. Unfortunately, this limited instruction is not very effective because more than ninety percent of the financial aid forms submitted for processing are returned because of errors and omissions. As a result, financial aid deadlines for submitting applications are often missed.

There is much more to be done besides just filling out the requested information on the financial aid forms and waiting for your award letters from the colleges. This approach is very costly, and the high schools do not have the time or the training to help you with *all* of the necessary college funding and financial aid strategy needs.

College Financial Aid Officers

Do not rely upon the college financial aid officers at the colleges to help you apply for financial aid. Asking the financial aid officer to help you get more money from his or her school is like going to the IRS and asking it to help you save money on your taxes. It is not in the college's best interest to show you how to get the most money from the school. It has a limited amount of funds to give out to a large number of students who request financial aid.

Professional College Planners

Many families mistakenly believe that they can manage the college experience on their own. This is because they lack knowledge about the enormity of the college planning process, which requires comprehensive and coordinated activities being taken on by both the student and the parents. They also do not realize how costly mistakes made can be. Doing it yourself using free advice may be cheap, but paying for competent, good professional advice can be a wise investment.

You probably would not hesitate to pay a tax advisor for help to lower your tax liability or pay a lawyer to avoid losing money from a lawsuit. So, why would you not consider using a qualified college planning professional to help lower your out-of-pocket financial commitment for college—especially because the financial commitment to attend college can be as much as $18,000 to $45,000 a year? By starting the college planning process early and relying upon the *right* kind of guidance, the fee charged should more than pay for itself many times over.

What should you look for in a professional college planning advisor?

Unfortunately, college planning advisors are an unregulated group, and some are loaded with defrauding schemes to take your money in exchange for providing suspect results. These advisors have different forms, and one can be a commission-hungry insurance agent whose college planning agenda centers on selling you a cash value life insurance policy or an annuity as a way to exclude accumulated money from being calculated in the financial aid formulas. This agenda is lucrative for them and costly for you.

Another form of advisor comes in the form of financial aid and scholarship search companies that promise and guarantee to obtain money for families with college-bound students. These firms are typically not reputable and use official-sounding names in order to appear professional and legitimate. Just about all families with a college-bound student receive unsolicited enticing letters from them saying "Your student has been selected" or "We guarantee to get thousands of dollars in financial aid and scholarships." They typically require that an up-front fee be paid and offer a full money-back guarantee if the promised results are not produced. However, in the end, these supposedly reputable firms either vanish or do not deliver on anything, including their guarantee to return your money. ***Never pay anything to anyone making these kinds of offers.***

As discussed, a comprehensive financial planning approach is required for effective college planning. That is what you need to look for in a college planning advisor: one who is a ***fee-only*** advisor and not biased with advice that is motivated for pushing financial products to earn a commission. Also, be aware that the term "fee-based advisor" implies fee-only and can be misleading. Fee-based means that the advisor charges fees but is also licensed to sell financial products and receive commissions as well. At the end of Chapter Fifteen, you will be shown how to find a competent financial advisor who can guide you with a comprehensive approach to the college planning process.

Once you get through managing and paying for the college experience, it is all too short a time before the reality of retirement comes into focus. The next two chapters will cover how to afford retirement in a manner where you can feel financially independent and secure about not running out of money when you stop earning an income.

Quiet Millionaire® Summary

■ Use the 529 college savings plan, Coverdell education savings account, Roth IRA, and taxable investment account to intelligently save for college.

■ Avoid using the minor's account, annuity, cash value life insurance, U.S. Government EE bond, bank certificate of deposit, and savings account to save for college.

■ Consider the alternative ways to make college more affordable if you have not saved enough.

■ Apply to a sufficient number of schools.

■ Do not apply for early-decision acceptance for college.

■ Understand the financial aid system and how it applies to you, and then plan and apply for financial aid accordingly.

■ Use student loans, not parent loans, to fund your "gap" between the cost of attending college and what you have saved and received in free financial aid.

■ Know where to find and use a competent and comprehensive college planning professional if you are not fully prepared and willing to knowledgeably complete the process on you own.

■ Do not jeopardize funding your other lifetime objectives such as retirement by paying too much for college.

CHAPTER FOURTEEN

Retirement Part I:
How to Quit Working as a Quiet Millionaire® and *Not* Run out of Money

Did you know that prior to the twentieth century, retirement was only a wishful dream and not a reality? Most people worked until the day they died. Then, by the 1950s, the percentage of people working after age sixty-five dropped to fifty percent, and by the 1990s, that percentage was down to only sixteen percent of workers not retiring. However, times are changing again, and now an increasing number of people over age sixty-five are continuing to work. If the quiet millionaire® works beyond normal retirement age, it is by choice. For many others, it is to maintain their standard of living or just to survive financially.

The meaning of the word "retirement" is different for all of us. What does retirement mean to you? Being free to do what you want without working and without worrying about the money? Being financially independent and feeling secure enough about not outliving your money? Being able to do something that you really want by starting a new and exciting second career?

Maybe you will never retire per se. If so, hopefully it will be for the right reasons. Consider this story about Jody, who lived according to an accustomed upper-middle-income lifestyle most of her adult life.

> *Jody is a lovely woman, always smiling and conversational, who, with her blonde hair tied in a ponytail, looks younger than her sixty-six years. Frequently, I take time to chat with Jody as she sweeps litter from the sidewalk outside our office in the city. "I never thought I'd ever be doing something like this in my older years," she sighed to me one hot summer day. "I lived pretty well until my husband suddenly died ten years ago, one month after our youngest daughter graduated from college."*
>
> *Today, with very little savings, Jody lives on a $465 per month Social Security check and earns about $25,000 a year as building custodian. "Thank goodness my employer provides me with an apartment to live in. It's great, but I don't know what I am going to do when I can't work here anymore."*
>
> *I asked her, "How did you get in this situation? Why didn't you and your husband save more?" She replied, "I ask myself that all the time. We could have, but there was always something more to buy that we really didn't need. My husband and I planned to save for our retirement once our two daughters graduated from college, but then ...*
>
> *"My two married daughters don't like what I'm doing and want me to live with one of them and not worry about money. But, they have their own lives, and it's too hectic for me, and I prefer my own privacy. Most of all, I really don't want to have to depend upon them."*

Unfortunately, Jody's situation is becoming more and more common, and sadly her ill-fated outcome could have been avoided with some intelligent retirement planning. However, when it comes to planning for retirement as well as other financial objectives, people seem to make costly and unnecessary mistakes through ignorance and procrastination.

Failing to plan and start early to save enough for retirement are the main reasons that most people cannot afford to retire. They dream and wish and hope rather than set specific goals and seriously work a

> QUIET MILLIONAIRE® WISDOM
> *Most people do not plan to fail, but they do fail to plan; the quiet millionaire® always plans.*

plan to achieve them. The quiet millionaire® knows that the failure to plan and save for retirement can become an overwhelming mistake because it is usually impossible to play "catch up" during the accumulation stage for retirement and there is no turning back once the actual retirement decision has been made. Keep in mind that retirement can be made by choice as planned or by circumstance, which may not always be on your terms.

Unfortunately, many high-income earners are irresponsible, extravagant spenders who typically allocate only a relatively small portion of each paycheck for retirement savings. They foolishly believe that the cost of not planning and saving for retirement is small and that it will take only a little bit of extra effort in the future to make up for lost time. Not knowing what needs to be done (lack of knowledge) and putting off what needs to be done (procrastination) make up a deadly combination that steals potential wealth.

This chapter will review the reasons and the dynamic trends affecting the affordability of retirement. Knowing these trends will alert you about the mounting obstacles and pitfalls associated with retirement planning and why you must start intelligent planning earlier and more diligently than the previous

322 ■ The Quiet Millionaire

generations of workers. You will also be shown how to determine whether you will be able to quit working when you want to and not run out of money.

Dynamic Trends Affecting the Affordability of Retirement

Pension income retirement plans are being replaced by employee contribution retirement plans

Historically, the pension *benefit* retirement plan funded by the employer provided the employee a lifetime of *certain* retirement income. Today, it is being replaced with the employee *contribution* retirement plan being funded primarily by the employee, which provides the employee an *uncertain* amount of retirement income.

It used to be commonplace that people remained with the same employer for their entire working life and in return the employer funded a **pension income retirement plan**, which provided the employees with income for their entire retirement life. The amount of the retirement income benefit was defined based upon the employees' length of employment and income level, and accordingly the pension plan in technical terms is referred to as a *defined benefit plan.*

Today, the structure and funding of retirement plans have changed to an **employee contribution retirement plan** because employees typically make multiple job changes and because the pension funding requirements have become too costly for employers. Instead, it is now the employees who are primarily responsible for funding their own retirement income needs by contributing a defined amount of their earned income to a retirement plan such as a 401(k), 403(b), SEP-IRA, or SIMPLE-IRA plan, which in technical terms is referred to as a *defined contribution plan.*

To illustrate the magnitude of this shift in retirement accumulation responsibility from the employer to the employee, consider the following examples, which, for simplicity's purpose, have no tax consequences factored in:

■ In order to replicate a pension plan that produces a defined annual retirement income benefit of $50,000 a year in today's dollars and that during retirement increases each year for inflation at five percent a year (assume twenty-five years of retirement), you must accumulate $843,000 and earn an eight percent average rate of return on your investments.

■ In order to accumulate the above required $843,000 (assume a twenty-year accumulation period before retirement), you must save $17,057 each year and earn an average eight percent investment rate of return during the accumulation period.

Unfortunately, most workers do not sufficiently save toward their retirement. Furthermore, the employee contribution retirement savings plans typically offer limited and often underperforming investment options from which to select. Moreover, even when employees are offered worthwhile investment options, many plan participants make poor selections for achieving the required growth.

Worst of all, some retirement plans encourage or require that employee investments be concentrated in the employer's company stock. This lack of diversification can be very risky even if the company stock is of a large publicly traded company. Just ask the thousands of Enron employees whose financial lives and retirement dreams were suddenly ruined in 2001 when Enron's stock, which was positioned inside the employees' 401(k) plan, plunged in value from $81.40 per share in January 2001 to a mere 40 cents per share by December of that same year. In terms of total dollars, $1 million vanished to become a paltry $4,914!

*People are living longer during retirement
and therefore need to accumulate more
money than ever before to last a lifetime*

Today, a sixty-five-year-old male can expect to live another sixteen years on average, while a female at age sixty-five can expect
to live another nineteen and a half years. This means that there
will be an increasingly large widowed population, especially
when you consider that most wives are younger than their hus-
bands. Therefore, women are even more likely to experience the
consequences of inadequate savings for retirement. Most workers
are not making the maximum contributions allowable to their
retirement plans. Even if they are saving the maximum allowable
in their retirement savings plan, that amount alone will usually
be far from sufficient to meet many accustomed standards of
living. Supplemental saving for retirement must also be done
beyond just retirement plans and IRAs.

However, research shows that the savings rate for average American workers as a percentage of their income is near zero. In
other words, they spend what they make. Most pre-retirees and
retirees do not understand how fast increases in the cost of
living, income taxes, estate taxes, and a catastrophic illness can
wipe out even substantial retirement saving accumulations. You
need to account for these things in order to plan and save adequately so you can know for sure when you can quit work.

*Because of poorly structured investment
management programs, it will take a longer time
and require larger amounts of money to be
accumulated in order to fund a secure retirement*

For overly aggressive investors, greed often turns to grief when
stock market adjustments cause devastating losses. Alternatively,
for overly conservative investors, their money is often not
working hard enough to grow and keep pace with inflation. Con-

sider the following, which, for simplistic purposes, have no tax consequences factored in:

■ With a *ten percent* average rate of return, in order to accumulate $1,000,000 over a twenty-year period, you must save $15,872 each year during the accumulation period.

■ With a *four percent* average rate of return, in order to accumulate $1,000,000 over a twenty-year period, you must save $32,290 each year during the accumulation period.

In this example, the lower four percent rate of return requires you to save more than twice as much *each* year in order to accomplish the same $1,000,000 result as the higher ten percent rate of return. By intelligently structuring your investment portfolio in accordance with your risk tolerance comfort level, you can let your money work harder for you instead of you working harder for your money.

Social Security alone will no longer be a reliable source of adequate income for retirement security

Social Security started in 1935 and was greatly liberalized between 1950 and 1975. Since then, the demographics have changed so that today the ratio of retirees collecting Social Security checks is increasing relative to the number of current workers who are contributing to the system. This has made the financial future of Social Security uncertain and unsound unless restructuring and additional funding is implemented.

Social Security presently represents about forty percent of the retirement income that the average retiree lives on. However, Social Security is becoming the primary source of retirement income for the increasing number of baby boomers who are retiring. This is because the private pension income retirement plan is disappearing, and the amount of savings being set aside by workers for adequately funding their retirement income needs is insufficient. As a result, the present structure of Social Security system will be challenged by the increasing demographic and financial demands being made upon it.

There have been various proposals made for fixing the Social Security system. One proposal is to increase the eligibility ages for collecting benefits. This would result in a lesser funding liability because of a longer contributing period by workers and a shorter withdrawing period by recipients. Although it is only a partial solution, it is reasonable because people are living longer and staying healthier, and more of today's jobs do not require physical labor.

In addition, it is likely that Social Security benefits will become indexed according to the retiree's total income level and financial need, which would phase out benefits entirely for the more affluent retiree. In fact, the current taxation of Social Security income benefits has already been rendering the benefits received insignificant for many high-income retirees.

More recently, personal Social Security retirement accounts have been proposed for younger workers whereby a portion of their payroll taxes could be allocated by them for placement in growth investments in order to achieve a higher (and lower as well) expected return. However, this proposal places more risk on the worker for receiving income from Social Security during retirement. Poor investment choices made by the worker and/or generally poor investment performance could ultimately require the government to fund in the future a costly bail out of the Social Security system and the desperate plight of retirees requiring income to merely exist.

College funding costs for educating children will delay or destroy retirement plans for an increasing number of families

Many married couples are starting their families later in life and will be paying for college close to traditional retirement ages. Consider the situation of Dan and Mindy.

Dan, age thirty-five, and Mindy, age thirty-four, live the good life. They both earn substantial incomes and spend money without concern beyond today. They have a big house and a jumbo mortgage, a leased BMW, and a newly financed Toyota Sienna minivan. Their financial mentalities are to spend impulsively for instant gratification, and they are fully dependent upon both their incomes to live their desired lifestyle. "We work hard and deserve to do what we want. Tomorrow will work out." They have two children ages five and three; next month, they are expecting their third child. This has caused them to think about opening 529 college savings accounts.

Both Dan and Mindy contribute five percent of their pay to 401(k) plans, and they plan to seriously start saving for retirement when the kids are out of college. Dan and Mindy, who were not committed to saving before they started a family, had evolved into a lifestyle beyond their legitimate financial means. Now, saving for anything is a built-in impossibility. They will be in their late fifties when their last child graduates from college, and retirement will be only a few short years away. There is inadequate time to plan and prepare for their retirement in the way they thought they could.

Dan and Mindy are now realizing the cold, hard facts about the serious consequences of not starting to save earlier and regularly for college and retirement.

Trying to catch up and save enough for retirement in the shorter time frame after the college funding commitment ends will severely impact your ability to retire. Consider the following examples, which, for simplistic purposes, have no tax consequences factored in:

■ If you are now age thirty-five and want to accumulate $1,000,000 for retirement at age sixty-five, you must save

$5,527 each year and earn an average ten percent investment rate of return during the thirty-year accumulation period.

■ If you are now age fifty-five and want to accumulate $1,000,000 for retirement at age sixty-five, you must save $57,041 each year and earn an average ten percent investment rate of return during the ten-year accumulation period.

Americans typically do not save enough for funding future major milestones such as college and retirement, and trying to catch up because of a delayed start usually does not work. Each year of delaying savings dramatically impacts your ability to meet future needs. Taking advantage of long-term *compounding* investment returns is a compelling reason for starting early and intelligently structuring a disciplined investment program for retirement. The challenge many families face to save enough for retirement is made difficult because parents have to divert money to pay for educating their children and then try to make up for lost time when that commitment is done.

> QUIET MILLIONAIRE® WISDOM
> *The most important element of a successful wealth accumulation program is time: time to gain from the compounding effect of investment returns.*

If you have children to educate, how old will you be when your youngest child graduates from college? Will you have to rob your retirement savings to pay for college? Remember, your retirement plan savings alone is probably not enough to financially secure your retirement. It is going to take a lot of money to retire. Do you know how much? By following the cost-reducing college planning strategies discussed previously, you will be able to allocate more money for retirement that otherwise will have to be used for college funding.

Failing health, rather than choice, will become the primary reason for retiring

An increasing number of people are working to age sixty-five and beyond for various reasons such as to retain their group health insurance coverage until they are eligible for Medicare at age sixty-five, to survive financially, or just because they enjoy working, which many quiet millionaires® do. As a result, many people continue to work until they physically can no longer commit to maintaining employment. This uncertainty of how long you can physically remain in the workforce before failing health forces retirement can complicate the financial planning analysis and cloud what preparation is required for adequate funding.

Long-term-care expenses, out-of-pocket prescription costs, and other medical expenses are becoming a major financial factor for accelerated depletion of retirement savings

Long-term care can devastate retirement resources. Most people do not incorporate quantified "what if" medical expense scenarios into their retirement cash flow analysis. A fact of reality is that more women than men will suffer the consequences of not planning for high medical expenses during retirement. This is because wives are more frequently the surviving spouse, and furthermore the husband may have already seriously impacted the family's savings with a costly illness prior to death.

Retirees will have higher levels of debt than previous generations to repay out of their retirement cash flow

Credit cards did not exit for previous generations of retirees, and auto and consumer credit loans were not available to anyone without earned income. Furthermore, it was considered intelligent retirement planning to pay off a mortgage before retirement. However, during a low-interest-rate environment, this may not be the best strategy to implement. If the mortgage debt interest rate is low relative to the expected rate of return on investments, maintaining a mortgage during retirement could be an intelligent leveraging strategy for additional retirement capital. In addition, the mortgage interest deduction can offset the income tax liability incurred as money is being withdrawn from tax-deferred retirement plans.

Using low-interest-rate borrowed money that a mortgage can provide enables you to utilize the spread or differential in interest rates. This is what skilled lenders such as bankers do very profitably, and for pre-retirees and retirees, it is an opportunity to utilize the lender's money for a more profitable retirement. With a fixed low-interest-rate mortgage, the monthly repayment amount remains the same (**significantly, a mortgage payment does not increase with inflation**) while the interest cost steadily decreases each month. Meanwhile, the residence's market value continues to appreciate whether or not there is a low-interest mortgage loan outstanding.

The home equity money becomes available for investment instead of being dead or wasted retirement capital, which, outside the house, could be providing compounding investment growth in order to extend the length of time before retirement money might run out. Furthermore, if desired, the invested home equity money is available to reduce or pay off the mortgage balance at any time.

Caution: This intelligent mortgage leveraging approach should be done only with the careful guidance of a comprehensive financial advisor. As with all debt management, there are many planning considerations that need to be discussed and evaluated, and it is not recommended as an appropriate strategy for everyone.

Extracting cash from home equity with a reverse mortgage *and from a permanent cash value life insurance policy with a* viatical *or* life settlement *will become more prevalent as a source of supplemental retirement income*

Reverse Mortgage

Many retirees have a large amount of money that is tied up in their home equity that they could use to provide them with additional retirement income. However, using traditional mortgage financing to extract home equity for cash to pay for living expenses during retirement might be either not affordable or not available at all. Alternatively, if the house is sold to obtain cash, they still have to live somewhere. Therefore, another form of mortgage, termed a **reverse mortgage**, is becoming readily available for retirees. A reverse mortgage enables retirees to continue living in their home and access the equity value that is tied up in the house in order to use it for living expenses.

With a reverse mortgage, the roles of lender and borrower are *reversed* from that of a traditional mortgage; the lender pays you instead of you paying the lender during the life of the mortgage. You remain the owner of your home, and are responsible for paying property taxes, homeowner insurance, and maintenance expenses. The amount of money advanced depends upon the borrower's age and the value of the home equity. There are financing fees and ongoing interest costs, which are added to the loan balance and repaid when the loan is over. The loan is over when the last surviving borrower dies, sells the home, or permanently moves out of the home. The amount owed equals all the loan advances, plus all the interest that has been added to the loan balance. If the total amount owed is less than what the home is worth, then you (or your estate) keep whatever amount is left over. Furthermore, you can never owe more than what the house is worth at the time that the loan is repaid, and the reverse mortgage lender cannot seek repayment from your income, other assets, or your heirs.

In order to determine whether a reverse mortgage is appropriate for you, be sure to work with a reputable independent financial advisor to help you evaluate the merits and pitfalls and direct you to a trustworthy reverse mortgage provider. Additional information about reverse mortgages can be found at *www.reversemortgage.org* or *www.aarp.org*.

Viatical and Life Settlements

While reverse mortgages can be used to extract money from home equity for retirement income, it is now also possible for retirees to use viatical settlements and life settlements to extract a lump sum cash amount from their life insurance for use during their lifetime. **Viatical settlements** are offered to the terminally ill, while **life settlements** are offered to those people who are still healthy. In essence, both of these financial tools provide the retiree a discounted lump sum cash advance against their insurance policy's death benefit. In exchange for the cash advance, the future proceeds from the death benefit are assigned to the company or individual that makes the death benefit advance.

The amount of cash advanced is determined by the size of the death benefit available and how long you are expected to live, but typically the advance against the death benefit is severely discounted. For example, a $1,000,000 life insurance policy might provide a lump sum cash advance of only $300,000. Upon the insured's death, the cash advance provider, which has been assigned the life insurance policy's death benefit proceeds, receives the full death benefit amount regardless of whether the death happens in one month or thirty years. Whenever the death occurs, survivors receive none of the life insurance proceeds that would have otherwise been available.

In both instances, you have to watch out for scams and abuses when considering a viatical or life settlement, and they should be considered only as a last resort. In order to be certain whether either is appropriate for you, be sure to work with a reputable independent financial advisor who can help you evaluate the merits and pitfalls and direct you to a legitimate provider.

Multigenerational living patterns will become a more prevailing way of life, returning to the way it used to be before financially independent retirement living became feasible

Today, an estimated twenty-two percent of the American population is categorized as the "sandwich generation," meaning they are parenting their own children and taking care of their parents at the same time. Some estimates project that in the next ten years, nearly two-thirds of working families will be required to take care of an elderly parent. This can cause major stress on family finances, emotions, and relationships and can affect the sandwich generation's ability to plan and accumulate money for their own secure retirement.

Fortunately, research also shows that for the majority of families that establish multigenerational coresidency households, with good communication and cooperative family dynamics in place, several generations under one roof or nearby can provide positive outcomes. The benefits experienced include enhanced well-being and better care for grandchildren as well as for grandparents, more love and caring responsibility being exchanged through chores and activities, and the joy of family closeness, which has been lost in recent generations.

How to Save for a Worry-Free Retirement

The quiet millionaire® knows that any way you save for retirement is good; the main thing is to do it and start early. Many people work for employers that sponsor group retirement savings plan such as a 401(k), while other people have no group plan offered by their employer and instead have to save for retirement using an individual retirement savings vehicle such as an individual retirement account (IRA). Some people also save beyond their retirement plan by investing money in an individual taxable investment account. Most people will have to use some combination of group and individual retirement savings plans as well as individual taxable investment accounts in order to accumulate enough for having a secure retirement lifestyle. This section discusses all of the different options that are available to save for retirement, some of which are better than others.

Group Retirement Savings Plans

Group retirement savings plans are sponsored by employers and should be the starting point for a retirement accumulation program, especially if the employer makes some form of matching contribution to the employee's contribution. There are certain employer-sponsored group plans that are approved by the IRS as *qualified* for certain favorable tax benefits and savings incentives, while others are termed *nonqualified*, with less tax benefits and incentives for the employee to save for retirement.

As mentioned before, the structure of today's employer-sponsored group retirement plans has shifted the responsibility to have enough money for retirement from the employer (pension income plan) to the employee (retirement savings plan). If your employer sponsors and makes committed contributions to a pension income plan on your behalf, you are one of a decreasing fortunate few. Today, employers more typically make some form of matching contribution to a group retirement savings plan such as a 401(k) or 403(b), and/or the employer makes a discretionary contribution to a profit sharing plan if the company's profitability warrants it.

It is a "no-brainer" that as an employee you should contribute to a retirement savings plan whatever amount is necessary in order to receive your employer's matching contribution if there is one.

Not all employers make matching contributions, but if they do, it is a gift of money that you should always take advantage of.

Regular 401(k) and 403(b) retirement savings plans (pretax contributions, tax-deferred investment growth, taxable withdrawals)

In simple terms, the 401(k) plan is a group retirement savings plan sponsored by a private company employer, while the 403(b) plan is a retirement savings plan in the form of a tax-sheltered annuity (TSA) sponsored by a nonprofit organization employer. Employees are allowed to contribute money via payroll deduction on a pretax basis, which increases the amount you can save and reduces your taxable income. There is an annual dollar limit on the employee's contribution amount, which as of 2006 was $15,000 and is adjusted upward annually for inflation. In addition, some 401(k) and 403(b) plans permit a federally legislated "catch up" provision, which allows participants that are age fifty or older to contribute an additional amount, which as of 2006 was an additional $5,000, and this too is inflation adjusted annually.

Employers may choose to match up to as much as fifty percent of the employee's contribution, but most will offer a much smaller match or no match at all. As stated before, if the employer does match a portion of the employee's contributions, the employee should always contribute enough to receive the full match amount, unless he or she does not expect to be with the employer long enough (usually three to five years) to have a vested interest in the match amount.

The pretax contributions made to a 401(k) or 403(b) retirement savings plan are allowed to grow tax deferred until being used in retirement, at which time the withdrawals are fully taxed at ordinary income tax rates. Accordingly, the more you take out in order to keep up with the increasing living costs during retirement due to inflation, the higher the dollar amount of taxes you pay will be. This double-barreled threat of inflation and taxes is often misunderstood and not properly accounted for in many retirement analysis projections, causing eventual financial hardship for retirees. Therefore, any retirement cash flow analysis must include assumptions about inflation and taxes as shown subsequently in the retirement projection example at the end of this chapter.

Roth 401(k) and Roth 403(b) retirement savings plan (after-tax contributions, tax-free investment growth, tax-free withdrawals)

Beginning in 2006, the IRS permits employers at their discretion to offer 401(k) and 403(b) plan participants the option of designating their contributions as *after-tax* Roth contributions instead of *pretax* regular contributions. The Roth designated contributions, unlike the regular, will not be taxed when the money is withdrawn during retirement because the contributions were made on an after-tax basis. The quiet millionaire® realizes the value of this Roth feature being added to the 401(k) and 403(b) because unlike the Roth IRA, which has earned-income limitations for being eligible to contribute, there are no such earned-income limitations for contributing to the Roth 401(k) and 403(b). As a result, high-income earners can now also participate in the ability to invest money that will not be taxed during retirement or ever again.

The quiet millionaire® will consider this new 401(k) and 403(b) Roth option instead of the regular pretax option if he or she anticipates a higher income tax bracket during retirement either because of high dollar amounts of annual withdrawals or because the current relatively low income tax levels will increase in the future. The quiet millionaire® is willing to give up the pretax benefit on the "seed," or the smaller contribution amount, in order to gain the tax-free benefit of paying no taxes on the "harvest," the larger dollar amount coming out during retirement.

Consider the following comparison of a regular 401(k) contribution program versus a Roth 401(k) contribution program for Aaron, who is currently age fifty and is in a twenty percent income tax bracket. He plans to retire in fifteen years at the age of sixty-five, and he anticipates being in the thirty-five percent income tax bracket at that time.

	Regular 401(k) vs.	**Roth 401(k)**
Annual Deferral	$20,000 pretax	$16,000 after-tax
Total Annual Contributions	300,000 pretax	240,000 after-tax
	($20,000 x 15 years)	($16,000 x 15 years)
Account Balance (15 Years)	700,000	560,000
(Average Return 10%)		
Tax Liability	- 245,000 (@35% tax rate)	0 tax-free
Net After-Tax	$455,000	$560,000

Because Aaron has planned intelligently by contributing to the Roth 401(k), he therefore has $105,000 more money ($455,000 for the regular 401(k) vs. $560,000 for the Roth 401(k)) either to spend during retirement or to transfer to heirs, completely free of any income taxation.

Furthermore, at Aaron's age 70½, the money in the regular 401(k) must start to be withdrawn and taxed annually during his lifetime according to the IRS required minimum distribution schedule (even if Aaron does not need the money), while the money in the Roth 401(k) can remain untaxed indefinitely. From an investment and tax planning standpoint, the quiet millionaire® believes that you cannot do better than to invest money that grows in value to be used whenever *you* decide and never to be taxed again.

However, Aaron's financial situation gets even better if he were to instead contribute each year to the Roth 401(k) the full allowable $20,000 a year on an after-tax basis for fifteen years (instead of the $16,000 a year on an after-tax basis shown on the prior page comparison).

	Regular 401(k) vs.	**Roth 401(k)**
Annual Deferral	$20,000 pretax	$20,000 after-tax
Total Annual Contributions	300,000 pretax	300,000 after-tax
	($20,000 x 15 years)	($20,000 x 15 years)
Account Balance (15 Years)	700,000	700,000
(Average Return 10%)		
Tax Liability	- 245,000 (@ 35% tax rate)	0 tax free
Net After-Tax	$455,000	$700,000

Now, at age sixty-five, Aaron has an additional $245,000 ($455,000 for the regular 401(k) versus $700,000 for the Roth 401(k)), which he can grow, spend, or transfer to heirs completely tax free and never be taxed again.

Simplified Employee Pension Plan (SEP-IRA) (pretax contributions, tax-deferred investment growth, taxable withdrawals)

A SEP-IRA retirement plan is a form of a profit sharing plan that is especially appealing for small business employers because the use of readily available IRS-approved prototype plan documents is permitted. Therefore, setting up the plan is easy, and the administrative costs are kept low because of reduced paperwork and minimal ongoing reporting requirements to the IRS.

The employer's annual profit sharing contribution depends upon the company's profitability and affordability. Therefore, each year the employer can use its discretion whether to make a profit sharing contribution directly to the individual employee's SEP-IRA retirement account, the amount of which can vary each year or be discontinued at any time.

The contribution made for each employee is made on a per-centage of annual pretax income basis, and the percentage rate must be the same for all plan participants. For example, if the percentage of pretax income contribution rate is determined to be ten percent in a given year, the employee who earns $100,000 receives a $10,000 contribution, while the $25,000 employee receives $2,500. In another year, the determined rate could be reduced to five percent, whereby the contribution amounts would be $5,000 and $1,250, respectively.

Some SEP-IRA plans also allow the employee to contribute annually in addition to the employer's profit sharing contribution. However, by law, there is a maximum allowable contribution amount that can be made for each plan participant. The combined annual contribution by both the employer and employee can be no more than twenty-five percent of the employee's pretax income, with a maximum allowable dollar limit of $42,000 per year (adjusted annually for inflation).

Because each employee has his or her own separate tax-deferred retirement account, he or she can choose among the plan's available investment options in accordance with individual tolerance for risk. The investments grow tax free, and all accumulated amounts can be rolled over for continued tax deferral to a regular IRA if the employee leaves the company for any reason. Any withdrawals are subject to the same restrictions and taxation as regular IRAs, and borrowing against the account is not permitted.

SIMPLE-IRA Plan (pretax contributions, tax-deferred investment growth, taxable withdrawals)

The SIMPLE-IRA is similar to the SEP-IRA in that it is simple to set up and administer. However, its sponsorship by employers is limited to companies with fewer than one hundred employees. The contributions to a SIMPLE-IRA plan are made primarily by the employee, who may contribute one hundred percent of his or her annual pretax income up to a maximum of $10,000 per year, and as of 2006, an additional $2,500 annual "catch-up" provision became available for participants who are age fifty or over.

For all eligible employees who voluntarily elect to participate in the SIMPLE-IRA plan, the employer must match the employees' contribution dollar for dollar up to three percent of their compensation. The matched percentage can be lowered to one percent for any two out of every five years. No match is required for the employees who do not participate. As an alternative to the three percent match, the employer can instead elect to contribute two percent of all eligible employees' salaries, whether they want to be in the plan or not.

The contribution limits for a SIMPLE-IRA plan are significantly less than those of a qualified 401(k), 403(b), or SEP-IRA. Effectively, the most that a very highly compensated employee (including owners) can contribute annually is $16,000 maximum, $10,000 from salary reduction (without the $2,500 catch up) and $6,000 from the company's match, assuming that the match is three percent and the salary is $200,000 or more per year.

Therefore, the SIMPLE-IRA plan is not a sufficient way to save enough money for retirement, and the company cannot offer any other type of retirement plan as long as the SIMPLE-IRA is being contributed to as an active plan. Plan participant accounts are always one hundred percent vested immediately, which includes the salary reduction amount and the employer's matching contribution. The employee can choose from the plan's available investment options as he or she sees fit. Loans are not permitted, and there is a two-year waiting period before the money can be rolled over tax free into a regular IRA. Then, if you meet certain earned-income limitations for eligibility, you can subsequently do a taxable conversion from the regular IRA to a Roth IRA.

Individual Retirement Savings Plans

Employer-sponsored group retirement plans are not always available for individuals to save money toward their retirement. Furthermore, if a group retirement plan is available, the contribution amounts allowed are limited by law and are not adequate to fund a financially secure retirement. Therefore, accumulating enough money for retirement often requires using *individual* retirement plans, which can be done on both a tax-deferred or taxable account basis.

Regular or traditional individual retirement account (IRA) (pretax or after-tax contributions, tax-deferred investment growth, taxable withdrawals)

A regular IRA allows contributions that are tax deductible, and the investment earnings can grow on a tax-deferred basis until retirement, at which time the withdrawals are subject to federal income tax. Annual contributions allowed for the regular IRA are limited to a maximum of $4,000 or one hundred percent of your annual earned income, whichever is less. A total of $8,000 can be contributed per married couple, provided at least that amount of income has been earned by one or both of the spouses. Furthermore, each person age fifty or older may make a "catch-up" contribution of an additional $1,000. However, even if you contribute each year the maximum allowable pretax contribution amount to a regular IRA during your entire working career, the financial accumulations will not be sufficient to fund a comfortable retirement lifestyle. Other supplemental savings must be done.

If neither spouse participates in an employer-sponsored group retirement plan, the contributions are fully tax deductible regardless of the amount of adjusted gross income, and the withdrawals made during retirement are taxable as ordinary income. However, if one or both of the spouses participate in an employer-sponsored group retirement plan, be aware that there are various adjusted gross income levels for the different tax filing statuses that determine how much of the contribution is tax deductible.

Generally, high-income earners who participate in employer-sponsored group retirement plans are not permitted to make tax-deductible contributions to a regular IRA. Specifically, this restriction applies to a married couple earning $160,000 or more annually, and if they file separate tax returns, the earnings limitation reduces to a mere $10,000. For single tax payers, the earnings restriction is $110,000. There may be circumstances when although you are restricted from making pretax contributions to a regular IRA, you are allowed to make after-tax contributions. This causes a different taxation result to occur when you make withdrawals from the regular IRA during retirement.

With after-tax contributions, when withdrawals are made, only the investment gains are taxed, as opposed to with pretax contributions, both the contribution amounts and investment gains are taxed on withdrawals. However, making after-tax contributions to a regular IRA is not recommended because it is better to instead make an after-tax contribution to a Roth IRA, which results in no taxation when you make withdrawals.

Withdrawals from a regular IRA without penalty can start at age 59½ and are subject to ordinary income taxation. Withdrawals made before the age of 59½ will be subject to an additional ten percent early-withdrawal penalty fee except where certain allowable exceptions apply. Withdrawals are required to begin no later than April 1 of the year following the year in which you reach age 70½. The rules for regular IRA withdrawals are complex and loaded with pitfalls, and it is recommended that you seek the advice of a qualified professional in order to avoid a costly mistake.

Roth IRA (after-tax contributions, tax-free investment growth, tax-free withdrawals)

The Roth IRA, named after the late Senator William Roth, has a powerful tax advantage over the regular IRA when withdrawals are made during retirement. Although the investments inside both types of IRAs can grow without taxation, withdrawals made from a Roth IRA are **not** subject to taxation, while withdrawals made from a regular IRA are taxed as ordinary income. Unfortunately, the quiet millionaire® typically cannot contribute to the Roth IRA because it has the same earned income limitations as the regular IRA ($160,000 married filing joint, $10,000 married filing separate, $110,000 single filing).

The maximum amount of annual contribution allowed for the Roth IRA is the same as for the regular IRA ($4,000 per person, $8,000 per married couple filing joint), and for persons age fifty or older, an extra $1,000 a year "catch-up" contribution is allowed. The contribution limit applies to the total combined contributions that are made to both types of IRAs. However, the contribution limit is not reduced by contributions that are made to other forms of retirement plans.

Individual annuity (pretax or after-tax contributions, tax-deferred investment growth, taxable withdrawals)

Individual annuities are offered by insurance companies and by some banks, and for federal tax purposes, individual annuities are classified as either qualified or nonqualified. The investments inside both can grow on a tax-deferred basis, but an individual *qualified* annuity is subject to the same regulations and restrictions as the regular IRA and therefore qualifies for pretax contributions. Accordingly, when the annuity owner makes withdrawals, both the contribution amount and the investment gains are taxed as ordinary income and are subject to a pre-age $59\frac{1}{2}$ ten percent early-withdrawal penalty as well.

An individual *nonqualified* annuity does not qualify for pretax contributions, and therefore the contributions are made with after-tax dollars and are not tax deductible for federal income tax purposes. Accordingly, when the annuity owner makes withdrawals, only the investment gains, not the contribution amounts, are taxed as ordinary income, and the ten percent early-withdrawal penalty is applied only to the investment gains. Unlike the qualified annuity, the nonqualified annuity does not have limits for eligibility with respect to earned income or contribution amounts.

The downside for using annuities of any kind for investing is that annuities typically have high internal costs, which reduces your investment returns and offsets the proclaimed tax-deferral benefits. Furthermore, withdrawals from annuities are taxed as ordinary income and have heavy penalties and surrender charges if you make early withdrawals. Annuities are popular with financial salespeople because they pay out large commissions, which drive up the costs you incur. For these reasons, although there may be special circumstances that are appropriate for buying an individual annuity, most times they do not merit being used as a savings vehicle for retirement or any other purpose. In particular, IRA annuities should be avoided because of their high internal administrative and mortality costs, which can be eliminated by using the nonannuity regular IRA instead.

Taxable investment account (after-tax contributions, taxable investment growth, taxable withdrawals)

In some instances, making pretax contributions and deferring taxes when saving for retirement may not be as beneficial as saving in a taxable account. This is because the present fifteen percent tax rate for capital gains is low relative to higher ordinary income tax rates, which can be twice as much. Therefore, withdrawals from retirement plans, which are taxed at ordinary income tax rates, could be double the amount of taxes paid on a taxable investment account, which can be managed to pay the lower capital gains tax rate.

Certainly, you should always contribute an amount to a retirement savings plan that takes the maximum advantage of any employer's match. Never forego that gift money. However, because a taxable growth investment portfolio can be structured in a tax-efficient manner, it should be part of an intelligent savings program. In Chapter Six, the discussion about taxes explained how harvesting investment tax losses can offset investment capital gains, which can effectively lower the fifteen percent capital gains tax rate. In addition, an ongoing, proactive, tax-efficient investment program that emphasizes capital appreciation more so than dividend and interest income keeps taxes low.

Furthermore, not only can money invested in a taxable retirement account be structured for lower tax consequences when making retirement withdrawals, but also the money is more readily available without IRS penalties in the event of taking an early retirement prior to the age of $59\frac{1}{2}$. In order to avoid a ten percent IRS-imposed penalty for pre-$59\frac{1}{2}$ retirement withdrawals from a retirement plan, a customized IRS-approved periodic distributions program has to be established. Otherwise, the added ten percent penalty on top of the ordinary tax can cause a nearly fifty percent hit on every retirement dollar withdrawn. This big difference between fifty percent and fifteen percent is another compelling argument for balancing your retirement savings program between tax-deferred and taxable accounts.

Last, money situated within a tax-deferred retirement plan may have a required concentration in your employer's company stock. This lack of investment diversification presents an unjustifiable amount of higher risk. However, it can also provide you with a tax reduction opportunity upon your retirement by using the IRS net unrealized appreciation (NUA) rule for retirement plan assets consisting of highly appreciated employer company stock. It may be more beneficial to withdraw the company stock from the plan and pay lower capital gains taxes on the increased value instead of rolling over the company stock portion of the plan to an IRA for subsequent higher taxation at the ordinary income tax rates.

In summary, there are a number of informed choices you have to make in order to save and preserve money for a worry-free retirement. Furthermore, there are very costly and unforgiving mistakes that can be made because of all of the IRS rules and regulations that you must address correctly. The quiet millionaire® knows this and therefore wisely works with a qualified financial advisor to provide a guided safe path.

Cardinal Rules for Tax-Deferred vs. Taxable Savings Plans for Retirement

Here are several cardinal rules for deciding whether to contribute to a tax-deferred retirement plan or to save in a taxable investment account for retirement.

Rule One

Never contribute *after*-tax dollars to an employer-sponsored group tax-deferred retirement plan, regular IRA, or insurance company sponsored annuity.

Rule Two

If eligible, always contribute the maximum allowable amounts to a Roth IRA. This money will never be taxed when withdrawals are made if you abide by the rules.

Rule Three

If you are in a lower tax bracket during the retirement accumulation period than you will be during the retirement withdrawal period, then evaluate saving in a taxable account vs. a tax-deferred retirement account. This increasing tax bracket circumstance can occur if an increasingly affluent lifestyle is occurring and will not decrease during retirement.

Most pre-retirees have no idea when they can actually retire, and they do not know how much they need to live on and not run out of money. Without specifically quantifying their retirement objectives, pre-retirees often have no idea what amount is required for funding a wishful retirement and living the life they want.

> QUIET MILLIONAIRE® WISDOM
> *Know specifically how much money is required for you to live a secure retirement according to your accustomed standard of living and not run out of money.*

The double-barreled negative effect of inflation and taxes during retirement is often underestimated

The following story about Grandma Jo illustrates the devastating effects of inflation and taxes:

Grandma Jo did not want to take any risk with her money. Like many retired seniors, she thought that banks were the safest place for her money with their FDIC "guaranteed" protection. So, she bought five $100,000 CDs at five different banks, which paid an average rate of four percent interest.

In addition to the interest earned on her CDs, Grandma Jo also had retirement income from Social Security, two pensions, and an IRA, which combined put her in a twenty-five percent tax bracket. This meant that the effective after-tax rate on her bank CDs was actually three percent. Accordingly, with her living expenses going up five percent every year because of inflation, Grandma Jo's CDs are losing money because of a yearly negative two percent loss in purchasing power as follows:

4%	$500,000 annual CD interest	**$20,000**
−1%	Annual taxes (25% tax bracket)	**− 5,000**
3%	Net after-tax annual interest	**15,000**
−5%	Annual inflation	**−25,000**
−2%	Annual loss	**−$10,000**

This means that after twenty years, Grandma Jo's $500,000 in CDs has lost $200,000 in purchasing power ($10,000 x 20 years), and her $500,000 becomes worth only $300,000 in purchasing power without her having spent a cent. In effect, the low-interest-rate CDs have effectively built in a -40% (-$200,000) guaranteed total loss of principal, which is a sure way for Grandma Jo to run out of money during her retirement.

QUIET MILLIONAIRE® WISDOM
Annual increases in the costs of living and taxes present a higher risk for retirement security than is often anticipated by pre-retirees.

The Department of Labor's published inflation rates are a myth compared to reality. The Consumer Price Index (CPI) indicates that the inflation rate has averaged about 2.25 percent for the past twenty years and is currently in the two percent range. Calculating the actual inflation increases for basics such as food, housing, energy, automobiles, gasoline, and health care reveals that the CPI is a dangerous and financially damaging statistic to use for the retirement planning process.

For example, a fully loaded new Jeep Cherokee in 2005 cost approximately $38,000, while in 1985 a fully loaded new Jeep Cherokee cost $15,000. If you use the CPI inflation figure of 2.25 percent for the past twenty years, the Jeep should cost only $23,500 in 2005, which is off by $14,500. In reality, the true inflationary rate increase is 4.8 percent.

Let's look at gasoline prices. Remember in 1985 when gasoline cost as low as 70 cents a gallon? You did not even have to get out of your car to pump it, and you had the added benefit of having your oil checked and the windows washed by a friendly attendant, all for that low price. In 2005, at various times, gasoline cost more than $3 a gallon, *and* you have to get out of your car and do everything yourself. The CPI says you should have paid only $1.09 a gallon in 2005. At that price, who would mind having to do self-serve?

Most dramatically, nursing home costs have skyrocketed. In 1985, the monthly cost for nursing home care was approximately $1,000 per month. If you believe in the government's CPI, it should cost only about $1,600 per month in 2005. However, in 2005, a high-quality facility actually costs $6,000 per month. At this *actual* 9.5 percent rate of increase, a nursing home stay will cost nearly $15,000 per month in only ten years from now!

But why would the government misrepresent the true rate of inflation? One very big reason is that the annual cost of living increases for federal employee pensioners and for Social Security benefits are based on the CPI. If the government was honest about inflation, the annual increases for these government-funded retirement programs would have more than doubled.

Most financial advisors typically use three to four percent as the average annual rate of inflation in their retirement planning assumptions. On the basis of the true inflation rate, those assumptions are too low. It is more realistic to use a five percent inflation factor in preparing retirement cash flow projections and thereby leave room for any margin of error with that higher presumed inflation rate. Better to err on the side of caution and have an excess of cash than to come up short at the end. And, if the retirement cash flow analysis works successfully on paper, you know that it is more likely to succeed in actuality.

Now think about this: If the cost of living keeps going up during retirement and you expect to maintain your accustomed standard of living, how does this affect the amount of taxes you pay during each year of retirement? Remember that all pretax contributed money inside of a tax-deferred retirement plan has never been taxed. So, *all* the money that you withdraw will be subject to ordinary income taxes. Accordingly, as the cost of living goes up each year, it follows that you will have to withdraw more money in order to keep up, and this will create a *higher* tax liability each year, which is contrary to most people's common belief.

Consider the following story about Phil and Mary, who are both age fifty:

> *Phil has been a sales manager for the past eleven years at a Fortune 500 consumer products company, and he earns <u>before</u> taxes $200,000 a year. He and Mary want to retire in ten years at age sixty, when both children will be finished with college. They want to live comfortably during retirement on* **$100,000 a year <u>in today's dollars after taxes,</u> for which the dollar equivalent at their age sixty is $162,888 per year.**

> *Currently, Phil has $500,000 saved in his 401(k) plan and contributes five percent ($10,000) annually in order to receive his employer's maximum fifty percent matching contribution of $5,000. And, his intention is to continue doing this until his planned retirement at age sixty.*

> *Phil and Mary believed that their retirement objective and the amount of money being saved toward it seemed pretty reasonable. In order to be certain, the below <u>preliminary</u> retirement cash flow analysis was prepared, presuming a five percent inflation rate, a ten percent average rate of investment return, and a twenty percent tax rate.*

> *The projection showed that with contributions and growth over the next ten years, Phil's 401(k) plan would be valued at $1,382,664. Phil and Mary thought that this was enough money to retire at age sixty along with their*

projected Social Security benefit of $37,301 per year starting at age sixty-two.

Let's see whether Phil and Mary are on track to hit their goal of retiring at age sixty.

Phil and Mary's *Preliminary* Retirement Cash Flow Analysis Detail

Age	Social Security	Portfolio Earnings	Total Income	Living Expenses	Taxes Paid	Total Expenses	Net Cash Flow	Portfolio Balance
59								$1,382,664
60	0	118,720	118,720	162,888	32,578	195,466	(76,746)	1,305,918
61	0	110,068	110,068	171,032	34,206	205,238	(95,170)	1,210,748
62	37,301	103,106	140,407	179,584	37,409	216,993	(76,586)	1,134,162
63	38,047	94,441	132,488	188,563	39,234	227,797	(95,309)	1,038,853
64	38,808	83,852	122,660	197,991	41,151	239,142	(116,482)	922,372
65	39,584	71,090	110,674	207,891	43,162	251,053	(140,379)	781,993
66	40,376	55,881	96,257	218,286	45,272	263,558	(167,301)	614,692
67	41,184	37,919	79,103	229,200	47,488	276,688	(197,585)	417,107
68	42,007	16,864	58,871	240,660	49,812	290,472	(231,601)	185,506
69	42,847	0	42,847	252,693	45,670	298,363	(255,516)	0

In reviewing the above *preliminary* analysis, at age sixty Phil and Mary will need to start living on $162,888 a year after taxes just to maintain the purchasing power of $100,000 after taxes in today's dollars. Furthermore, they will have to withdraw additional money from the 401(k) each year beyond their living expenses in order to pay taxes, which initially start at $32,578 for the first year.

Notice that their cash flow is immediately negative beginning the first year at -$76,746, and it increases each year thereafter as they have to keep up with funding increasing living expenses and resulting higher taxes. The higher tax bill each year occurs because the money that was contributed to Paul's 401(k) plan has never been taxed. As more money is required to be taken out of the 401(k) to live on, the amount of taxes that has to be paid each year also increases.

QUIET MILLIONAIRE® WISDOM
Just because you earn a high income and do not spend more money than you make does not mean that you do not have a cash flow problem.

This double-barreled blast of inflation and taxes is destructive to retirement cash flows. In Phil and Mary's case, you can see how devastating this plan is as they run out of money entirely at age sixty-nine, merely nine years into retirement. Needless to say, they had to rethink their hopes for quitting work at age sixty.

However, by making several planning adjustments in Phil and Mary's retirement objectives, an *adjusted* retirement cash flow was prepared for them to consider. The following adjustments were made in their retirement objectives:

■ Social Security start age increased to age sixty-five from sixty-two.

■ Retirement age increased to age sixty-five from sixty.

■ Retirement spending lowered to $75,000 after taxes in today's dollars from $100,000.

■ Total 401(k) contributions per year increased to $23,000 from $15,000. This increased amount is permitted because of an IRS allowed "catch-up" provision.

Now let's look at the results of the *adjusted* retirement cash flow analysis for Phil and Mary.

Notice how by delaying their retirement age until sixty-five instead of age sixty that their retirement portfolio increased from $1,382,664 (at the *beginning* of age sixty) to $2,542,172 (at the *beginning* of age sixty-five), which represents an eighty-four percent increase of $1,159,508. As a result, their net cash flow does not turn negative until they reach age eighty-three, which enables their investment portfolio to continue to grow until then. Now, they will not run out of money until they reach age ninety-five instead of age sixty-nine.

Phil and Mary's *Adjusted* Retirement Cash Flow Analysis Detail

Age	Social Security	Portfolio Earnings	Total Income	Living Expenses	Taxes Paid	Total Expenses	Net Cash Flow	Portfolio Balance
64								$2,542,172
65	39,584	254,217	293,801	155,918	32,767	188,685	105,116	2,647,288
66	40,376	264,729	305,105	163,714	34,358	198,072	107,033	2,754,321
67	41,184	275,432	316,616	171,900	36,028	207,928	108,688	2,863,009
68	42,007	286,301	328,308	180,495	37,779	218,274	110,034	2,973,043
69	42,847	297,304	340,151	189,520	39,617	229,137	111,014	3,084,058
70	43,704	308,406	352,110	198,996	47,206	246,202	105,908	3,189,966
71	44,578	318,997	363,575	208,946	49,678	258,624	104,951	3,294,917
72	45,470	329,492	374,962	219,393	52,287	271,680	103,282	3,398,199
73	46,379	339,820	386,199	230,363	55,008	285,371	100,828	3,499,028
74	47,307	349,903	397,210	241,881	57,875	299,756	97,454	3,596,482
75	48,253	359,648	407,901	253,975	60,899	314,874	93,027	3,689,509
76	49,218	368,951	418,169	266,674	64,089	330,763	87,406	3,776,915
77	50,203	377,692	427,895	280,008	67,452	347,460	80,435	3,857,350
78	51,207	385,735	436,942	294,008	71,001	365,009	71,933	3,929,282
79	52,231	392,928	445,159	308,708	74,670	383,378	61,781	3,991,063
80	53,275	399,106	452,381	324,143	78,527	402,670	49,711	4,040,774
81	54,341	404,077	458,418	340,350	82,581	422,931	35,487	4,076,261
82	55,428	407,626	463,054	357,368	86,840	444,208	18,846	4,095,107
83	56,536	409,511	466,047	375,236	91,309	466,545	(498)	4,094,609
84	57,667	409,461	467,128	393,998	95,861	489,859	(22,731)	4,071,878
85	58,820	361,640	420,460	413,698	100,605	514,303	(93,843)	3,978,035
86	59,997	349,830	409,827	434,383	105,348	539,731	(129,904)	3,848,131
87	61,197	334,318	395,515	456,102	110,043	566,145	(170,630)	3,677,500
88	62,421	314,602	377,023	478,907	114,994	593,901	(216,878)	3,460,622
89	63,669	290,164	353,833	502,852	119,795	622,647	(268,814)	3,191,808
90	64,942	260,419	325,361	527,995	124,564	652,559	(327,198)	2,864,610
91	66,241	224,744	290,985	554,395	129,013	683,408	(392,423)	2,472,188
92	67,566	182,439	250,005	582,115	133,252	715,367	(465,362)	2,006,826
93	68,917	132,736	201,653	611,221	137,163	748,384	(546,731)	1,460,095
94	70,296	74,802	145,098	641,782	140,588	782,370	(637,272)	822,823
95	71,702	7,734	79,436	673,871	143,316	817,187	(737,751)	85,071

These retirement cash flow exercises illustrate what every pre-retiree should do. It helped Phil and Mary realize that they needed to seriously address the inflation and tax challenges affecting their retirement and plan accordingly so they would not run out of money. Of course, no one can accurately project with one hundred percent certainty what will happen in the future. Fortunately, today's computer technology enables experienced retirement planners, using appropriate assumptions and intelligent data input, to improve the predictability for achieving desired retirement objectives. If retirement is doomed for failure, it is better to find out on paper and plan for success rather than live with flawed expectations and run out of money.

However, be aware that data put into a computer can produce false expectations, and this is a risk you cannot afford. Be realistic, honest, and accurate with your numbers. Furthermore, be cautious about relying upon the results produced from using do-it-yourself computer retirement programs because they are too simplistic and therefore are not accurate enough for such an important decision that cannot be reversed once the retirement commitment is made.

For a reliable confirmation of your retirement cash flow analysis, you might want to seek professional guidance from a competent advisor. However, be diligent about who you select because selecting the wrong advisor can also put your retirement security at risk. You will probably be best served by working with an independent, comprehensive *fee-only* financial advisor whose advice is not biased with motivation to sell you an annuity or some other form of financial product for a commission.

Do not wait to plan for your retirement until you are ready to retire. In order to ensure a worry-free, financially independent retirement, you need to correctly position yourself and then monitor and adjust your planning as both personal and external dynamics continue to change during your lifetime.

Quiet Millionaire® Summary

■ Intelligently plan for retirement and other milestones.

■ Understand and know your own retirement plans provided through your employer and any group savings plans, as well as the pros and cons for all the various ways to save for retirement.

■ Know the realistic dynamic trends affecting the affordability of retirement in order to plan and manage your finances intelligently.

■ Become familiar with the Social Security system as well as with long-term health care possibilities.

■ Use the Cardinal Rules for successful retirement.

■ Understand the effects of college planning, failing health, and long-term health care on your retirement plans.

■ Learn how to overcome the double-barreled negative effects of inflation and taxation both before and during retirement.

■ Understand and utilize the various retirement savings plans.

■ Periodically (at least annually) perform a detailed retirement cash flow analysis to determine and monitor whether you will run out of money during your lifetime.

CHAPTER FIFTEEN

Retirement Part II: How to Maximize Retirement Assets and Transfer Estate Wealth

In retirement, the primary financial objective for most people shifts from accumulating and growing their wealth to preserving and protecting their wealth. However, the quiet millionaire® knows that it is just as important during retirement to still grow assets as well as preserve and protect them in order to keep up with the increasing living costs and to manage the uncertainties that can occur with today's long retirement duration. The biggest uncertainty of all is how long you are going to live.

Some people have an unrealistic estate planning goal of "bouncing the last check." However, the quiet millionaire® has a more ambitious estate planning objective. Instead, the quiet millionaire® wants to transfer the maximum possible amount of his or her remaining wealth to survivors. The quiet millionaire® also knows that the only way to have control in achieving this goal is to plan in advance. This will also make the transfer easy and assure that the wealth is distributed in accordance with the way he or she intended.

Retirement Part I discussed how to make certain you can quit working without running out of money during retirement. Retirement Part II discusses some of the best ways to preserve, protect, and grow your assets in order to live on during retirement and then pass on the remainder during the estate settlement process. This chapter will complete your journey through the Financial Management Review process, and at the end of the chapter, you will be shown where to find a sample of a completed Financial Management Review.

QUIET MILLIONAIRE® WISDOM
Accumulating and keeping wealth require that informed planning and skilled financial management be performed with persistent discipline.

In order to preserve, protect, and grow your assets during retirement and pass on the remainder during the estate settlement process, you cannot allow procrastination, false beliefs, and negligence to rule. Without proactive intelligent planning, all of your retirement wealth will become very costly taxable income while you are living and/or burdensome estate taxation upon death. In addition, you will cause unnecessary and upsetting hardship for the people you care about the most.

The Best Ways to Preserve, Protect, and Grow Your Retirement Assets

Proactively develop a retirement funding game plan that optimally coordinates the taxation incurred when taking retirement money from all financial sources

The amount of taxation for money that you use during retirement depends upon your work career and how you accumulated the money for retirement. Some retirees have their money in tax-deferred retirement accounts and annuities that have never been taxed but that will be subject to costly taxation as withdrawals are made. Many retirees also will receive taxable income from Social Security, and some will receive taxable income from a company pension plan as well. Retirement money that is located outside of tax-deferred retirement plans in taxable accounts, rental properties, and business interests is also subject to taxation when withdrawn.

Taking money from all the various sources of retirement money requires a well-thought-out optimization strategy or else a significant amount of accumulated wealth can vanish because of taxes both during and after your lifetime. For example, the IRS has a required minimum distribution (RMD) schedule that forces you to withdraw money from tax-deferred retirement plans and IRAs (except Roth IRAs) starting at age 70½ for the remainder of your expected lifetime. If you should die before completing the IRS required schedule for lifetime withdrawals, the federal and state governments will be there to collect the remaining income taxes owed on the deferred money as well as any estate or inheritance taxes owed.

It *is not* in your best interest to remain on cruise control when traveling the complicated and confusing road of retirement and estate taxation because as much as ninety percent of your wealth can be lost to taxes, leaving only ten percent for you and your survivors to use. It *is* in your best interest to work with a professional advisor who can safely guide you through and around all of the financial road hazards you may encounter before it is too late to avoid them.

Account for catastrophic long-term-care costs in your retirement cash flow planning analysis and determine how you will manage and pay for this risk

A major threat to your security during retirement is the financial devastation that catastrophic long-term-care costs can cause your investment portfolio. In Retirement Part I, you were shown an illustration of how the retirement cash flow analysis for Phil and Mary was adjusted so they could make critical planning decisions to avoid running out of money during their lifetime.

One of the most important parts of any retirement cash flow analysis is to include performing a "stress test" for catastrophic long-term-care expenses. This is done by hypothesizing specific "what ifs" for your retirement cash flow analysis that compare the different investment portfolio outcomes that might occur *if* you:

■ Use your investment portfolio to pay premiums for long-term-care insurance in order to fully or partially limit your exposure to the potential out-of-pocket costs for catastrophic long-term care and protect your financial security.

■ Use your investment portfolio to fully or partially self-insure your exposure to the potential out-of-pocket costs for catastrophic long-term care. Going broke and relying upon Medicaid (medical welfare) is not an acceptable option for the quiet millionaire®. If your retirement cash flow analysis reveals that your investment portfolio is more financially secure by paying affordable insurance premiums, then you should avoid shouldering the financial risk of long-term care and pay the premiums to insure.

Maintain a well-diversified investment portfolio that will continue to keep you ahead of inflation

The reduction of your money's purchasing power as a result of inflation is an investment risk you cannot afford at any time and especially during retirement when you are living off of your investment portfolio. Having a bank certificate of deposit (CD) mentality during retirement erodes the value of your money for paying living expenses. Another valuable aspect of the retirement cash flow analysis is the process of inputting various assumptions for investment rates of return in order to determine how detrimental it is by getting too "safe" with an investment program during retirement. Remember, as discussed in the previous chapter, you must keep your eye on the net after-inflation, after-tax investment rate of return in order to make your retirement money last longer.

By having a well-diversified investment portfolio during retirement that grows faster than the rate of inflation, you lessen the risk of running out of money. Furthermore, with a well-structured investment portfolio, you can comfortably withdraw money to live on when difficult investment performance periods occur without

QUIET MILLIONAIRE® WISDOM
A diversified investment portfolio does not require that you be right about every decision one hundred percent of the time (only most of the time) in order for it to grow and be well protected.

permanently harming the portfolio's overall value. The advantage to this circumstance is that no matter when money is taken out, there are always some parts of a diversified portfolio to access that are performing relatively well and having their "time in the sun," and the more downtrodden portions of the portfolio do not have to be invaded. Then, when the clouded portions shine again, they are intact to regain value and make a major contribution to overall growth.

Strategically, during difficult investment times, certain asset classes such as the fixed income portion of an investment portfolio can be made somewhat overweighted in order to steadily anchor the portfolio and defend it against downside risk. Then, when economic and investment conditions improve and regain momentum, certain other asset classes can become strategically overweighted in order to capture maximum growth opportunities. This is not market timing, but rather it is asset class "tuning" to make sure that you "win by not losing."

Understand annuities and their pitfalls and how to manage them for best results

An annuity is an insurance product that is the reverse of a life insurance policy and is sold as a tax-deferred investment vehicle that provides income. There are two basic types of annuities: fixed and variable. The money placed in fixed annuities is invested and managed by the insurance company in a fixed-income bond portfolio that pays interest, which is adjusted at least annually. Alternatively, with variable annuities (VA), the money is invested by the owner of the annuity in a diversified array of mutual funds sponsored by the insurance company. VAs are intended to provide more growth than fixed annuities but with more consumer responsibility and risk than fixed annuities.

When issuing a *life insurance policy*, the insurance company determines how long you are expected to live and accordingly charges a premium for underwriting a *death benefit*. With an *annuity*, the insurance company also determines how long you are going to live and, according to how much money you invest, will *guarantee* to pay you a fixed *income benefit* for the remainder of your lifetime from the time that you start the income payments (annuitize).

However, there are pitfalls if you choose a lifetime fixed income payment (annuitize). The payment amount always stays the same and does not keep pace with inflation, and if you die after receiving as little as one income payment, the insurance company gets to keep all of the remaining money you invested. With life insurance, you "win" if you die early, while with an "annuitized" annuity, the insurance company wins if you die early. Neither arrangement seems good.

Depending upon the annuity policy, there may be other alternatives besides a "guaranteed" lifetime fixed-income benefit that you can select. One option might be to elect a fixed-income benefit for an *agreed certain period* of time such as five or ten years.

This way, if you die before the agreed income period is up, your survivors will receive the benefit amount still owed for the remaining unused period.

Another option is to instead *withdraw* your money as needed from an annuity without being "guaranteed" a stipulated fixed-income amount. The advantage to making the withdrawal election is that you can be flexible about how much and when you take money out. The pitfall is that you give up any form of "guaranteed" fixed-income benefit, but the positive side is that by letting the invested money inside the annuity continue to grow, you may be able to take out larger payments as needed and better keep up with inflation. Another advantage to the withdrawal program is that the annuity's survivor beneficiary(s) do not lose receiving any investment amount remaining inside the annuity if you die before using it all.

In most instances for reasons already discussed, the withdrawal program is usually the best option to elect. However, be aware that an unannuitized annuity in the withdrawal mode can present an income tax hardship for the named survivor beneficiaries, which can be avoided by investing money instead in a taxable account and forgoing the tax-deferral benefit. This is because any money remaining inside an annuity does not "step up" for income tax purposes to the value at the date of death, and therefore survivors have to pay income taxes on the gains that have been tax deferred over the years, whereas survivors inheriting a taxable account do not have to pay any taxes on the gains because the investment value is "stepped up" to the dollar value that exists at the date of death.

Annuities are sold by financial salespeople as being a great tax-deferred savings vehicle for retirement and/or college funding. What they do not tell you is that annuities have high fees and internal costs and onerous surrender charges and penalties, and they also do not tell you that they get paid an exorbitant commission for selling them. One of the biggest travesties involving annuities is the sale of an IRA annuity, which is entirely unwarranted because a less costly nonannuity regular IRA already offers the same tax-deferred investment benefit.

So, if people attempt to sell you an annuity as an investment for retirement, college funding, or any other reason, just remember that they win and you lose. The best decision is not to purchase an annuity in the first place, but if you already have an annuity, there is a transaction you can do to improve your situation. Specifically, it is an IRS-approved transaction termed a "1035 tax-free exchange," which allows you to transfer the money from one annuity to another without income tax consequences. But, you have to be careful because this transaction is often abused by persons selling annuities in order to gain another commission being paid on the money being transferred, and there may be costly early-surrender charges incurred for the annuity being replaced.

Therefore, if you already own an annuity and choose to do a 1035 exchange, be sure to fully understand how to make sure it is in your best interest. Also, make sure you realize all of the costs involved and make sure that you are moving to an annuity that pays no commissions (no-load), has no surrender charges, and is immediately available for you to use any time you want your money. Annuity pitfalls can be ugly, but the storyline for buying them can sound beautiful.

Consider and evaluate converting
a regular IRA to a Roth IRA

If you have money situated inside a regular IRA and in any given tax year your modified adjusted gross income (MAGI) is $100,000 or less, you are eligible and should evaluate whether converting your regular IRA to a Roth IRA makes financial sense for you. In particular, during retirement, without any earned income, you might be able to plan your income flow in order to stay under the $100,000 threshold. Be aware that if you convert your regular IRA to a Roth IRA, it can be done either on a full or partial conversion basis in order to control the amount of income taxes you are required to pay on the dollar amount converted. However, the dollar conversion amount is not included as income in the calculation for determining the $100,000 MAGI limit and therefore does not affect your conversion eligibility.

Regardless of whether you decide to convert all or part of your regular IRA to a Roth IRA, it is important that you pay the taxes owed with money from outside the regular IRA in order to avoid paying additional taxes and possible penalties. If you use the regular IRA funds to pay the taxes incurred on the conversion, that amount used to pay the taxes is considered a withdrawal and is also subject to taxation, which reduces the conversion benefits. Even more costly is if you are under age 59½ and use the regular IRA funds to pay the taxes because that amount used is considered to be a premature distribution and is also subject to a ten percent early-distribution penalty.

Retirees who determine that they will not need to use all of their regular IRA money during their lifetime will find the Roth IRA conversion opportunity to be especially attractive. This is because once the money is converted to a Roth IRA, you are no longer forced to start making withdrawals at age 70½ as the IRS mandates be done with regular IRAs. Making it even more attractive is the fact that neither you nor the beneficiaries you name for the Roth IRA will ever have to pay taxes on withdrawals once the conversion process is completed. Invested money can grow and never be taxed again, and you will never have to be concerned about income tax rates going up in the future. Doing the Roth IRA conversions the right way can be tricky, but gaining from the potential payoffs can be a wealth building and preservation bonanza.

How to Transfer Your Estate's Wealth for Maximum Value and in the Most Private, Least Difficult Manner Possible

The quiet millionaire® knows that estate planning is a financial area where many costly, negligent errors occur and therefore stays current about how to transfer the most amount of wealth to survivors with the least amount of hassle for them. The following are some of the major activities that should be done to accomplish that objective.

Legally prepare, execute, implement, and maintain proper estate planning documentation

Most people do not want to think about their own mortality, which is an uncertain certainty. When in good health, everyone expects to live a long life, but it does not always turn out to be that way. Estate planning is not just for the ultra wealthy, and documentation must be established during your lifetime in order for your intentions to be legally effective upon your incapacity, incompetence, or death.

As a basic minimum, everyone should have a simple will prepared by an attorney, and it should definitely not be a do-it-yourself document. If there is no documentation, there is no family control of the estate settlement process. Rather the process is in the control of a probate judge who has no idea about your true desires and who abides by a set of state laws that might not match your actual intentions. Often, family members who were once close are torn apart by disputes, frustration, and greed. In other words, you left a confused mess resulting in unnecessary hardship. No family is immune to the consequences of money disputes.

Another important aspect of estate planning that is often neglected by not having prepared a valid will is what happens to minor children in the event that both parents are tragically gone.

Without proper documentation, a judge will have to decide issues such as who will have custody of the children and who will be responsible for the children's money and welfare. It might not produce the same decisions you would have made, and this could mean additional hardship for the children.

Other important documents to have in place include a living will and durable powers of attorney for health care and financial decisions. Your attorney in conjunction with the will preparation should also prepare these documents. In addition, all beneficiary designations for life insurance, retirement plans, IRAs, etc., should be reviewed and maintained up to date for accuracy.

If you have a potential federal estate tax liability (remember all of your life insurance counts in the estate tax calculation), then you should also have a revocable living trust to increase the amount of assets that can be distributed estate tax free. In addition, having trusts in place keeps the estate settlement process private because the court-supervised probate process can be avoided.

It is mandatory that assets be transferred into a trust in order for the assets to be considered legally incorporated and shel- tered by the trust. Furthermore, in order to avoid or reduce poten-

> **QUIET MILLIONAIRE® WISDOM**
> *Signed trust documents are just worthless pieces of paper until the assets are titled in the trust's name.*

tial federal estate taxes, the trust assets of a married couple must be properly balanced in value between the trusts of each spouse. Unfortunately, some attorneys are not diligent about properly funding trusts and balancing trust asset values once the trust documents are prepared and signed. So, make certain that you hire only an attorney that will diligently follow up for completion of the implementation required after the trust documents are signed.

All documentation must abide by the state laws where you legally reside. If you relocate, the documents must be reviewed again to assure they conform to the laws of the new state of residence. You should also maintain an up-to-date *non*legal document termed a "final letter of instructions," which details such things as funeral arrangements and the location of important documents, insurance policies, investments, cash, safe-deposit boxes, etc. Because life is full of unexpected events, it is important that there be open and detailed communication with ultimate survivors even if the need for their estate settlement role is expected to be a long way off.

There are also other numerous complex estate planning issues and strategies too comprehensive for the scope of this book that require many specific forms of legal documentation to implement. The purpose of this information is to make you aware that having even the basic documentation is very beneficial and to recommend that you initiate action with a comprehensive financial advisor working together with a competent estate planning attorney. This should be done even if you do not have a potential estate tax liability in order to remain in control of the distribution of your assets and to clearly and legally communicate your intentions to survivors. Moreover, family survivors who will be responsible for settling your estate should be introduced to your financial advisor and attorney during your lifetime in order for the family to be more prepared in the event that something happens.

Stay up to date with changes in the federal income and estate tax laws and update your tax reduction planning strategies throughout the year

In particular, the federal estate tax laws are in a state of disarrayed change and confusion that requires constant monitoring in order to be updated and informed about changing estate planning strategies. One example of the importance of monitoring is that as of 2006 through 2008, if your estate's net worth is two million dollars or more, including all investment accounts, retirement plan assets, real estate, life insurance, etc., it is subject to federal estate tax as high as fifty-five percent. Even worse, when income taxes are added on top of the estate tax, as much as ninety percent of your estate over two million could pass on to the federal government instead of being transferred to intended heirs. In addition, most states also impose an inheritance tax on remaining estate assets.

The good news is that the federal estate tax might be on its way to being repealed. In 2009, the estate tax exemption amount increases to $3,500,000 from $2,000,000, and then in 2010, the estate tax is repealed entirely for one year as part of what is termed a "sunset" provision. Then at the dawn of 2011, any estate over a mere $1,000,000 is again subjected to the high federal estate tax. However, there are also indications that all of these scheduled changes will be replaced by a $5,000,000 estate tax exemption. This political fickleness is why estate planning is a confusing moving target that must be monitored in order to protect your accumulated wealth from taxes.

Have sufficient estate liquidity for paying all taxes owed at death

If your estate plan does not provide enough cash to cover final expenses such as outstanding debt and taxes owed, then valuable assets may have to be sold immediately and frequently for much less than their actual market value. Planning should be done in advance in order to avoid this scenario that robs survivors from retaining hard-earned accumulated family wealth. One planning tool can be life insurance that provides proceeds for the required liquidity at death. In addition, life insurance proceeds are not generally subject to income taxes and when properly structured in advance may not be subject to otherwise applicable estate taxes.

Establish a lifetime gift-giving program to reduce taxes and provide income

Each year, an individual can gift up to $12,000 (adjusts for inflation) to any person without incurring federal gift tax. Married couples can gift up to $24,000. This is a good way to reduce the value of your estate and transfer it over time. For parents and grandparents who may want to reduce the size of their estate and educate children, the college savings 529 plan offers a unique opportunity because it enables them to accelerate five years' worth of the annual exclusion amount into one year. For example, married grandparents can transfer $120,000 out of their estate to each grandchild and avoid gift tax consequences.

Best of all, the 529 plan is the only estate planning device available whereby a monetary gift is considered an irrevocable completed gift for tax for estate tax reduction purposes, but in fact the gift can be revoked in the event the money should be subsequently needed or if the student becomes unworthy of the gift. However, if the money is taken back, there is an income tax liability and ten percent penalty incurred on the earnings and appreciation. The ten percent penalty is waived if the student beneficiary becomes disabled or is deceased. It is also waived if the student receives a scholarship and the withdrawal of funds equals the amount of the scholarship.

The family limited partnership (FLIP), grantor-retained interest trust (GRIT), grantor-retained annuity trust (GRAT), and the grantor-retained unit trust (GRUT) are some of the other estate and gift tax reduction entities used to maximize the transfer of wealth to family members. However, the description and best ways to effectively use these techniques are extensive, but you should be aware that they exist and may warrant your consideration.

Use appreciated investment assets to make monetary gifts

One way to use this strategy is to shift a tax liability from a higher to a lower income tax bracket by gifting an appreciated asset such as a stock or mutual fund to someone who is in a lower tax bracket than you. This way, the appreciated asset can be sold without any tax liability to you and with a smaller tax liability being incurred by the person receiving the gifted appreciated asset. For example, the lower tax liability can be created when a grandparent makes a gift to a grandchild. However, watch out for something called the "kiddie" income tax, which occurs when the child is under age eighteen. Also, be cautious to abide by the limited $12,000 gift tax exclusion in order to avoid possible gift tax consequences.

Even more tax beneficial is to gift an appreciated asset to a charitable or religious organization or to any other IRS-approved non-profit entity that is excluded from having to pay any tax on the gain in value for the donated appreciated asset. Making gifts to a charitable or religious organization with appreciated investments instead of cash can leverage the size of your contribution while at the same time reducing your tax liability. For example, assume that you own a mutual fund that you paid $10,000 to purchase and that has grown in value to $30,000. If you were to sell it, you would have to pay a fifteen percent capital gains tax totaling $3,000 ($20,000 gain x 15% tax). If you wanted to donate the net proceeds ($27,000) to a charitable organization, you could, but there is a better way. Instead, donate the appreciated $30,000 mutual fund to the charity, let it sell the fund tax free, and remove all your tax liability. In addition, the amount of your contribution is increased by $3,000, and your income tax deduction is larger by $840 (assume 28% of $3,000). This represents a nice *additional* $3,840 (38%) gain on your original $10,000 investment.

A more sophisticated planning idea using this appreciated asset planning concept is to establish a charitable remainder trust

(CRT), which provides you the added benefit of receiving lifetime income, the amount of which depends upon the size of the contribution amount. Sometimes, business owners having a highly appreciated value for their business use the CRT to avoid paying a huge tax on the gain business value and to reduce their estate tax liability, get a large charitable deduction, and create a source of lifetime income for their retirement.

Establish stretch IRAs to maximize remainder wealth for heirs

The stretch IRA is an estate planning technique that allows you to *stretch* out the time that your leftover IRA money can remain untaxed and be paid out to children or grandchildren. The following story about Jim and Sara's smart estate planning is an example of how the stretch IRA works.

Jim is a quiet millionaire® with $500,000 in a traditional IRA. Both he and Sara at age 70 know that with $3,000,000 in another separate traditional IRA, they will not need to spend any of this $500,000 IRA money during their lifetime. However, starting at Jim's age 70½, the IRS will require that he take taxable distributions from both his IRAs according to an annual schedule that completely pays out the total $3,500,000 over his expected lifetime. However, he can take the annual required minimum distribution amount from his other IRAs and leave the separate $500,000 IRA as the last IRA from which to take his required lifetime distributions.

Jim originally designated Sara as the primary beneficiary for both IRAs without naming a contingent beneficiary. As currently planned, this meant that if he died, Sara as his surviving spouse would have the option of either continuing the forced payout over Jim's required minimum distribution schedule by the IRS or rolling the inherited IRA into her name and having the IRS required distribution schedule change according to her remaining life expectancy. Either way, Jim and Sara's surviving son, Tom, a successful physician, was going to have to pay taxes on the entire remaining IRA balances if his parents died before their life expectancy. Furthermore, Tom is financially secure and so will not need to inherit that IRA money and pay unnecessary taxes.

So, with some intelligent advice from their financial advisor, Jim, instead of designating Sara as his primary IRA beneficiary on the separate $500,000 IRA, named their twenty-five-year-old grandson, Kyle, as the primary beneficiary, and their other twenty-one-year-old grandchild, Tammy, as contingent beneficiary. This now means that when Jim dies, the payout and taxation of the remaining separate $500,000 IRA balance will be stretched out according to his grandson Kyle's life expectancy, which could be as long as sixty years if Jim were to die prematurely while Kyle is age twenty-five.

Jim and Sara's situation is just one of many circumstances that warrant establishing a stretch IRA. Now that you are aware of the stretch IRA concept, it is recommended that you work with a competent financial advisor in order to make sure that all of the IRS requirements are met and that the stretch IRA is set up properly. You should also make sure that the custodian for you IRA permits you to set up a stretch IRA because not all do. In addition, you should prepare a retirement cash flow that determines whether you will need to use all of your retirement assets.

Would you just jump into a car or take an airplane to go wherever without planning your trip? If so, you would likely wind up somewhere other than where you

QUIET MILLIONAIRE® WISDOM
Your future depends upon how well you manage your financial life now.

intended if you had planned your course. Nevertheless, this is how many people plan their travel through life. In essence, they are counting on a miracle to reach their desired destination. Your financial success is not in the hands of some "fickle finger of fate" or fortunate changes in the economy; it is completely up to you to plan and manage the course of your life and to fulfill your dreams.

"If one advances confidently in the direction of their dreams, and endeavors to live the life which they have imagined, they will meet with a success unexpected in common hours."

—**Henry Thoreau**

How to Advance in the Direction of Your Dreams

■ Know where you are today relative to where you want to go. Do not be uninformed about your situation and what it will require to get to your destination.

■ Set specific goals for where you want to go. A goal remains only a dream if it is not specific. We all should have dreams, but in order to be terrific, you must be specific!

■ Formulate and implement workable strategies for achieving your goals. Carrying out successful strategies requires making informed decisions about issues such as tax reduction, investing for growth in a comfortable risk tolerant manner, purchasing financial products, and evaluating which financial products are most appropriate and from whom to purchase them.

■ Manage your financial plan both proactively and responsively to your dynamically changing personal circumstances, i.e., changes in employment, earned income, health status, and family life transitions such as education funding commitments, retirement, etc. Adjust to shifting external events such as changes involving economic conditions, tax laws, inflation, and investment returns, etc.

■ Monitor and measure the progress relative to your plan assumptions and expected outcomes. For example, are your assumptions about investment rates of return and inflation increases holding up? Are you maintaining the discipline to accumulate the amounts required for meeting your specified financial goals? Stay alert for when and how to best fine-tune and adjust for any changes in your personal circumstances and outside events.

■ Overcome procrastination. Think things through, and then follow through.

Now that you have seen how the Financial Management Review is assembled and the information is used, you are ready to see a sample of a completed Financial Management Review, which is shown in Appendix A and at *www.quietmillionaire.com*. Keep in mind that everyone's review has different components included and that the illustrated review is just a sampling for you to get an understanding of how the review is comprehensive yet concise as a useful tool for following up and monitoring your progress.

How to Decide Whether to Hire a Professional Advisor or Do It Yourself

When you look at what is required to achieve wealth building success, you have another important decision to make, whether to do everything diligently on your own or work with the help of an objective and competent professional advisor. Either way, there are all sorts of resources available to you, many of which seem reliable and are convincingly trustworthy but which actually can be irreparably harmful. Most painful could be that you might not even realize financial damage has been done until it requires anxious adjustments and unexpected financial realignments to your lifestyle. Therefore, it is important that you discern the good advice from the bad.

■ Avoid mass media noise from television, magazines, the Internet, etc., which can be especially harmful because it indicates credibility but primarily communicates unregulated hype that is more intended to attract your attention and sell wares than to provide you with intelligent solutions. At best, the mass media offer rules of thumb and generalities that may not be applicable or appropriate for your particular situation.

■ Be suspicious about subscription newsletters that play upon greed and ignorance with enticing claims about secret strategies for easy financial success. Warning: There are no get-rich-quick schemes to replace an intelligent ongoing financial management program. At best, the scheme maybe works for a designated period that the schemer chooses to show you for substantiating the claim of success.

> QUIET MILLIONAIRE® WISDOM
> *Even if you are able to discern the value of financial information and are capable of managing your own finances, it might not be the most economically productive use of your time.*

Time is worth money, and you should use it most productively to increase your net worth. It does not make economic sense to be a financial do-it-yourselfer unless you are able to devote the necessary time to do it consistently and competently without making costly mistakes that need to be undone, often when it is too late to rectify. Maybe you would be better off focusing on earning more income or freeing up more time to enjoy life.

In addition, while you may believe that you have the financial shrewdness and tools and are doing what is best, you might be missing valuable opportunities for maximizing your wealth. Significantly, in the event the primary family financial management decision maker suddenly is no longer around, survivors would benefit by having trustworthy continuity with a financial advisor who was selected mutually by all parties involved during their lifetimes.

Having Professional Advice Can Be Your Best Investment

The quiet millionaire® uses professional help and realizes that "good advice is seldom free" and that "cheap advice is likely cheap in value." Often, advice can be self-serving for the provider, and it can also be downright incompetent and inappropriate. Moreover, do not be foolish enough to believe that the descriptions for financial service providers as "big" and "well known" and "reputable" will assure that you are getting the best direction for your situation. This is why there are so many regulatory watchdogs required to guard the financial terrain.

On the other hand, if you work with the right advisor, it takes only a few tidbits of good, sound advice to make a professional fee worth paying. Consider this: If during a down market, your $500,000 investment portfolio would have dropped twenty-five percent ($125,000) under your control, but because of the investment advisor's structure, it decreased only ten percent ($50,000), would a $5,000 investment advisory have been a cost or a good investment? Furthermore, if while you are withdrawing money for funding retirement, the same advisor, included in the same fee, showed you ways to reduce taxes by $5,000 a year, plus provided other value-added financial planning and management services, would paying the $5,000 fee for such comprehensive advice be worthwhile to you?

This book has advocated the merits of working with a *fee-only* advisor because the commission-only and fee-based advisors can be biased and motivated by commission compensation to sell financial products as part of their agenda. Also, be realistic about working with investment consultants or advisors employed by well-known and, therefore, perceived reputable brokerage firms and banks. Realize that they too can be biased to direct you toward the financial products and services offered by the firms they represent rather than objectively representing you as their deemed employer.

Unbiased advice is more likely to be received from an entrepreneurial, independently owned and operated, *fee-only* advisory firm. Furthermore, the advice is usually superior to that received from commission-earning salespeople and from salaried employees representing large, multilayered bureaucratic financial firms. Importantly, receiving unbiased, competent professional advice also helps you to avoid making uninformed or emotional financial decisions.

However, the method of compensation does not guarantee advisor competency, and you should go through a careful due diligence advisor search and interview process. This process, if done properly, should produce a successful advisory working relationship that lasts a lifetime.

Be cautious about relying too heavily upon references. While they are important and should be a part of the search process, it could turn out to be a situation of "what is good for the goose might not be so good for the gander." Furthermore, advisors are going to provide you with only references that they know will respond positively to your inquiry. You need to evaluate objectively and first hand the competency, trustworthiness, and rapport with the prospective advisors produced by your search process.

Any concluding decisions about which financial advisor to hire should be made by *both* spouses in a married household, even if one spouse usually takes the lead in the family's financial decision making. The deferring spouse may turn out to be the survivor who then must assume more responsibility for the financial situation.

For further information about what to consider when looking for professional help, you can visit *www.quietmillionaire.com* or call 1-800-542-4198 for a free report titled "Ten Questions to Ask a Financial Advisor *Before* You Hire Them."

How to Find and Hire the Right Financial Advisor for You

The following is a procedure you can use for conducting your due diligence process to find a financial advisor. For your convenience, *www.quietmillionaire.com* has links to the referenced Web sites.

■ Visit the Financial Planning Association (FPA) Web site *www.fpanet.org* for a listing of Certified Financial Planners™ (CFP®) located in your geographic area.

■ Visit the National Association of Personal Financial Advisors (NAPFA) Web site *www.napfa.org* for a listing of *fee-only* advisors located in your geographic area.

■ Visit the individual advisor's Web site as well as the Web site of the local Better Business Bureau for awareness about any adverse complaints involving the advisor.

■ Contact the individual advisors under your consideration for a free, no-obligation introductory interview. Make a final selection for establishing a working advisory relationship.

Be in control of your life and be "the quiet millionaire®"

Work to discover the true you and to define specifically what the important achievements and goals are for your life. This will form a solid and motivating base from which to plan and manage your finances. Intelligent financial management will enable you to accumulate money for financial security and independence and to maintain control of your path through life. Your destiny should not be a matter of circumstance but rather a matter of choice and achievement.

Quiet Millionaire® Summary

■ Know the best ways to preserve, protect, and grow your retirement assets.

■ Learn how to transfer your estate's wealth for maximum value and in the most private, least difficult manner possible.

■ Legally prepare, execute, implement, and maintain proper estate planning documentation.

■ Determine whether you will take action on your own or with the help of a financial advisor.

■ Conduct an informed due diligence search process in order to find a trustworthy and competent financial advisor who is right for you.

■ Be in control of your life and be the quiet millionaire®.

APPENDIX

Sample Financial Management Review™

T his sample Financial Management Review™ (FMR) is intended to help you visualize how the information data gathering process is used to produce a comprehensive, coordinated report. Each FMR is customized for the client and not prepared from a template. The FMR serves as an agenda for the advisor/client meeting and serves as a checklist for follow-up requirements. Each FMR is supported by other reports, which are referred to throughout the FMR meeting, such as a current financial statement, cash flow analysis, tax projections, insurance reviews, retirement projections, etc.

This sample FMR is based upon actual situations, but it is fictional for confidentiality purposes. Also, keep in mind that the sample does not provide for every financial management circumstance. Some of the analysis shown has been condensed, and the names of financial product providers and organizations are fictional.

John and Mary Sample

Financial Management Review – January 2007

Background Information

John birth date: November 21, 1942 (age sixty-three); employment: professor, Cape University, twenty years.

Mary birth date: June 14, 1941 (age sixty-four); employment: high school teacher, Marie School, eighteen years.

Cash Flow Management

(See 12-31-06 cash flow statement for further details)

Income: John paid monthly, cost of living increases occur annually in October effective on a fiscal year basis. Mary paid twenty-one times annually, no cost of living increase expected in 2007.

Current Cash Flow: Cash flow is positive, but higher expenses are expected for new house purchase. Revise and review 2007 cash flow to reflect expenses associated with new home expenses.

Cash Management Tools: Uses 2007 Quicken Deluxe to track expenses. Direct deposit paychecks into Big Bank joint checking account, which is used for living expenses and investment of excess cash flow. Use the online bill pay option and have a debit card. Also, maintain a local Small Bank joint checking account.

Personal Asset and Liability Management

(See 12-31-06 financial statement for further details)

Primary Residence

Purchased new home July 2006, cost $950,000. Sold previous home October 2006 for $500,000. New home equity $550,000: cash down payment $100,000 plus $450,000 net equity from previous home sale. Mortgage financing: lender Independent Federal, mortgage amount $400,000, loan to house value 44%, interest rate non-jumbo 5.55%, thirty-year fixed, monthly principal and interest payment $2,284 per month, property taxes $903 per month, homeowner insurance $217 per month. Automatic monthly payment program established for payments from Big Bank account.

Financial Management Strategy: *Do not prepay low fixed mortgage; mortgage interest deduction provides current tax savings and future tax savings when withdrawing from retirement plans subject to taxation. Mortgage allows diversified investment assets to grow at an average rate that should exceed 5.55% mortgage rate. Thirty-year mortgage can be paid off early at anytime or after ten to fifteen years when the interest tax deduction is no longer as beneficial. Home is titled in name of Mary's trust to avoid potential estate taxation.*

Home Equity Line

$100,000 line at Big Bank reestablished with new home equity, interest rate prime minus ¼%. Financial Management Strategy: Utilize for short-term working capital needs in lieu of maintaining high checking/savings account balance. Objective: Remain fully invested in diversified portfolio as described in the investment section of Financial Management Review.

Automobiles

John: 2003 Honda Accord, 78,000 miles as of January 2007. Three-year auto loan in lieu of cash used to finance purchase, loan interest rate 0%, fully repaid.

Mary: 2000 Jeep Grand Cherokee, 90,000 miles as of January 2007, previously used tax-deductible home equity line to finance auto purchase, paid off within three years from date of purchase.

Financial Management Strategy: *Intention is to first replace 2000 Jeep Grand Cherokee, with either a low-mileage used or a new vehicle. Will compare cash purchase vs. financing options with low-interest auto loan vs. with home equity line auto loan. Leasing is not a recommended option because of preference to own cars long term and expectation to exceed allowable lease mileage. General rule: Lease new, buy used (shop in advance of need). Recommend auto financings not exceed 36 months unless 0% finance rate. Home equity line used if preferable financing not available.*

Credit Cards

Three cards: Visa $20,000 limit, MasterCard $15,000 limit, American Express (used only for foreign travel purposes). Paid off monthly in full, no interest charges incurred.

Potential Financial Exposure Risk to Financially Assist Other Family Members

Parents

John:

- *Father,* deceased 1999.

- *Mother,* age eighty-five, poor health, Alzheimer's, resides in the Montvale Nursing Home, no long-term-care insurance. Monthly expenses $6,000 per month, receives Social Security income $750 per month, and deceased husband's survivor pension income $500 per month. Monthly cash flow shortfall $4,750 funded from $250,000 remaining investment portfolio expected to last approximately three to four years. Montvale accepts Medicaid payments if it becomes necessary. Has will and other estate planning documents, executed 1999.

- **Financial exposure risk:** possible but currently appears low.

Mary:

- *Mother,* deceased 1996.
- *Father,* age eighty, failing health, heart disease, resides alone in own private residence in Cleveland area, market value $150,000, no mortgage. Father refuses to discuss his financial situation with family, monthly expenses presumed to be approximately $2,000 per month, receives Social Security income presumed to be approximate $800 per month, no pension income, investment assets unknown, father only states "enough to survive." Family concerned about failing health and affordability of assisted living or nursing home facility, no long-term-care insurance, no known will or other estate planning documents.
- **Financial exposure risk:** unknown.

Siblings

John:

- *Brother,* age sixty-one, resides in Cleveland, attorney, married, three adult children. Financially secure.
- **Financial exposure risk:** none.

Mary:

- *Brother,* age sixty-one, married, financially secure, two adult children, resides in Cincinnati.
- **Financial exposure risk:** none.
- *Sister,* age fifty-nine, divorced, no children, resides in Atlanta, recently diagnosed with multiple sclerosis, now forced to retire as flight attendant, will have no health insurance, will apply for Social Security disability. $40,000 in 401(k), no pension income. May be necessary to reside with John and Mary as a dependent.
- **Financial exposure risk:** high.

Children

Two sons, both married, reside in Cincinnati, financially independent, John and Mary recommending to sons that they also become clients.

Financial exposure risk: none.

Grandchildren

One grandchild, Jane Elizabeth Sample, birth date May 3, 2004.

Tax Reduction Management

(See tax returns and tax projection report for further details; tax returns reviewed annually for accuracy and potential tax reduction opportunities. 2001–2005 reviewed and filed)

2005: Married filed separately lowered overall tax liability; John AGI $130,589; federal tax $28,671 with $3,018 AMT; owed $4,314; effective rate 22%, AMT credit carry forward $983; capital loss carry forward to 2006 $2,318; state tax $6,564, refund $2,265 applied to 2006 taxes; rate 5%; local 1% rate, $1,409 liability but $0 due (gets credit for other local taxes paid), refund $181. Mary AGI $109,516, federal tax $21,129 with $70 AMT, owed $4,571, effective rate 19%; state tax $5,153, owed $1,398, rate 4.7%; local rate 1%, $851 liability but $0 due, $1,114 refunded.

2006: Return currently being prepared by Roger Smith, CPA.

Financial Management Strategy: *CPA to calculate married file joint vs. married file separate. Investment tax loss harvesting saved $10,000 in federal and state income taxes and will continue to reduce future year tax liability. Mortgage deduction for new house will provide initial estimated annual tax savings of approximately $6,500 per year.*

2007: Projection assuming married file joint, federal joint tax $54,517 with $2,952 AMT, withhold plus estimated payments $43,905, project owe $10,612. State married file joint $15,270 w/$12,563 withhold. Safe Harbor calculation: assume married file joint 90% of projected total 2006 tax − for 2007 $49,100 federal and $13,243 state.

Pretax Retirement Contributions

Recommended all 403(b) contributions be stopped because John and Mary have approximately $2 million in tax-deferred investments, which constitutes 54% of total investment assets. This amount is likely to grow significantly. At age 70½, IRS Required Minimum Distributions (RMDs) will force withdrawal of tax-deferred account funds based upon life expectancy, and *ordinary* income taxes will be paid at potentially higher marginal rates (current reduced rates expire 2010). While minimizing current taxes by maximizing retirement plan contributions is an option, the long-term effects must be considered. The current tax rate structure is expected to change, with ordinary income tax and capital gains tax rates increasing to higher levels. RMDs decrease flexibility in portfolio planning as assets must be sold, perhaps at an inopportune time, to meet the IRS withdrawal requirements. John and Mary, with high-value tax-deferred retirement accounts, face a potential tax liability time bomb. *In today's current tax environment* of relatively low income and capital gains rates, increasing contributions to taxable investment accounts for retirement is preferable to contributing money to high-value tax-deferred investment accounts.

Financial Management Strategy: *Analysis indicates that by age 70½ John and Mary's combined RMD from all tax-deferred accounts will result in excess income taxed at ordinary income rates. During John's expected lifetime, over $600,000 in income taxes will be paid on unneeded IRS required withdrawals. Therefore, it is recommended that tax-deferred contributions be* *stopped, annually strategies be implemented to reduce taxes involving the taxable investment accounts.*

Roth IRA Contribution Status

Not eligible to contribute because of high adjusted gross income and married file separate tax reduction benefit. Monitor conversion opportunities, but probably not allowable for foreseeable future because of high retirement income level expected.

Flexible Spending Account

John: 2007 election $750.

Financial Management Strategy: *Annually project out-of-pocket medical expenses; if greater than $500, elect to make pretax contributions to the FSA. Make sure to use it, or you lose it.*

Affordable Housing Tax Credits

This is a possible financial tool to help alleviate tax on ordinary income on tax-deferred withdrawal during retirement.

Financial Management Strategy: *Currently subject to alternative minimum tax (AMT) while employed. May avoid AMT once one or both are retired. Revisit at that time. Consider (a) credits cannot be used in year with AMT but do carry forward and (b) living expenses associated with new home will require higher withdrawals for income that may trigger AMT in future years. If evaluation indicates credits as a useful tool, then recommend tiered entry to stagger credits and diversify among offerings.*

Financial Planning and Investment Advisory Fee

100% of advisory fee being deducted from IRA account and therefore paid with pretax dollars because it is not considered a taxable distribution and will help mitigate required minimum distribution during retirement. This is more tax advantageous than the limited use as a personal itemized deduction, which also raises the alternative minimum tax.

Long-Term-Care Policy Premium

Personal tax deductible subject to 7.5% AGI level; S-Corp can take deduction based on age of insured. In 2006 up to $2,600 each in premiums deductible.

Financial Management Reduction Strategy: *Current tax law contains favorable capital gains and dividend income treatment, but a multitude of conditions must be met to take advantage of them. Every investment account must be closely monitored to ensure these conditions are met to achieve tax savings under the new law. Retirement living expenses must be forecast each year and withdrawals managed from taxable and tax-deferred accounts to efficiently manage the current and future tax burden. See other tax-related recommendations within other Financial Management Review sections.*

Retirement Financial Management

Retirement Objectives

John plans to retire from the university at age sixty-five and stop outside consulting at age sixty-six; Mary plans to retire at age sixty-five or sixty-six. **Retirement income objective: $92,000 per year in today's dollars after taxes** (includes revised spending plan for new home).

Financial Management Strategy: *Review retirement cash flow annually. Using 8% average investment rate of return assumption, objective is achievable, and estate planning is required to reduce taxation. The income tax effect from required minimum distributions during retirement has been illustrated, also reviewed retirement cash flow with paying long-term-care insurance premiums vs. fully self-funding the potential out-of-pocket costs of long-term care.*

Ohio State Teachers Retirement System Pension Income Benefits

Both John and Mary contribute to OH-STRS 10% of gross pay annually, and their employers contribute 14%. Retirement pension income benefit calculation is based upon an 8% rate of return. STRS determines benefit based upon highest three years of earnings and performs two calculations: one based on credited service and one based on combined employee and employer contributions; the higher amount is used for the pension benefit. 3% cost of living adjustment is applied each year, *simple compounding*, based on actual first month retirement benefit. Reduction factors applied for less than thirty years' service or retire prior to age sixty-five. In years when the investment performance exceeds assumed 8% rate of return, a thirteenth monthly check may be issued. Partial lump sum payment (PLOP) is available, which essentially returns employee contributions and then pays a reduced annuity benefit. Upon death, remaining employee contributions with interest are paid to beneficiaries. Joint annuity option with reversion allows return to higher payment single life annuity if spouse dies first. Note: operates on July 1 to June 30 fiscal year basis for service credits.

Projected STRS Pension Income Amounts:

- **John:** STRS (OH) at planned January 2008 retirement, age sixty-five, 50% joint survivor monthly pension income benefit with reversion $4,423/month. PLOP maximum $171,108. If John retires March 2008, receives credit for full year service and benefit increases $150 per month for 50% joint and survivor benefit with reversion.

- **Mary:** STRS (OH) July 2007 retirement, age sixty-five; 50% joint survivor monthly pension income benefit with reversion $3,194. PLOP maximum $124,668; retire age sixty-five get max multiplier. January 2008 retirement benefit $3,238, July 2008 benefit $3,333.

Social Security

Background information: The Social Security Windfall Elimination Provision (WEP) and Government Pension Offset (GPO) will be triggered when John and Mary receive their OH State Teachers Retirement System pension income. WEP affects the Social Security income benefits received by the primary recipient, while GPO affects the Social Security received by the spouse.

Social Security Income Amounts:

- *John* has attained forty plus credits; eligible at age sixty-two for $1,100 per month, at age sixty-five plus ten months $1,443 per month. Review analysis indicates that John has thirty plus years of substantial earnings to qualify for exemption from windfall, and his eligible Social Security income benefit should not be reduced.

- *Mary* also attained forty plus credits; eligible at age sixty-two $584 per month, at age sixty-five plus eight months $725 per month. Mary has thirteen years, and her Social Security benefit will be reduced to approximately $428 per month at age sixty-five; Mary will receive no benefit from John's Social Security because of GPO. Apply for benefits three months prior to collecting Social Security.

Medicare

Both John and Mary qualify for Medicare benefits.

Financial Management Retirement Planning Strategy: *Monitor retirement planning and investment program in order to outpace inflation and to minimize income and estate tax consequences during retirement.*

Investment Management

(See December 31, 2006, financial statement and investment report for current account values and further supporting details)

Account Listing as of December 31, 2006 (Tax-Deferred)

John

Retirement Reserves Variable Annuity: Nonqualified tax-deferred annuity with Big Insurance Company. Because of high surrender charges until June 2009, recommend retain annuity until eliminated and monitor fund investment selections. Third Party trading authorization is in effect to monitor account online direct. Primary beneficiary: Mary. Contingent beneficiary: John revocable trust.

IRA Rollover: This IRA account is a consolidation (for administrative simplification and diversified investment management) of previously separate accounts consisting of: a contributory IRA, a dormant 403(b) account, a dormant business money purchase/profit sharing plan, and an IRA annuity. Primary beneficiary: Mary. Contingent beneficiary: John revocable trust.

403(b): Per recommendation, has stopped contributing to plan because of required minimum distribution tax issues during retirement. Note: This retirement savings plan offers very limited diversification options; all of the equity fund options are large cap growth funds because of similar top ten holdings, and all are lagging S&P Index. Therefore, recommend that the 403(b) be rolled over to a diversified traditional IRA upon retirement. Subsequently, monitor for Roth conversion opportunities. Primary beneficiary: Mary. Contingent beneficiary: John revocable trust.

Mary

IRA Rollover: This IRA account is a consolidation (for administrative simplification and diversified investment management) of previously separate accounts consisting of: two dormant 403(b) accounts (recommended no further contributions be made to a 403(b) plan), a rollover IRA, and an IRA annuity. Primary beneficiary: John. Contingent beneficiary: Mary revocable trust.

No-Load Variable Annuity: Nonqualified annuity with Low Cost Insurance Company resulting from 1035 tax-free exchange of $8,000 cash value from a $10,000 whole life policy. Primary beneficiary: John. Contingent beneficiary: Mary revocable trust.

Account Listing as of December 31, 2006 (Taxable)

John

Business Investment Account: Used for investing business consulting profits. Reregistered John Sample and Associates to reflect S-Corp status instituted in July 2005 from sole proprietorship for liability protection. Monitor and implement strategy to diversify from existing low-basis stock mutual funds.

Revocable Trust Account: Cost basis accurate on investment reports; diversification program fully implemented.

Mary

Revocable Trust Account: Cost basis accurate on investment reports; diversification program fully implemented.

Investment Risk Tolerance and Profile

Reviewed updated risk tolerance questionnaires dated December 2006; both John and Mary indicate reduced risk tolerance since December 2005 assessment. Portfolio risk and return targets for the investment portfolio changed accordingly. Revised the investment policy statement to reflect changes. Monitor results vs. expectations. Investor Profile completed and reviewed.

Financial Management Investment Strategy: Maintain Modern Portfolio Approach to diversify and reduce portfolio downside risk. Continue using investment advisor's current custodian for consolidating custody of investment assets, accessing low-cost, tax-efficient institutional mutual funds and I shares across a variety of asset classes for improved diversification, reduced taxation, and increased efficiency and easier control and monitoring.

Risk Management (Insurance Planning)

Current Health Insurance

Health Status: Both in good health, nonsmokers. Current coverage for both through John's **Cape's** STRS group plan, Health Company PPO insurance, $0 deductible, minimal co-pays, premium $662 per month of which $612 is reimbursed tax free; remaining $50 is paid by John as pretax deduction.

Retirement Health Insurance

Upon retirement, it is important to coordinate Medicare coverage and STRS retiree health insurance. Both John and Mary qualify for Medicare. As long as John is full-time employee, Mary continues to be covered by his plan; Mary should contact Social Security Administration to inform she will not enroll in Medicare at age her age sixty-five because of existing group coverage. This will defer the start for her Medicare B initial enrollment period and avoid any late-enrollment penalty. Once John retires, both should enroll in Medicare Parts A and B, and STRS will be the Medigap policy. STRS reduces coverage for Medicare-eligible participants who do not enroll for Medicare coverage. STRS subsidizes the Part B premium 3% per year of service credit up to 90% (2006 Part B premium is $88.50). STRS premiums for retiree medical coverage increase if there is no Medicare coverage. Furthermore, the status of the STRS health insurance program could change, and retirees may be required to pay the full premium in the future. Using STRS retiree medical as a MediGap policy is the safest course of action. STRS requires copy of Medicare card within ninety days of sixty-fifth birthday. Mary should inform STRS that she has group coverage and does not require enrollment in Medicare at this time. STRS does not subsidize spousal Medicare A & B plan premiums.

Current Life Insurance

John

Employer group: 1x salary $114,520 (2007 estimate), employer paid with imputed income. No spousal coverage. No coverage upon retirement. Primary beneficiary: John revocable trust.

Adjustable life policy: Reliable Insurance Company (AA credit rating), policy #0000000, $116,000 death benefit, issued November 10, 1987, Option 1 level death benefit, current cash value $25,760, no premiums being paid. Current 6% interest rate carries policy to John's at age ninety-six. Primary beneficiary: John revocable trust.

Financial Management Strategy: *Retain policy, no premium payments are required.*

Mary

Employer group: 1X salary, $84,200 (2007 estimate). Primary beneficiary: Mary revocable trust. No coverage upon retirement.

Financial Management Strategy: *Life insurance for John and Mary is purely an estate planning issue, not a capital needs issue. Capital needs analysis indicates no need for survivor income replacement life insurance. Determine their concern of estate tax liability diminishing their estate value.*

Disability Insurance

STRS group coverage for both until age sixty-five, 60% of salary replacement grandfathered under pre-1992 program, employer pays entire premium, benefit taxable.

Long-Term-Care Insurance

Long-term-care insurance (policy #1818181) with Long-Term-Care Insurance Company purchased December 2005. John and

Mary each have $4,500 monthly benefit, ninety-day elimination, 5% compound inflation, forty-eight months coverage, no other riders. With preferred and joint couple discount, premium for John $1,800 per year, Mary $2,430 per year.

Property & Casualty Insurance

All P&C insurance is through Safe Insurance Company.

Homeowner: Recommend $1,000 deductible for new home coverage to reduce insurance cost.

Auto: Comprehensive deductible $100; collision deductible $500.

Personal Liability: $2 million umbrella, premium $470 per year.

Business Liability Insurance: Evaluate liability risk potential for consulting business, which is now structured as an S-Corp.

Financial Management P & C Strategy: *Current P&C insurance company is acceptable and competitively priced. Evaluate annually.*

College Planning and Gifting for Grandchildren

Grandchildren: First grandchild born May 3, 2004, Jane Elizabeth Sample. Established 529 plan January 2004, $10,000 initial contribution; Mary owner and John contingent.

Background information re: options for college gifting:

529 College Savings Plan

Advantages: Can jointly gift $24,000 annually or $120,000 lump sum without triggering "gift tax," maintain ownership (control), removed from estate, grows tax free under current law if used for college, no federal/state taxes due for qualified higher education expense withdrawals (until 2011 pending congressional action), can reclaim money but taxes due on gains, money transferable to other family members for college.

Disadvantages: Limited investment choices, money must be used for higher-education expenses to take advantage of tax-free withdrawals, possible "sunset" in 2011 for federal tax purposes, colleges now offset financial aid awards with money invested in 529.

Coverdell Education Savings Account

Advantages: Maintain control, removed from estate, beneficiary changes allowed, transfer to beneficiary at age eighteen is discretionary, can be used for any educational expense (including private high school tuitions), federal income tax free (subject to 2011 sunset), unlimited investment choices unlike 529.

Disadvantages: Maximum annual contribution limit $2,000 with adjusted gross income limits for contributors ($160,000 married file joint in 2006), must be used by beneficiary by age thirty or beneficiary incurs income tax liability, noneducational use triggers taxes and penalty, entire value counts against student for financial aid.

UGMA

Advantages: Maintain control until age of majority for beneficiary, removed from estate, can be used for any purpose by beneficiary, unrestricted investment choices, can gift appreciated investments for sale at minor's lower capital gains rate.

Disadvantages: Money belongs to beneficiary, at age of majority lose control, no tax deferral, earnings subject to "kiddie" tax, can adversely affect student financial aid calculation.

Crummy Trust

Advantages: Can control how and when assets are spent, unrestricted investment choices, no restriction on use by beneficiary unless dictated by trust, assets removed from contributor's estate.

Disadvantages: Significant setup and maintenance costs, complicated and cumbersome administration, no tax deferral, beneficiary can access current contribution immediately (but not previous contributions), annual crummy letter(s) requirement. Note: Other type trusts for minors can be "raided" by the beneficiary within ninety days of reaching the age of majority.

Financial Management Strategy: *Use 529 plan to save for future college needs of grandchildren in tax-efficient manner, reduce gross estate, maintain control of investment, and minimize adverse effect upon financial aid. Will exceed AGI limits to contribute to Coverdell Education Savings Account if file taxes separately; married file joint limit is $180,000 AGI. Planned gift currently does not warrant cost of trust.*

Estate Tax Reduction & Distribution Management

Current Documentation: All estate documents reviewed and properly executed in October 2006. The funding of the joint estate is completed and evenly balanced. Successor trustees for both John and Mary are both sons, with bank as corporate trustee. Both John and Mary have executed pour-over wills, living wills, with durable power of attorney for health care and financial. All documents prepared by JD Attorney, Esq., at B & B law firm. All accounts are properly titled, and beneficiary designations are up to date and filed. Letter of Instruction has been prepared and provided to the successor trustees.

Financial Management Strategy: *Despite the increased federal estate tax exemption and the establishment and funding of revocable trusts, implementing further estate tax reduction strategies is a priority planning issue. Also, expected future increases in total estate asset size including life insurance death benefits should be monitored going forward relative to future changes in the tax laws. Some preliminary ideas for discussion include:*

- *Disclaimer of IRA upon first death.*
- *Gifting of assets during lifetime outright, or in a Crummy Trust.*
- *Charitable gifting of taxable assets or bequests of IRA assets.*
- *Irrevocable Life Insurance Trust (ILIT)—fund trust with second-to-die life insurance to pay income and estate taxes payable on IRAs.*

Business Planning

John Sample and Associates, Consulting

Legal structure planning strategies: Switched to S-Corp from sole-proprietorship effective January 1, 2005, to reduce personal liability exposure and self-employment taxes.

Tax Strategy: S-Corp tax benefits are reduced as salary increases. An initial salary of $5,000 was coordinated with Small Business CPA Associates to limit payroll taxes and establish a level of compensation that avoids IRS concerns. Recommended use IRS mileage allowance for business purposes. A profit sharing plan was established but deliberately unfunded because of required minimum distribution factors previously indicated. Monitor for Roth 401(k) possibility.

Financial results: Tax return prepared by CPA; gross income $40,000, John salary $5,000, $28,000 net income after expenses flowed to personal tax return. 2007 is projected $42,000. John plans to stop consulting in 2008.

Cash Management: Business account established for all business transactions.

Benefit Programs: Although eligible for a qualified retirement plan, will not establish because of required minimum distribution tax issues. However, long-term-care policy is tax-qualified, and premiums paid by the S-Corp are deductible subject to IRS age limit rules (up to $2,600 John and Mary each in 2006).

Coordinated Comprehensive Financial Management Summary

Coordinated, comprehensive financial management plan: Implement and monitor for expected results. Prevent loss of wealth typically resulting from four primary sources: bad investments, uncontrolled spending, poor tax planning, and lawsuits.

Goal setting: Establish congruency of money goals with money values. A **goal** is quantifiable money milestone such as: "We want to retire at any age of choosing starting now, annual retirement income of $92,000 per year in today's dollars after taxes." A **value** is a nonquantifiable feeling, such as: "We want to maintain and improve our quality of life upon retiring."

Identity theft: Protect assets from potential of identity theft. Review credit report annually at *www.annualcreditreport.com.* Look for errors such as false delinquencies and accounts that may not belong. Check for incorrect personal information including name, address, birth date or age, and past or present employers, which, if incorrect, is a clue either to identity theft or improperly merged information from lenders to the reporting agency. Use a heavy-duty paper shredder before discarding all confidential information.

Index

F

I

Want to order more books of
The Quiet Millionaire?

If you would like to order additional copies of *The Quiet Millionaire*, visit the website *www.quietmillionaire.com*, telephone 1-800-542-4198 or complete the below order form. *(If you are not completely satisfied with your purchase for any reason, you may return the books for a full refund, less shipping & handling).*

Please send me _____ copies of *The Quiet Millionaire* to the below address.

NAME _____

ADDRESS _____

CITY _____ STATE _____ ZIP CODE _____

TELEPHONE (_____) _____ E-MAIL _____

(Information only used if need to clarify order)

Copies _____ @ $18.95 each $_____

Sales tax @ 7% per copy (OH residents only)   _____

Shipping & handling @ $4 first book, $2 each additional   _____

                                              TOTAL $ _____

Enclosed is a check for $_____ made payable to FMG Publishing, Inc. or charge my

❏ Visa   ❏ MasterCard # _____ Exp. date _____

Mail order form to: FMG Publishing, Inc., 10979 Reed Hartman Hwy., Suite 209, Cincinnati, OH 45242 or call 1-800-542-4198 for faster processing.